The
COMPLETE ANCHORING HANDBOOK

The COMPLETE ANCHORING

HANDBOOK

Stay Put on Any Bottom in Any Weather

Alain Poiraud, Achim Ginsberg-Klemmt, and Erika Ginsberg-Klemmt

International Marine / McGraw-Hill

Camden, Maine • New York • Chicago • San Francisco • Lisbon • London • Madrid • Mexico City
Milan • New Delhi • San Juan • Seoul • Singapore • Sydney • Toronto

The McGraw·Hill Companies

1 2 3 4 5 6 7 8 9 DOC DOC 0 9 8 7

Library of Congress Cataloging-in-Publication Data
Besser ankern. English
    The complete anchoring handbook : stay put on any bottom in any weather / Alain Poiraud, Achim Ginsberg-Klemmt, and Erika Ginsberg-Klemmt with a contribution by Alain Fraysse.
        p.   cm.
    Includes index.
    ISBN: 978-0-07-147508-2 (pbk. : alk. paper)
    1. Anchors.   2. Seamanship.   3. Heavy weather seamanship.   I. Poiraud, Alain.   II. Ginsberg-Klemmt, Achim.   III. Ginsberg-Klemmt, Erika.   IV. Title.
    VM791.B47 2007
    623.88'1—dc22   2007001135

ISBN 978-0-07-147508-2
MHID 0-07-147508-7

Questions regarding the content of this book should be addressed to
International Marine
P.O. Box 220
Camden, ME 04843
www.internationalmarine.com

Questions regarding the ordering of this book should be addressed to
The McGraw-Hill Companies
Customer Service Department
P.O. Box 547
Blacklick, OH 43004
Retail customers: 1-800-262-4729
Bookstores: 1-800-722-4726

Photographs and illustrations courtesy the authors unless otherwise noted. Page ii: Billy Black (bottom left), Onne van der Wal/Bluegreen (middle), Spade (bottom right). Page iii: Gary John Norman/Bluegreen (bottom).

Contents

Foreword

by Jimmy Cornell, *Aventura III*

The technique of sailing has changed enormously in recent years, but one area that has remained virtually unchanged from the early days when humans first ventured afloat in a hollowed-out tree trunk is that of anchoring. GPS, radar, electronic charts, and other such aids have vastly increased the safety of sailing, but they are all primarily concerned with movement.

When I was asked to write a foreword to this book, I looked back at the various accidents among cruising boats that have come to my attention during my recent circumnavigation and was amazed to find that the majority were the direct consequence of poor anchoring. In the not too distant past, the major cause of groundings in areas such as the South Pacific was poor navigation; nowadays, boats are often lost or damaged because they are anchored in the wrong way and in the wrong place. And I say that not just from my observations of others but also from hard-gained personal experience! I will never forget some sticky moments, especially in my early sailing years, when we were one step from serious trouble by not having paid due attention to anchoring properly.

As more boats and sailors take to the seas, *The Complete Anchoring Handbook* is a welcome and timely addition to yachting literature. As the ideal combination of sailor, boatbuilder, inventor, and engineer, Alain Poiraud is in a unique position to deal with the art of anchoring in both theoretical and practical ways. After all, Alain has shown that he knows more about anchors and anchoring than probably anyone else in the world by designing and producing the most successful anchor for yachts in recent years: the universally acclaimed Spade anchor. Thousands of boats all over the globe are now cruising safely because of that anchor.

In order to ensure that this book presents an objective and comprehensive picture of all anchor types and anchoring techniques, Alain has secured the collaboration of coauthors Erika and Achim Ginsberg-Klemmt, whose thoughtful comments based on their rich cruising experience have added a valuable dimension to this book, as well as the expertise of Alain Fraysse and the mathematical equations he has contributed (see Appendix 1). Their collective effort has produced a book that is so comprehensive in its scope that it should satisfy the demands of both weekend sailors and hardened professionals.

Acknowledgments

This book is a product of work done on five continents, in three different mother tongues, by three authors. It has gone through many revisions and has withstood scrutiny from engineers, mathematicians, physicists, inventors, and all kinds of seafaring people. We thank our families and friends who have patiently supported and encouraged us as we sculpted the manuscript.

We would like to especially thank Jimmy Cornell, Chuck Hawley of West Marine, Ulli Kronberg of Palstek, Ole Pfeiler, Steven Paley of Navimo USA, Coby Smolens, Professor Knox, and Alain Fraysse. Erika especially thanks all of the baby-sitters, and all three authors are grateful to the many cybercafés on the planet. Finally, we are especially grateful to Bob Holtzman, our editor, who was able to dig through the weeds and grab hold of the substance.

Introduction

by Erika Ginsberg-Klemmt

What a great thing it is to be aboard a boat. It's even better, however, if you actually leave the dock once in a while, and better still if you go farther than your local bay and stay aboard longer. Going somewhere with your boat is wonderful, especially when you can stay awhile. And what better way to stay than at anchor? Most sailors dream of setting their anchor in the crystal-clear waters of a beautiful, isolated bay to enjoy swimming, snorkeling, or fishing, or just to lie back, have a good meal, and take it easy. It is a fantastic way to enjoy all the delights of the water and the beauty of the coastline surrounding you.

During the sixteen years that Achim and I cruised on our sailboats, our best times were when we were anchored off breathtaking coastlines. Anchoring is one of the most rewarding experiences of navigation and yet one of the most overlooked maneuvers, in terms of its complexity.

With the growing number of vessels navigating under power and sail, anchoring has become an increasingly tricky aspect of boating. Anchorages and marinas are crowded, especially during the high season. As the prices of transient berths continue to skyrocket, the boating kitty takes a nosedive. Financially speaking, even the best and most expensive ground tackle can pay for itself in just a few days. Perhaps more important, anchoring offers a critical measure of safety. With the proper ground tackle and a skilled crew, anchoring provides safety in adverse weather and will keep your boat off the rocks in case of engine or equipment failure.

The more we have studied the subject of anchoring, the more we have come to realize how much there is to know—and just how riddled contemporary anchoring techniques are with myth and misconception.

People invariably ask whether or not we are scared out there. "What if something happened to you out on the big wide ocean, with nothing but miles of empty water around you?" What most landlubbers don't realize is that "out there" is where it's quite safe; it's in harbors and anchorages where Murphy's Law rules. Dragging, collisions, grounding, and angst abound near land. Anchoring is perhaps the hairiest of all boating maneuvers, yet it often gets the least attention.

This book is the product of a multilingual and multicultural collaboration. The core of the text was written in French by Alain Poiraud, and Achim and I were brought aboard originally as translators. When we read the newfangled concepts in Alain's work that had been heretofore neglected, we offered to expand the book with our observations, gathering data and the experience of other experts. This book purposely avoids the nautical vernacular found in many seamanship publications. This may irritate some traditional skippers, but our hope is that this approach will make the subject matter accessible to a wider audience.

The result is a collaborative effort. The tests and observations Alain Poiraud made in conjunction with the National School of Engineers of Monastir (ENIM) in Tunisia, and the force diagrams compiled from those tests, inform the methods and approaches this book advocates. In addition, over the past decade, other objective, comparative tests have helped us and others develop a more rational approach to anchoring technology and methodology. We have assimilated the results of tests conducted by independent engineering organizations and boating magazines, including *Practical Sailor*, *Yachting Monthly*, *Practical Boat Owner*, *Bateaux*, *Voile Magazine*, *Loisirs Nautiques*, and *Voiles et Voiliers*.

With all this practical and experimental evidence behind it, *The Complete Anchoring Handbook* is not afraid to take issue with accepted anchoring wisdom. We hope this book will entertain and inform, but we also hope it will dispel at least ten misconceptions about anchoring that sailors have both promulgated and suffered for centuries:

1. **Anchoring, like sailing or fishing, is an art—and you either have a talent for it or you don't.** As in sailing, fishing, *and* art, study and practice improve your ability to anchor excellently and safely. However, the laws of physics and the design of your anchoring equipment have much to do with your success. There is a learning curve, but with routine practice, once you understand the main principles, you can become an expert without elevating anchoring to an art form.

2. **Anchoring is a science based solely on physics.** The notion that scientific knowledge and muscles are all you need, and that the rest is merely fluff, is no more accurate than the attitude spelled out in the first misconception. Anchoring is a learned skill in which theoretical knowledge should be combined with educated decision making. The information presented in this book can help you understand how and why

certain methods work better than others, but every time a skipper anchors a boat, his or her acquired experience contributes invaluably to success. Physical strength and expensive equipment can help, but they cannot replace technical knowledge, patience, communication skills, and most of all, practice, practice, practice.

3. **Most how-to boating books already include a chapter on anchoring. Why would sailors ever need a whole book on the subject? Besides, how is reading about anchoring going to help me anchor? All you have to do is throw the darn thing overboard and you're anchored!** This book covers many aspects of anchoring that other how-to guides may only touch on, including modern anchor types, chain-rode combinations, onboard ground tackle design and configuration, and techniques for anchoring in any weather. What's more, by understanding seafloor characteristics, the loads and forces working on your ground tackle, and various strategies for dealing with difficult anchoring environments, you can feel more secure when you leave the safety of the harbor for adventures unknown. Then again, you can take your chances and just throw down the hook and hope for the best—and may the force be with you.

4. **I'm just a pleasure boater, and I only go out for a few hours to fish, daysail, or water-ski, so I don't need to master** anchoring maneuvers. Most of the time, sailors anchor their vessels not because they need to but because they want to. Many times, thankfully, there is almost nothing to it; otherwise, who other than daredevils would ever have the guts to anchor? But even the most worry-free situation requires some understanding of regulations, etiquette, and technique. Then, unfortunately, there are those times—as in the case of a fire aboard, or the failure of an engine, propeller, or sailing rig—when anchoring is an emergency maneuver necessary to avoid discomfort or disaster.

5. **The heavier an anchor, the better.** This statement seemed true for centuries, although it was never very good for the orthopedic health of the crew or for the performance of the boat. Fortunately, our understanding of physics has evolved—and so has anchor design. We can have very efficient anchors that are a fraction of the weight of traditional anchors. This is the first book that deals with these new-generation concepts in detail.

6. **Plow anchors with hinged flukes dig in and turn with the shift in direction of pulling force better than fixed-fluke versions.** This deep-rooted belief is not supported by evidence. Many boaters who dive to check their anchors have found their hinged plows lying sideways on the seafloor. Read Chapter 3, Anchor Selection, to understand why

more and more mariners are trading in their articulating anchors for fixed shanks.

7. **If you want to be really secure, an all-chain rode is the way to go.** We do not share this point of view and tell you why in Chapter 4, Anchor Rode.

8. **You can never use too much scope.** In general, holding power increases significantly with scope, up to a 10:1 scope. Beyond that, paying out more rode will give only a very small increase in holding while increasing swing radius, which is not a particularly desirable effect in a crowded anchorage or near a rocky shoreline. You have to weigh the diminishing returns against the negatives of excess scope, including having to weigh all that rode back aboard.

9. **Two anchors in tandem (on one rode) hold better than one anchor**

alone. We show that this is rarely the case in Chapter 7, Advanced Anchoring Techniques.

10. **To know what kind of ground tackle to use, look at everyone else. To know where to anchor, look at everyone else.** This is the *moutons de Panurge* phenomenon: if the lead sheep jumps off a cliff, all the others blindly follow. Just because someone has chosen a particular piece of equipment or a particular spot in an anchorage doesn't make that the right choice for you. It is interesting to observe what others are doing—but it is even more interesting to understand why before following suit.

Once *The Complete Anchoring Handbook* is in print, the anchoring world will continue to evolve. We welcome interaction from readers and look forward to improving, expanding, and updating this publication in the future.

CHAPTER 1

Seabed Characteristics

Most discussions on anchoring begin with the anchor itself, but we believe it makes more sense to look first at the seabed in which you want your anchor to hold, and then look at the forces that can make your anchor drag or dislodge. This is how we have approached the discussion in this book, and we hope the first two chapters provide a solid context for the discussion in Chapter 3 on anchor selection.

The seafloor is one of the most overlooked aspects of anchoring. No responsible skipper disregards visible problems, such as a loose cleat or a worn link in an anchor chain, but what remains unseen is often ignored. What you can't see, however, can of course hurt you, so it's essential to pay attention to the nature of the bottom in which you hope to set your anchor.

Unfortunately, not all anchorages offer large areas with excellent holding ground in dense clay or fine sand. Seafloor characteristics can vary greatly within a few feet. Two boats side by side in an anchorage may easily have their anchors in different sediments, and even when the sediment itself is homogeneous, you may encounter a slippery forest of dense weed just a few feet from a very good-holding sand patch. Asking your neighbor how the holding is in a particular anchorage may contribute to your decision making, but you can never really know the quality of any given anchor ground with absolute certainty unless you retrieve a sample or dive down and look for yourself!

Sometimes crystal-clear water will offer a view of what you're sinking into, even in deep water. Most seasoned mariners learn to read the chiaroscuro mosaic below, aiming for the lighter patches of sand between the dark boulders, seaweed, or other impenetrable spots.

But your eyes will only help so much. A good view of hard, compact sand may look the same as the loosely packed spot a few feet away. What's more, even with an excellent view of your anchoring field, that's only the upper layer. Once an anchor has pierced the bottom surface, it should dig itself into the subsurface layer. A sandy surface may only be a few inches deep, hiding an impenetrable rock plate below.

If you can see your anchor safely tucked in the seabed, you may feel safe in your bunk bed, too. But be aware that even a completely

Once you've lowered your anchor, whether it holds depends on many factors, not least of which is the quality of the seabed where it lands.

This Spade anchor has just fallen upon a bed of fine sand, an excellent type of holding ground, and is ready for full penetration during the rode pull.

buried anchor is no guarantee; soft mud, seashells, and pebbles offer only precarious holding.

Nautical charts, cruising guides, and pilots often give helpful information on seabed characteristics in a particular area, so you should always check your chart when preparing to anchor to see what it says about the type of bottom; see Table 1-1 for a list of abbreviations. This information, however, may be inaccurate or may not represent your exact anchoring spot. So if you don't want to get out your mask and snorkel, do what the ancient mariners did: heave a sounding line.

TABLE 1-1. SEAFLOOR ABBREVIATIONS IN NAVIGATIONAL CHARTS

Types of Seabed	NOS/NIMA[1]	IHO[1]/International Charts
Sand	S	S
Mud	M	M
Clay	Cy; Cl	Cy
Silt	Si	Si
Stones	St	St
Gravel	G	G
Pebbles	P	P
Cobbles	Cb	Cb
Rock; Rocky	Rk; Rky	R
Coral and Coralline algae	Co	Co
Shells	Sh	Sh
Two layers (e.g., sand over mud)	S/M	S/M
Weed (including Kelp)	Wd	Wd
Qualifying Terms	**NOS/NIMA**	**IHO/International Charts**
Fine	f; fne	f
Medium	M	m
Coarse (only used in relation to sand)	c; crs	c
Broken	bk; brk	bk
Sticky	sy; stk	sy
Soft	so; sft	so
Stiff	stf	sf
Volcanic	Vol	v
Calcareous	Ca	ca
Hard	h; hrd	h

[1]NOS = National Ocean Service; NIMA = National Imagery and Mapping Agency; IHO = International Hydrographic Organization.

A *sounding line* or *lead line* is a length of rope with a lead weight at the lowered end. Used to measure depth, this handy device also allows you to check seafloor characteristics. Put tallow, wax, or grease on the bottom of the lead weight to pick up traces of mud, sand, or shingle from the seabed. If you don't have a lead line, put some grease on your anchor, lower that, then bring it back up to see what's sticking to the flukes. This will work, but a lead line is much easier!

TYPES OF SEAFLOORS

Thanks to the meticulous work of cartographers, surveyors, and marine geologists, we have access to fairly accurate data pertaining to the seafloor sediments near the coastlines of the world. Geologists have classified the seabed into four major categories by particle size: muds, sands, gravels, and rocks. Keep in mind that these classifications are complicated by the fact that seafloors rarely have a homogeneous surface. Sand can be muddy, covered in algae, or contain a greater or lesser proportion of shell or coral fragments. The various types of seafloors differ in their penetrability and their capacity for holding anchors.

Mud

Geologists define mud as consisting of particles smaller than 62.5 microns in diameter. We can't see a particle this small with the naked eye, since it takes 1,000 microns to make 1 millimeter and 25.4 millimeters to equal 1 inch. Mud is subdivided into clay particles, which are smaller than 4 microns in diameter, and silt particles, which are 4 to 62.5 microns.

A semiliquid mixture of water and sediment, mud is soupier and lighter than pure clay, and less sticky. The softer and soupier mud is, the weaker its holding capacity will be.

Sand

Sand is comprised of rock that has been abraded by wave action into particles, or granules, ranging in size from 0.063 mm (63 microns) to 2 mm. Sand can be further subclassified as fine sand (0.06 mm to 0.2 mm), medium sand (0.2 mm to 0.6 mm), and coarse sand (0.6 mm to 2 mm). A mixture of fine and medium sand is considered dense sand for purposes of holding (see Table 1-2). Note that even the coarsest grain of sand is no more than a tenth of an inch in diameter.

Some sands are made up of the skeletal material of marine organisms. Coral sand is created not only by wave action but also by bio-erosion. For example, parrot fish bite off

pieces of coral, digest the living tissue, and excrete the inorganic component as silt and sand. Coral sand is one of the better materials in which to sink your anchor. Long live the parrot fish!

Gravel and Rocks

The next coarser sediment class above sand is gravel, with particles ranging from 2 mm to 60 mm (i.e., from $^1/_{10}$ inch to roughly 2.5 inches). We can subclassify gravel into granules (2 mm to 6 mm), pebbles (6 mm to 20 mm), and stones (20 mm to 60 mm). Since it has little cohesion, gravel is one of the worst materials in which to anchor. It can also prevent an anchor from setting even when it covers a more desirable sediment such as fine sand. You can only hope that if your anchor digs itself in deeply enough, the sheer weight of the gravel will keep it in place.

Above 60 mm (2.5 inches) in diameter, we have rocks, then boulders. (In the United Kingdom, cobbles are considered larger than pebbles and smaller than boulders, in the size range of stones and rocks.) Rock bottoms offer no holding power at all, unless you get lucky enough to hook a fluke under a boulder or in a crevice, in which case you will need equal luck to unhook the chain or anchor when the time comes to leave. A *trip line* for retrieval is recommended when dealing with a rocky bottom (see Chapter 7).

Table 1-2 compares the holding power of various bottom sediments relative to dense sand. For example, based on the holding coefficients listed, an anchor that would normally provide a holding capacity of

TABLE 1-2. ESTIMATED HOLDING COEFFICIENTS FOR VARIOUS TYPES OF SEAFLOORS

Material	Dense Clay	Dense Sand	Silt	Soft Mud	Coarse Sand	Pebbles	Rocks
Particle size	<4 μ	0.06–0.6 mm	6–20 μ	4–63 μ	0.6–2 mm	6–20 mm	>20 mm
Holding coefficient	1.50	1.00	0.65	0.45	0.40	0.35	0.00

1,000 pounds when properly set in dense sand would hold 1,500 pounds in dense clay, but only 400 pounds in coarse sand. Dense clay is the most secure of all sediments, but only if your anchor will set properly. If your anchor will set in sand but not clay, you're better off anchoring in sand—a subject we'll return to.

Modern anchors are endowed with high holding power relative to weight, and we might therefore be inclined to select an undersized one. But although a small anchor might function well in excellent holding grounds, it may fail in poor conditions. From Table 1-2 we can estimate that to achieve the same holding power in soft mud as in dense sand, we would need an anchor with more than double the holding power.

Knowing as much as possible about your chosen seafloor will give you an edge for sinking your anchor in and staying put. When an anchor slips, many are quick to find fault with their tackle or tactics, but ignoring the characteristics of the seabed is tantamount to "plug and pray." Even the best anchors may offer poor holding on a hard, compact seafloor or soft mud. No matter how "ideal" the anchor, rode, and tactics might be, one type of anchor will stab at or slide along the top of a hard surface, while another will rake through an ultrasoft soup of ooze and weeds. We will illuminate why in the next chapters.

CHAPTER 2

The Forces on an Anchor

Sir Isaac Newton contributed to the science of anchoring in more ways than one. For one, his work on gravity provided the basis for understanding the effects of the moon and the sun on the tides. For another, Newton's three laws of motion describe the relationship between the motion of an object and the forces acting on it. We turn to the first two laws to help describe the effects of various forces on anchor gear.

Newton's first law of motion states that a body at rest will remain at rest unless acted upon by an external force. Thus, a vessel floating in calm waters—completely unaffected by wind and current—would stay put with no anchor at all. In practice, of course, this is never the case for long.

The second law describes how the velocity of an object changes when it is subjected to an external force. It states that the acceleration of an object is directly proportional to the magnitude of the net force acting on the object and inversely proportional to its mass. Thus the equation:

$$F \text{ (force)} = m \text{ (mass)} \times a \text{ (acceleration)}$$

Put another way, force is defined as a change in momentum (mass × velocity) per unit of time. This law gave rise to the *newton* (N), the unit of force required to accelerate a mass of 1 kilogram by 1 meter per second per second. We will use the *decanewton* (daN; i.e., 10 newtons) to quantify the force exerted by wind on a vessel and thus on its anchor (1 daN = 1.02 kg or 2.25 lb. of force).

For a boat at anchor, the force in question is the load exerted on the anchor by wind, wave, or current acting on the boat—or by a combination of these. The load due to the pressure of wind on the boat is relatively easy to approximate. It is much more difficult, however, to determine the intermittent loads on anchor gear that result from wave action. Even in a midsize vessel, the forces involved can reach several thousand pounds, which explains things like broken ground tackle connectors and bent anchor shanks.

Wave action causes a boat at anchor to pitch and roll. Gusts of wind cause it to sheer back and forth on its rode, falling off first one way and then the other. The bow is blown off until the rode comes taut, snubbing the bow back into the wind. Then the boat surges forward, responding to the weight and elasticity of the anchor rode, until the next gust blows the bow off once more. An important factor in this horsing tendency is the location of the boat's *center of effort* (CE)—the geometrical center of its exposed wind-surface area without sails relative to its *center of lateral resistance* (CLR) below the waterline.

The schooner in the left illustration shows a CE that is aft of the CLR. A wind gust at anchor will thus tend to turn this boat's bow into the wind, counteracting the undesired swaying motion of the vessel.

On the other hand, a catboat with stowed sails has its center of effort forward of the center of lateral resistance. Wind gusts at anchor

will tend to turn the bow of this boat away from the wind, amplifying the swaying motion and exposing a larger area of the hull and cabin to the wind. This horsing behavior puts additional strain on the anchor gear.

By setting a small supporting sail—known as a *riding sail*—at the stern of a vessel, or a reefed mizzensail on a ketch, sheeted amidships, a skipper can move the CE farther aft to counteract the swaying of the boat and induce it to lie more quietly to its anchor.

Another way to minimize the swaying of a boat is to form a *bridle* for the anchor rode. When you've paid out most of the scope you think you need (see the Importance of Scope section in Chapter 6), attach a secondary line to the anchor rode with a rolling hitch. Then

Center of Effort (CE)

Center of Lateral Resistance (CLR)

When the CE is aft of the CLR, a wind gust at anchor will tend to turn this schooner's bow into the wind, resulting in an uncomfortable horsing movement.

Center of Effort (CE)

Center of Lateral Resistance (CLR)

Wind gusts at anchor will tend to turn the bow of this catboat away from the wind, amplifying the swaying motion and putting additional strain on the anchor gear.

pay out the last of your needed scope so that the rolling hitch is a boat length or so from the bow roller. Take the other end of the secondary line aft—say to the primary cockpit winch—and put some tension on it. The result is an asymmetrical bridle, and the more tension you place on the secondary line, the more you will misalign your boat's keel to the wind direction. Keeping your vessel slightly misaligned with the wind can tone down its swaying motion substantially.

WIND FORCES

The force of the wind on an anchored boat—and thus the wind-induced load on ground tackle—depends on two factors: the wind speed and the exposed surface area of the boat. While wind speed is easily measured, exposed surface area is more difficult to discern. From the boat's length, beam, and height above the waterline, we can derive a first-order estimate, but design and gear play a large role as well. A sailboat equipped with roller furling, a large pilothouse, or a bimini—or a power cruiser with a canvas-enclosed flying bridge or a tuna tower—will clearly present more surface area to the wind than similar boats without such appurtenances. A powerboat will generally have more windage than a sailboat of equal length due to its higher freeboard, greater beam, and larger house structures.

But even a precise calculation of exposed surface area, were we able to derive one, would be insufficient for a precise calculation of wind forces on the anchored boat. We need to know the frictional drag induced by the boat's exposed surfaces, and that depends on the shapes of the surfaces and their orientations to the wind as well as their areas. In an effort to quantify this effect, aerodynamicists assign a drag coefficient (C_d)—a dimensionless measure of aerodynamic sleekness independent of size—to an object, usually after wind tunnel experiments. It would be very useful to know the drag coefficients of your boat with the wind blowing from ahead or at angles up to, say, 30° off the bow; but since most of us do not have an America's Cup budget to spend on aerodynamic research, we will try to approximate the actual C_d value for a given vessel with a "best possible" guess.

A sleek car has a drag coefficient of about 0.30; a flat surface erected square to the wind (picture a sheet of plywood) has a C_d of 1.98. For the hull and superstructure of an average sailing yacht with the wind blowing from ahead, we can assume a value of 0.7. For an average motor yacht, we can assume 0.8.

Where does this leave us? We can calculate forces exerted, or load, due to wind (F_w) on a given vessel by means of the formula:

$$F_w = \frac{1}{2} \times \rho \times C_d \times A \times V^2$$

where

ρ = density of air (1.225 kg/m^3)

C_d = drag coefficient

A = frontal surface exposed to the wind

V = wind speed in km/h

More practically speaking, we can take a conservative estimate of the likely wind-induced loads on our boats from a table like Table 2-1, which was developed by the American Boat & Yacht Council (ABYC) and takes into account the surface area an anchored

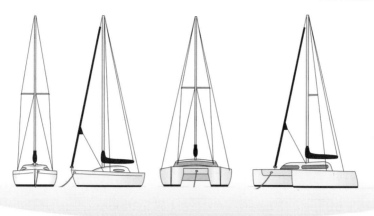

The exposed surface areas of a monohull and a multihull, with the wind blowing directly onto the bow and with the vessels swaying sideways. Note the higher windage profile of the catamaran.

boat presents to the wind when it is sheering back and forth on its ground tackle at angles of up to 30° from the wind.

Table 2-1 shows the immense increase in anchor loading as the wind rises. The load on an exposed surface increases by a factor of four if the wind speed doubles. If the wind speed triples, the load will be nine times higher.

To use the table, select your boat's length and beam and read off the corresponding values to get an idea of what kind of loadings your anchor and ground tackle should be able to cope with. If your boat's beam is greater than that indicated for its length overall (LOA), drop down to the next line.

TABLE 2-1. ESTIMATED AVERAGE WIND LOADS ON AN ANCHORED BOAT

Boat Dimensions (ft./m)			Wind Load, F_w (lb./daN)		
Length	Beam, motorboat	Beam, sailboat	Beaufort 7 (30 knots)	Beaufort 9 (45 knots)	Beaufort 11 (60 knots)
15/4.5	6/1.8	5/1.5	250/110	500/225	1,000/450
20/6.0	8/2.4	7/2.2	360/165	720/325	1,440/650
25/7.5	9/2.75	8/2.4	490/225	980/445	1,960/890
30/9.0	11/3.35	0/2.75	700/320	1,400/635	2,800/1,275
35/10.5	13/3.95	10/3.0	900/410	1,800/820	3,600/1,640
40/12.0	14/4.3	11/3.35	1,200/550	2,400/1,100	4,800/2,200
50/15.0	16/5.0	**13/3.95**	**1,600/730**	**3,200/1,450**	6,400/2,910
60/18.0	18/5.5	15/4.5	2,000/910	4,000/1,800	8,000/3,640
69/21.0	20/6.0	17/5.2	2,800/1,225	5,600/2,500	11,200/4,910
82/25.0	22/6.7	19/5.8	3,600/1,600	7,200/3,250	14,400/6,400

Adapted from a table courtesy ABYC

For example, for a 40-foot (12 m) sailboat with a width of 13 feet (3.95 m), enter the table as if for a 50-foot sailboat (we have bolded the appropriate figures in the table to illustrate this). For a 30-knot breeze, the horizontal load on your anchor due to wind alone will be 1,600 pounds, or 730 daN. If the wind increases to 45 knots, the load will double.

WAVE FORCES

Table 2-1 assumes that the water is flat. If the effects of wave surge are factored in, the intermittent loadings could be double or more. Still, independent calculations have shown that the values in the table are conservative enough to account for modest wave action.

Sheltered anchorages are usually protected from ground swell, but you cannot always avoid wind-induced waves of more local origin. What can happen when we are unable to prevent wave-induced shock loads on our anchor gear?

Let's imagine lying-to the hook in a popular anchorage that is protected from almost all directions. We have a heavy plow anchor deployed on an all-chain rode with 5:1 scope—a classic combination—and the weather looks quite good. We are enjoying a peaceful sundowner in the cockpit after a successful but grueling five-day passage to the Canary Islands from Gibraltar when—oops!—the weather forecast announces the expected arrival of a scirocco (a hot desert wind) during the night. After a moment of uncertainty we decide to put out more chain to increase our scope but not so much as to risk swinging into our neighbors, who seem to be making a similar decision. Sun and sun-

downers disappear while the clouds on the horizon come closer. The wind changes direction and slowly increases in speed. Then a few stronger gusts show up, but we are still confident that this thing will be over soon, and we are worn out from the passage.

Unfortunately the wind direction keeps changing until the wind jet acceleration zone of the gigantic cliff of the neighboring island reaches our formerly idyllic anchoring spot. We suddenly understand why the island just south of us is called Fuerteventura; we are in for an adventure, all right, and in dire need of good luck.

We now find ourselves anchored on a lee shore with the waves quickly building. Our anchor chain is jerking extremely taut because the weight of the chain can no longer soften the violent jolts of the bow riding up on the waves. It feels almost as if our boat is hitting a concrete wall backward, over and over. Fearing the anchor might start to drag, the skipper decides to weigh anchor, and he goes forward to operate the windlass. His hand is almost cut off by the chain when he loosens the chain stopper, and then he discovers that the load on the windlass is more than it can handle: the circuit breaker cuts the current every time we engage the windlass.

We wonder how high the strain on the chain must be at this point. Will our anchor hold? What about the chain and the bolts holding the chain stopper on deck? The jolts at our anchor gear become heavier and heavier. It is time to start the engine and try to relieve this load, but the engine will not start. Suddenly our bow turns and the heavy jolts subside. We are adrift.

With no time to make sail, we broadcast a Mayday on VHF Channel 16, and the Spanish Coast Guard confirms our position and dispatches a rescue vessel. It will arrive in 45 minutes, but we have only 30 seconds before we hit the rocks at the shoreline. Our rudder hits first, followed immediately by a gush of water into the aft cabin. Then the entire hull is aground. The agonized scraping of the hull on the rocks soon becomes weaker as the water inside the cabin rises. Thank heaven we can all jump ashore relatively unharmed.

In reality, we (Erika and Achim) can thank heaven that we only witnessed the above scene and didn't have to experience it with our fellow cruisers. Having crossed from Gibraltar to the island of La Graciosa, northwest of Lanzarote in the Canary Islands, we uncharacteristically opted for the no-frills protection of the Caleta de Sebo docks, wanting to ease our reentry into the bluewater lifestyle by having easy shore access at this

landfall. As it turned out, the choice was fortuitous.

A violent scirocco blew through that night, and the next morning Achim climbed above Playa Francesa to document the scene with our camera. All it had taken was for one anchor to slip, and others had followed suit. Two sailboats were laid over on the rocks, their owners wringing their hands on the shoreline. Four other cruising yachts limped into the harbor after having sustained dings and breaks. We heard all their horror stories; in each case, unfortunate circumstances had made it impossible to flee the anchorage and escape damage.

Locals said this was a regular occurrence for visiting boats. It's almost impossible to know whether or not an anchorage will be safe. The best you can do is to consider the worst-case scenario when choosing whether to anchor or tie up.

Let's take a closer look at the forces involved when your boat surges and pitches

Off La Graciosa in the northern Canary Islands, the anchors of these two boats slipped and did not reset, with the result that both yachts drifted onto the rocks.

at anchor. The boat's accumulated kinetic energy can generate peak loads on ground tackle of up to several tons when the anchor rode becomes taut. The relevant formula is:

$$E = 0.5 \times M \times V^2$$

where

E = boat's kinetic energy in joules
   (1 joule = the work done by a force of 1 newton acting through a distance of 1 meter)

M = weight of the vessel in kilograms

V = velocity in meters per second
   (1 knot = 0.515 m/s)

When a 40-foot, 20,000-pound (9,000 kg) boat is hurled back on its ground tackle at 2 knots in a 30-knot breeze, the resultant momentary force is 4,770 joules or 3,500 foot-pounds.

$$4,770 = 0.5 \times 9,000 \text{ kg} \times (2 \times 0.515)^2$$

The best way to combat a force of such magnitude is to find a way to dampen it.

Picture a wave hitting an anchored boat. This results in a backward and upward movement of the hull, and the anchor rode comes taut and slows down the vessel's surge. In order for the ground tackle to immobilize the vessel, however, it must completely absorb this kinetic energy, and an anchor chain can only absorb kinetic energy when it is not already taut. To avoid short-term, dangerous peak loads on the anchor rode, we try to apply a negative acceleration in the opposite direction, first with the weight of the chain

catenary (the sag in the chain) and then with the nylon rode or snubbing line's elastic deformation. Having plenty of sag in the rode decreases shock loads and helps the anchor remain embedded by lessening the angle between the rode and anchor. When the anchor rode is flat on the seabed, all pulling force is horizontal, which is called the *ideal angle of zero*. As the load increases, it overcomes the weight of the rode and the angle becomes positive. This positive angle rode tugs on the anchor, trying to pull it out. If the load continues to increase, the catenary becomes a straight line, ultimately dislodging the anchor (see Appendix 1).

A well-dimensioned anchor rode will convert the entire kinetic energy of the surging vessel into potential energy. When the wave passes, the vessel accelerates forward again, propelled by the weight of chain and the elastic recovery of the nylon rode or snubber, and as it does potential energy is converted back into kinetic energy. Repetitions of this cycle result in a boat's characteristic back-and-forth motion at anchor.

A taut anchor chain without the influence of an elastic line section stops a boat's movement very abruptly, making the folks on board feel as if they've hit a harbor wall at a speed of 1 to 2 knots (see Table 2-2). In the worst cases, the shock load on the anchor gear exceeds its capacity, jerking the anchor out of the seafloor or breaking the chain or even the deck cleat. On a lee shore, this can lead to the loss of the boat. A length of three- or four-strand nylon rope added to an all-chain anchor rode will reduce the maximum shock load due to its elasticity.

The yacht on the right in the photo on page 11 was riding on this full-chain rode during the storm. Note the bent shaft of the CQR anchor on the right.

A simplified example shows how a boat's wave-induced kinetic energy affects the intermittent loads on its anchor and ground tackle. Imagine a 15,000-kilogram boat surging back on its anchor gear at a speed of 2 knots. Since $E = 0.5 \times M \times V^2$, the boat's kinetic energy will be 7,950 joules or 5,860 foot-pounds:

$$7{,}950 = 0.5 \times 15{,}000 \times (2 \times 0.515)^2$$

TABLE 2-2. KINETIC ENERGY (JOULES/FOOT-POUNDS) GENERATED BY BOATS SURGING AT VARIOUS SPEEDS

Weight of Boat (kg)	Speed (kn)			
	0.5	1	1.5	2
3,000	100/74	397/293	895/660	1,591/1,174
5,000	155/114	662/488	1,490/1,100	2,650/1,956
10,000	332/245	1,326/979	2,980/2,199	5,300/3,911
15,000	497/367	1,987/1,466	4,470/3,299	7,950/5,867

Suppose we're depending on a nylon rode section with a maximum stretch capacity of 2 meters to halt that surge. The relevant calculation then becomes:

$$\text{kinetic energy (joules)} \div$$
$$\text{distance (m)} = \text{force (newtons)}$$

The calculation for the additional load (over and above the wind-induced load) that must intermittently be withstood by the anchor, anchor rode, and deck gear is then:

$$7{,}950 \text{ joules} \div 2 \text{ m} =$$
$$3{,}975 \text{ newtons}$$
$$= 397.5 \text{ decanewtons (daN)}$$
$$= 895 \text{ pounds}$$

As if that weren't bad enough, the additional load due to the boat's kinetic energy would be twice as high with a nylon rode section that could stretch only 1 meter. It doesn't take an overactive imagination to picture an additional 1,790 pounds of load breaking out an anchor that is already under a load of, say, 1,600 pounds (see Table 2-1 for a wind of 30 knots blowing on a 50-foot boat), or perhaps even breaking the rode. Clearly, wave forces must be minimized, and these forces must be taken into account when we size an anchor and ground tackle, as we'll see in later chapters.

CURRENT FORCES

The loads exerted by currents are relatively insignificant. A 5-knot current (a rare occurrence in an anchorage) would impose a load of around 340 pounds (150 daN) on a 40-foot (12.2 m) boat.

Current loads deserve consideration, however, especially when you're anchoring in a river estuary or some other area subject to considerable tidal influence. When subjected to strong tidal currents, an anchored boat will swing successively in one direction, then the other. Checking tidal depth will allow you to ascertain if your boat will handle the swing at low tide without running aground.

Every anchor type reacts differently to directional changes in the drag force. Some anchors pivot in place without breaking free from the seafloor, realigning themselves to the new direction of pull. Others break loose but quickly reset themselves, while still others simply will not reset themselves efficiently once they have broken free. When the current changes direction, some anchors will foul their own rodes and lose most of their holding capacity. These factors will be discussed in the next chapter, where we compare the advantages and disadvantages of the most popular anchor models.

CHAPTER 3

Anchor Selection

Ever since humans started traversing treacherous bodies of water, they have also been trying to anchor their vessels with some sort of heavy object. At the same time, they have always been concerned with excess weight on board. The first anchors—discovered on Phoenician, Egyptian, and Polynesian wrecks dating back at least as far as the Bronze Age—consisted of a pierced rock with an attached line.

For millennia the holding power of an anchor was affected only by its weight; the

Anchoring is the best choice for ocean voyagers who want to avoid crowded marinas and keep their cruising kitty intact.

Polynesian anchor.

heavier the anchor, the better it held. Today we know that a modern aluminum anchor weighing 15 pounds (6.8 kg), when properly embedded, will provide the same holding power as a 1.5-ton block of concrete.

As ships increased in size, the need for lighter, more user-friendly, more efficient anchors increased as well, since passagemaking with a gigantic boulder on the bow was inconvenient at best. Innovative Phoenician mariners made the first technical advances in anchor design by placing pointed wooden rods on the bottoms of their stones. The result was the great-grandfather of the modern fluke

Phoenician anchor.

anchor, designed to hook into the seabed and thereby increase its holding power. Later, the wooden rods were replaced by iron stakes. Almost all of the later advances in portable anchor design have combined two elements: a penetrating point, or fluke, and a carefully modulated mass.

Cruising sailors and powerboaters should carry at least two anchors: a primary anchor that you trust to hold your boat in a challenging anchorage, and a secondary anchor to deploy as a backup when the primary won't do the job alone. While you're at it, it makes good sense to choose a different design for the secondary than you choose for the primary; that way, if the primary won't set properly in the anchorage, perhaps the secondary will. In addition, many boats carry a third, lighter anchor to use as a fair-weather "lunch hook," a stern anchor, a kedge anchor (deployed by dinghy), and for other occasional duties.

ANCHOR ANATOMY

All portable modern anchors have four parts in common:

1. One or more *flukes* (palms, arms, claw, or plow) to contact and dig into the seafloor.

2. A *shank*, the shaft or stem that is pulled to set (bury) the fluke (the fluke tip is known as the pee, point, or bill).

3. A *crown* (or base or heel) that connects the fluke(s) to the shaft.

4. The anchor *ring* (or eye or shackle), by means of which the anchor is attached to the rode.

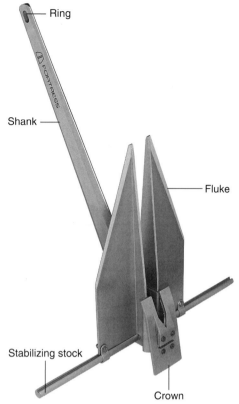

- Ring
- Shank
- Fluke
- Stabilizing stock
- Crown

The anatomy of an anchor.

Most modern anchors also have a tripping ring or eye, usually in the crown. A line fastened to this eye helps pull the anchor out of a fouled situation in the reverse direction.

Some anchors have a *stock*, a rod at the top of the shank that is situated perpendicular to the flukes. The stock provides roll stability and positions the flukes properly for entrenchment. Other models—such as the Bügel, Rocna, SARCA, and Manson Supreme—employ a roll bar to achieve the same goal. Ballast on the fluke tip can also help keep the fluke pointing downward for proper setting.

Many manufacturers claim that their anchors are highly effective on all seabeds, but the truth is that most anchors work better in some sediments than in others. Further, no matter how versatile an anchor is, it will not hold on an impenetrable, concrete-like seafloor. If the seafloor is very soft—such as mud with a high water content—almost any anchor will bury itself but may not hold well. If the seabed is hard sand, some anchors will skip and slide over the bottom, others will bury partially but not hold, and still others will bury themselves completely and hold to maximum capacity. Our objective in what follows is to show which anchors perform best in which bottom sediments, and why. An anchor's effectiveness and versatility depend on several characteristics:

- **Efficiency of setting.** A good anchor should fall on the seafloor properly positioned for ideal penetration. The directional pull of the rode should facilitate the anchor's proper setting in the seafloor, and the anchor should set as quickly and thoroughly as possible.

- **Holding power with unidirectional load.** Once well set in the seafloor, the anchor should offer sufficient holding power to resist heavy loads from the vessel due to wind and waves. If the load on an anchor exceeds the holding capacity of the sediment in which it is planted, the anchor should slowly "drift" through the sediment while maintaining its maximum holding power, never breaking free from the seafloor.

- **Holding power with multidirectional load.** If a shift in wind or current direction occurs, an anchor should remain buried while slowly pivoting to align with the new direction of load, rather than breaking free and then having to reset.

Further considerations include ease of stowage, ease of positioning on a bow roller, strength of construction, resistance to fouling, ease of freeing with a trip line if it becomes fouled, and—of course—price.

Table 3-1 provides an overview of major anchor categories and what we regard as their

TABLE 3-1. RECOMMENDED APPLICATIONS FOR REPRESENTATIVE ANCHOR TYPES

Category	Brand-Name Example(s)	Material	Recommended Application	Roll-Stable	Stowability
Classic, traditional, fisherman	Luke	Steel	Rock	Yes	Difficult
Plow	CQR	Forged steel	Mud, sand	No	Easy on bow roller
Plow	Delta	Steel	Mud, sand	Yes	Easy on bow roller
Plate	Danforth	Steel	Sand	No	Easy to stow on deck or in locker; difficult on bow roller
Plate	Bulwagga	Steel	Mud, sand, weed	Yes	Medium
Plate	Fortress	Aluminum	Sand	No	Easy to stow on deck or in locker
Concave	Spade	Steel or aluminum	Mud, sand, weed	Yes	Easy on bow roller
Concave	Sword	Steel	Mud, sand, weed	Yes	Easy on bow roller
Roll bar	Bügel	Steel	Mud, sand, weed	Yes	Medium on bow roller
Concave/roll bar	Rocna, Manson Supreme	Steel	Mud, sand, weed	Yes	Medium on bow roller
Claw	Bruce	Steel	Sand, weed	Yes	Easy on bow roller

suitable applications. Others might prefer to classify the Spade, Sword, Bügel, Rocna, and Manson Supreme as plow anchors, and they might prefer the term "pivoting-fluke anchor" to "plate anchor" when speaking of the Danforth, Bulwagga, and Fortress, but the method in our classifications will, we hope, become clear as this chapter unfolds.

TRADITIONAL ANCHORS

One way to survey the range of anchor types would be to explore each major category in turn, tracing the developments within that category. We have chosen instead to make a chronological survey across all categories, starting with the historical types and then tracing later developments and refinements more or less in their order of occurrence. By traditional anchors we mean those anchor styles that were available to boaters prior to the 1970s. Later we will turn to the new generation of anchors that has appeared since the 1970s and address in various ways one of the principal limitations of the traditional alternatives—their tendency to capsize, or roll, and thus to dislodge under strain.

Classic Stock Anchor (Fisherman)

Telemark skis, quill pens, kerosene lamps, stock anchors: this listing of iconic objects includes the anchor type that is tattooed on thousands of arms—and it's the one you see on beer labels, in jewelry, and on T-shirts. There is a place for the classic fisherman anchor (also called the yachtsman's anchor) in museums and in the hearts of romantic mariners worldwide.

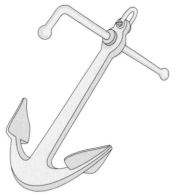

Classic stock anchor.

The fisherman employs a stock at the upper end of the shank that is perpendicular to the fluke arms as well as to the shank. The stock has a dual purpose. First, it prevents the anchor from settling on the bottom with its fluke points horizontal, which would discourage either fluke from digging in. Second, it is intended to prevent the anchor from capsizing under strain and thus releasing its fluke from the bottom. A variant of this anchor enjoyed an excellent reputation in the British sailing navy and came to be known as the Admiralty anchor. Other very similar variants include the Herreshoff and the Luke styles.

The fisherman is rarely deployed on large ships but is still seen on smaller craft. The ratio of holding capacity to weight in sand or mud is not high, but the fisherman can be useful on foul bottoms—rock, kelp, or heavy weed—that other anchors will fail to penetrate and "grab" into.

Historically, the fisherman anchors were often used as *kedge anchors*. A kedge anchor is usually smaller than a main anchor, and an unmotorized vessel could use a pair of kedges to move in and out of harbors and anchorages when there was no favorable wind. One kedge would be rowed away from the vessel in a longboat or rowboat and launched. The vessel could then be moved along by hauling in the anchor rode while the second kedge was deployed. The operation could be repeated as many times as needed until the vessel achieved its desired position.

Today, any anchor light enough to be deployed by a dinghy can be used as a kedge anchor. You might deploy a kedge abeam to windward so that your boat will rest more lightly on the windward face of a fuel dock, or you might deploy it as a second anchor under certain circumstances. You might also run a line from a kedge anchor to your masthead to try to heel your vessel enough to refloat it after a grounding (see Chapter 7).

There are lots of uses for a kedge anchor, but today's kedge is a lot more likely to be a plate anchor, as opposed to a fisherman. Its shape and weight make the fisherman difficult to handle over the bow, and it is prone to fouling on occasion. It can be disassembled, but even in disassembled form, it is rather cumbersome and a challenge to stow.

The stock anchor's symbolic value may far outweigh its comparative holding power. Still, in anchorages worldwide, you can always find a mariner who loves his trusty fisherman.

Modified Stock Anchor

Several variations of the stock anchor have been developed to improve burying, holding power, and convenience. One, the American-invented Northill, has a removable stock, which makes it easier to stow. Unlike the fisherman, the stock is at the crown end of the shaft with the flukes, rather than the opposite end. When used in mud or sand, the stock can act as an extra fluke, increasing the holding power of the anchor. This configuration does, however, make the anchor more difficult to deploy. It can foul anchor lines due to the projecting flukes, and, as with other stock anchors, it may offer insufficient holding in sand and mud due to its small fluke area.

The stainless steel Pekny comes disassembled, with two flukes sliding into a massive sleeve at the lower end of a round stock. The Pekny design allows for interchangeable flukes depending on anchoring conditions: flukes with sharp, reinforced edges are used for coral; extra-large flukes are used for mud bottoms; middle-sized flukes are used for most other conditions.

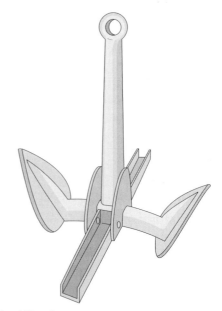

Northill anchor.

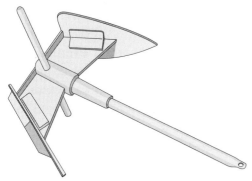

Pekny anchor.

Hall anchor.

Pivoting Stockless Anchors

Ruggedly constructed and of simple design, these anchors consist of a heavy head in which the crown, tripping palms, and flukes are forged in one piece. They do not have a stock (or crossbar)—hence the name *stockless*.

The design allows for relatively easy handling, hoisting, and stowing on a large vessel, since the stockless shaft can be pulled up through a hullside hawsehole. When the anchor is lowered and dragged across the bottom, the shoulders catch and push the flukes downward and into the bottom. Because an upward pull on the shank has a tendency to break out the flukes, a long scope of chain must be used to keep the pull horizontal when the anchor is set. Stockless anchors rely primarily on their tremendous deadweight and large amount of scope for holding power.

The first successful stockless pivoting anchor was the Navy stockless, introduced in 1821. Its fluke arms are articulated so as to pivot up to 45° from either side of the shank. The Navy stockless is still used today on large vessels and has inspired countless variations, among them the Hall and Pool anchors

shown here. These stockless anchors are not suitable for smaller vessels, since the required weight of the anchor would be prohibitive, but you may see a stockless anchor weighing anywhere from 110 pounds (50 kg) to 5,500 pounds (2,500 kg) on a large commercial vessel.

Another early stockless design, rarely used today, was the Porter anchor (see illustration next page). In this design the arms were formed in one piece and pivoted at the crown on a bolt passing through the forked shank.

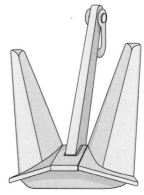

Pool anchor.

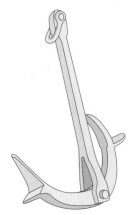

Porter anchor.

The CQR

Legend has it that in 1933, Cambridge professor Geoffrey Taylor conceived the first plow anchor, the CQR (the name being a faux acronym for secure), to outfit World War II hot-air balloon missions. This anchor's symmetrical twin flukes are shaped like back-to-back plowshares. The CQR offered improved performance over its predecessors and contemporaries; it penetrated more dependably than plate anchors like the Danforth (see opposite) and was less prone to capsize and dislodge under load.

CQR anchor.

Although the CQR performs well in mud, gravel, and sand, it relies primarily on static penetration of the bottom (see the How Anchors Set section later in this chapter) and often has difficulty penetrating weedy or compact seafloors. Many CQR owners feel that their anchors perform well in diverse bottoms—hooking rocks and penetrating loose sand and gravel—but fewer seem satisfied with the CQR's performance in weed or hard sand. Because it has no projecting flukes, the CQR is less prone than a plate anchor to foul anchor rodes. It usually breaks out quickly when desired, and a trip line can be added to the eye on the back of the horn to make breakout even easier in case of fouling.

Like other plow and claw anchors, including those that we classify as *concave-fluke* and *roll-bar anchors*, these anchors require bow rollers, without which they are awkward to handle and difficult to stow.

The CQR is distinguished from more recently developed plow anchors (discussed below) in part by the hinge at the base of its shank. This design was to allow the shank to pivot laterally in response to modest current and wind shifts while the flukes remain buried. The CQR and its numerous hinged-shank imitators (some better-designed and built than others) still enjoy immense popularity today. This originates from the fact that the CQR was the first serious alternative to traditional anchors for small boats, and as such the articulated plow won a dominant market share that lasted over fifty years. Even today its reputation as the "anchor of choice" is still hard to knock, particularly among traditionalists. But in our opinion, newer designs have rendered it out of date.

Pivoting-Fluke Stock Anchors

Also known as twin-points, the most famous variation of the Navy stockless was developed in the United States by Richard S. Danforth and Bob Ogg in 1939. The anchor was designed for use on seaplanes and to anchor the famous landing barges that stormed the beaches of Normandy on D-Day in World War II, so the Danforth anchor needed to be light enough not to overburden a small plane, and light enough for troops to deploy by hand on Normandy's shores while under withering machine-gun fire.

The Danforth was the first modern anchor to use plate flukes with a large surface area to increase holding power—and was thus the first in the category we call *plate anchors*. Relatively easy to manufacture, its thin twin plates (flat galvanized-steel polygons)

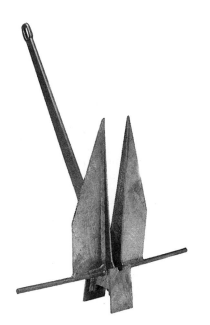

Danforth anchor.

bury readily in soft sand and mud. Instead of a stock through the head of the anchor, the Danforth has a round rod through the crown.

Since holding power depends largely on an anchor's embedded surface area, plate anchors offer high holding power with relatively low weight—but only when properly buried. These anchors are thus especially useful when they can be set by hand. They make fine kedge anchors in soft or sandy bottoms and can perform well when not subjected to changes of pulling direction—for example, when a boat is anchored Bahamian style or with anchors from both the bow and stern (see Chapter 7).

Due to their relatively shallow angle of penetration, however, pivoting-fluke anchors can be hard to set in compact sand or weedy seafloors, and if the flukes are caked with mud or clay the Danforth may take time to reset after being broken out of the bottom by a pitching boat, or may not reset at all. Because of its many protruding parts, the anchor may also foul its own rode, especially when only partially buried or when wind or current changes direction.

The Danforth's pivoting flukes make the anchor easier to stow flat in an anchor locker, but they also make the anchor awkward to handle. Just ask anyone who has handled a large Danforth on a pitching deck and has been hit in the shin by its dagger-like fluke. On the seabed, a small pebble or a piece of seaweed lodged between the pivoting flukes and shank is all it takes to block the fluke in one position, reducing the likelihood of proper setting.

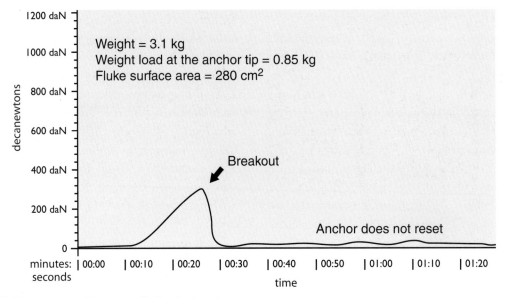

Holding power and breakout of a Danforth anchor.

Since the expiration of the Danforth patents, other notable variations of the stock-stabilized, pivoting-fluke anchor have emerged, among them the Seasense and the West Marine Traditional. One early derivative, the FOB, was created in 1956 by Armand Colin and FOB Forges et Outillages, in Brittany, France. A massive heel was added to this

Origin of the Anchor Holding-Power Diagrams

In the Mediterranean, most liveaboard sailors stow their sails during the winter and hibernate in one of the many marinas. In 1997, Alain selected the marina of Monastir in Tunisia, where he had the chance to meet Albert Tardy, an avid sailor and professor at the prestigious French engineering school, École Nationale Supérieure d'Arts et Métiers. Albert had been attached to the engineering school of Monastir, where they met and talked about anchors.

Alain showed Albert his new design, and he was very interested. They decided to execute a scientific, comparative test of anchors and compare that data to Alain's new design. This idea was given as a thesis subject to one student, and this was the first successful test of this anchor. A very small prototype (3 kg) was pulled in sand. It broke the 12 mm nylon rope several times. Using an 18 mm rope, the

anchor finally bent at 1,500 daN of holding. The Spade was born.

The diagrams in this chapter were done as a part of that study in conjunction with the École Nationale d'Ingénieurs de Monastir (ENIM), Monastir, Tunisia. The study, entitled "Analytical and Experimental Study of Marine Anchors," was performed on relatively hard sand. The anchors were set in the water and pulled nearly horizontally from the beach with 90 feet of hybrid rode.

In these anchor holding-power diagrams, using the one opposite that shows the holding power and breakout of a Britany anchor as an example, the Y-axis shows the anchor's holding power in decanewtons (daN) and the X-axis shows the drag time, which is proportional to the dragged distance. This anchor holds, dislodges, regains hold, and dislodges again to display an unstable "corkscrew" behavior. (Note that the Britany anchor is not available in the United States.)

Plate anchor with a substantial heel.

Older FOB model with a substantial heel.

anchor to lift the back of the fluke for a better penetration angle. In 1963, the stock disappeared, giving us the model that is still on the market today. This anchor type is still popular with small craft under 25 feet, especially when the main anchor necessitates deployment by hand.

In 1961, Colin created a second derivative called the Trigrip, which was followed by the Bigrip in 1962. The fluke shape on this anchor prevented small rocks from wedging between the flukes and the shank. In 1972 the Bigrip evolved into the Britany anchor, which, with slight modifications, is still

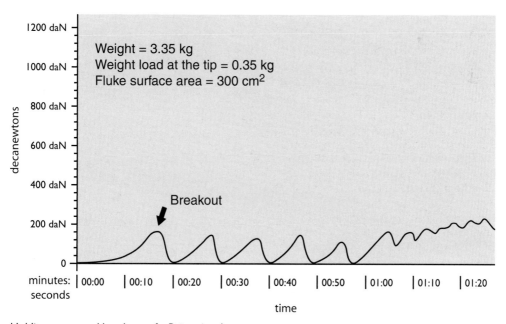

Holding power and breakout of a Britany anchor.

widely sold today, although it is not available in the United States.

Whether made of steel or aluminum, most pivoting-fluke or plate anchors (also known as *articulating anchors*) present similar virtues and problems, and looming large among the latter is *roll stability*. This is the anchor's tendency to break free of the bottom in a "corkscrew" manner when under load (roll stability is discussed later in this chapter). One anchor that attempts to solve the roll-stability problem of plate anchors is the Bulwagga. American engineer Peter Mele designed this odd-looking but clever anchor with a third fluke. The three flukes, set 120° from each other, ensure that at least two will always be embedded in the seafloor even if the anchor starts rotating under load. This

Bulwagga anchor.

anchor sets quite rapidly and offers a strong hold. It also seems to penetrate a weedy bottom better than any other plate anchor on the market.

Lightweight Anchors

Pivoting-fluke stock anchors made of light metal alloys rather than steel are known as lightweight anchors. The most renowned of

Fortress anchor. In its disassembled form, make sure to keep all five parts together! The angle of the fluke is adjustable from 32° to 45°.

these is the Fortress, produced in an aluminum/magnesium alloy and weighing about 40% less than a galvanized steel Danforth anchor of similar size. A few minutes with a screwdriver allow you to adjust the Fortress's fluke angle from 32° to 45°, which should optimize holding power for sand, shell, or soft mud bottoms. The Guardian anchor, manufactured by the same company, is a simplified, less expensive version of the Fortress without the adjustable flukes. As with the Danforth, the Fortress is popular among small craft, as it can easily be deployed by hand and stowed in a bow locker or on a pulpit.

Miscellaneous Anchors

This category includes anchors whose proper uses do not include securing boats of any size to the seabed. First among these are folding pocket anchors, which are easily broken down and stored. They work satisfactorily for small craft such as centerboard dinghies, tenders, and personal watercraft, but are not appropriate for boats any larger than that.

Grapnel anchors work on the ancient concept of a grappling hook: multiple points on separate hooked arms radiate from a common axis, so at least one point will always face the bottom. A folding grapnel, however, is not even an anchor in the strict sense of the word, and its holding power is comparatively weak. It may come in handy for temporary reef and wreck anchoring for a dinghy, but we do not recommend using one as the primary anchor even for your tender. Contrary to common belief, the grapnel is less effective than most other anchors on weedy bottoms. Many boaters still use the grapnel for small boats and inflatable dinghies, especially since the four-fluke design cannot puncture the fabric when folded.

When gunkholing in shallow waters or navigating in mangrove swamps, the grapnel can be wedged between tree trunks or roots,

Folding anchor.

Grapnel anchor.

between rocky slabs, or in thick brush. The grapnel is also very handy when you need to free your anchor rode from another anchor rode (see Chapter 7).

ROLL-STABLE NEW-GENERATION ANCHORS

Since the mid- to late 1970s there has been a proliferation of new and modified anchor designs. These developments have paralleled the growth of boating worldwide. As fiberglass production boats brought boating within the means of the middle class, the demand grew for anchors that were comparatively light, quick setting, easy to stow and handle, and reliable. In particular, most new-generation anchors are designed one way or another to be roll stable—that is, to resist capsizing and subsequent dislodging under load.

Claw Anchors

Contrary to popular belief, the only similarity between the U-formed, three-palmed scoop used by many pleasure boaters and the enormous anchors that have moored oil platforms in the North Sea is the name of their designer, Peter Bruce. This versatile design has become a popular option for smaller boats since its arrival on the boating scene in the late 1970s. Since the original Bruce anchor patent expired (the genuine Bruce anchor is no longer manufactured), the Claw, Horizon, Manson Ray, Super Max, and other claw anchors have appeared on the market.

A claw anchor buries similarly to a large scoop—just like a chisel does in wood (see the discussion of penetration angles later in this

Bruce anchor.

chapter)—and is known for the speed with which it penetrates the seabed. It is excellent for a variety of bottoms—even including rock, coral, and weed—but provides limited holding in soft sand and mud. It can be self-launched, free falling from a bow roller.

When deployed, the claw first rests on one side of its trefoil, and the subsequent horizontal drag then causes at least one fluke to embed. The anchor breaks out with relatively little effort due to the positive leverage of its design. Its one-piece construction includes no welds or movable points to bend, jam, or break, and it stows easily on a bow roller, though not on deck. It has a reputation for remaining embedded with tide or wind changes, slowly turning in the bottom to align with the new direction of load.

American Andy Peabody designed the claw-style Super Max with an adjustable shaft to optimize its penetration angle for various sediment types: 19° for compact sand or coral, 32° for mud, and 45° for soft mud and heterogeneous seafloors. Peabody has also developed a nonpivoting model, the Super

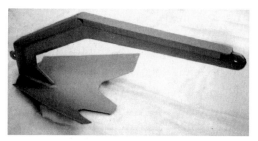

Super Max anchor.

FOB Rock anchor.

Max Rigid Anchor. This anchor penetrates and holds very well, and when the wind or current changes direction, it realigns itself readily without drifting or losing its hold.

New-Generation Plow Designs

The Delta anchor was created by Simpson-Lawrence (now part of Lewmar), manufacturer of the original plow, the CQR. Unlike the CQR, the Delta is a one-piece anchor with a nonarticulating steel shank. Thus the Delta is much lighter than the CQR, and it also offers improved penetration and setting performance due to its ballasted fluke tip. (Some 28% of the anchor's total weight is in the tip, one of the highest proportions on the

market.) Kept on a bow roller, the anchor can be deployed with an electric windlass, without manual intervention. When under heavy load, it drifts slowly through the sediment while maintaining an excellent hold.

The many Delta variations include the FOB Rock, the Kingston QuickSet, the Shark, the Davis Talon XT, and the Kobra. The Kobra is easy to stow under deck as the shank detaches from the fluke with one screw, making it practical for use on day boats that require a proper anchor but are short of storage space.

Concave-Fluke Anchors

Though similar in profile to plow anchors, and though frequently categorized as such, these anchors are distinguished from plows by the concave upper surface of their flukes.

Delta anchor.

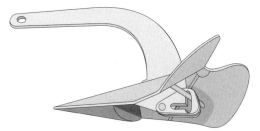

Kobra anchor.

This shape gives concave-fluke anchors—sometimes called scoop anchors—a high holding capacity and good stability. The fluke's penetration angle (similar to that of a wood chisel) and sharp edges allow these concave anchors to dig in readily even in such difficult seafloors as compact sand, coral, and seaweed mats. The Spade, for example, digs quickly into coral sand and does not have to be dragged a long distance across the seafloor before it gains hold. This is helpful when you are trying to anchor in a sandy spot between coral heads.

Developed by Alain Poiraud, the Spade has the most heavily ballasted tip of any anchor on the market, with approximately 48% of its total weight in the tip. Regardless of how it falls on the seabed, it positions itself for optimal penetration as soon as tension is put on the rode. The little skid at the root of the blade helps drive the penetrating edge of the fluke into the seabed.

The Spade's shank (with the exception of the 6 kg model) is fabricated from plate and is hollow. This is because, pound for pound,

a stronger shape can be constructed in this fashion than in the solid plate or cast steel shank used by other anchors. This helps place more of the anchor's weight in the tip.

The Spade is available in galvanized steel, stainless steel, and aluminum. The aluminum version offers identical holding power at half the weight but does not set as well as the steel versions in hard sand because of its lower tip weight. You can disassemble the Spade into shank and blade for long-term stowage, although it is best stowed on a bow roller.

The Sword anchor was also developed by Alain Poiraud and has the same concave fluke. In lieu of a ballasted tip, however, the Sword derives its tip weight and pressure from the fact that the shank is mounted closer to the tip. Its setting behavior is similar to a Spade.

The Sword also offers an adjustable setting angle for different sea bottoms—34° for sand and 45° for mud—without any changes to the anchor and without detaching the chain. To adjust the setting angle, you simply pass the chain through a second shackle located at a specified position along the curved shank of the anchor. The Sword's

Spade anchor.

Sword anchor.

This embedding sequence of a Sword anchor begins just after the anchor is set on the seabed. As soon as a pulling force is exerted on the shaft, the anchor turns with its tip into the seafloor. After a while the pulling force drags the anchor into the seabed until the blade disappears.

curved shank with its high vertical profile also helps roll the anchor into an upright embedding position.

Roll-Bar Anchors

These anchors, too, could be and often are categorized as plow anchors, but they are operationally distinct. The first roll-bar anchor, the Bügel, was conceived by German inventor Rolf Kaczirek to combine simplicity and efficiency. The trademark arch of a bar above its fluke is designed to prevent the anchor from inverting onto its back, and it orients the anchor to the correct attitude on the seabed. The fluke features a tapered, optimal chisel penetration angle. This anchor sets rapidly in most seafloors and generates a

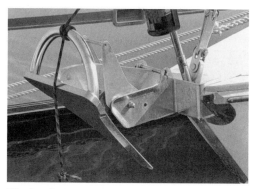

Bügel anchor.

holding power superior to that of unstabilized anchor models. Due to its lesser tip weight, however, it can be difficult to set properly in hard sand.

To penetrate, the Bügel relies mainly on the rode's pull on the anchor shank to generate torque, a rotating force on the blade. Under heavy loads that exceed its maximum holding capacity, a Bügel anchor drags slowly, without disengaging.

The Bügel is available in galvanized steel or stainless steel and enjoys an excellent reputation. It is particularly popular among European mariners. Owing to its simple construction, many homebuilt and unprofessional knockoffs abound and you must be careful to avoid purchasing a poor-quality version.

The illustration next page shows the holding power of a roll-bar anchor as a function of time when placed under heavy load. Notice the quick initial increase in holding power, reflecting efficient penetration of the seafloor. Under heavy load, the anchor drifts while retaining its holding power and without dislodging. This is an important safety asset.

The Rocna combines the Bügel's roll bar with the Spade's concave fluke. Its

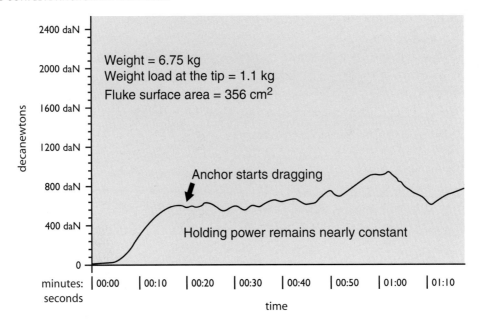

Holding power of a roll-bar anchor.

New Zealand designer, Peter Smith, considered tip ballasting inefficient; instead, he allocated the saved weight to the blade area, structural reinforcement, and the roll bar itself.

Like the Spade, this anchor also features skids on the heel of the blade, which are intended to aid during the setting procedure. They keep the heel elevated while the toe cuts into the seabed; this, combined with the rode pull, produces a turning moment that rights the anchor and causes it to bury quickly.

Instead of dedicated tip ballast, the Rocna employs heavier plate at the toe, which adds strength there.

The Rocna's shank is similar to that of a Delta, but its inside profile is slightly different in that the crown section creates a tight angle against your boat's bow roller. This is intended to ensure a snug seat on the roller and prevent movement at sea.

Rocna anchor. (Courtesy Rocna Anchors)

Other similar roll-bar anchors, including the Manson Supreme and the SARCA, incorporate a slotted shank, the purpose of which is to allow easy retrieval if the anchor gets jammed in a coral reef, under a rock, or under some other submarine obstacle. (Note: This should not be taken to imply that anchoring on coral reefs is *ever* acceptable. Anchoring on coral is illegal virtually everywhere in the world—and for good reason, given the massive worldwide coral reef die-offs. Try to imagine what even a perfect "reef anchor" could do to a protected Elkhorn coral.)

We are not big fans of the slotted shank for two reasons: it weakens the shaft, and the shackle may jam in the slot, decreasing the feature's effectiveness. Furthermore, it may work when you don't want it to—for example, when your boat drifts over the top of the anchor in the middle of the night and the wind pipes up from the opposite direction. Slotted shanks have been used on other

SARCA anchor.

anchors in the past, including Danforth variations—but never with much success.

The SARCA (an acronym for Sand and Reef Combination Anchor) is an Australian design. It is essentially a highly modified plow with a convex fluke. The SARCA's roll bar is thinner than that of the Bügel, and we wonder whether that will impede its performance in soft mud.

WHAT TO LOOK FOR IN AN ANCHOR

When selecting your main, or primary, anchor, choose one that handles a wide variety of bottoms. For changing winds and tides, your main anchor must be able to break free without fouling your anchor rode, and then be capable of resetting itself quickly. Other characteristics to consider include bow-roller fit, ease of stowage and transport, and ease of handling. In light of these considerations, we join Chuck Hawley (see the sidebar on page 36) in recommending a fixed-shank plow (such as the Delta) or a roll-stable plow derivative (i.e., a concave-fluke

Manson Supreme anchor. (Courtesy Manson Anchors)

or roll-bar anchor) as the primary anchor on any boat big enough to stow such an anchor on a bow roller. We recommend that this anchor be steel, simply because steel is stronger than aluminum.

For a boat that's too small to carry such an anchor on the bow, you'll probably choose a plate anchor (Danforth, Bulwagga, Fortress, or West Marine Traditional), despite its previously enumerated limitations, for its light weight, high holding-to-weight ratio,

and ease of stowing in an anchor locker. Again, however, you'd do well to make your primary anchor steel.

You'll want a secondary anchor for those times when the primary anchor either can't do the job alone or can't seem to set in the seabed. For serious cruising your secondary ought to have as much holding power as your primary, in case you lose your primary or have to cut it loose in an emergency. It makes sense to choose a different type for your

A spare anchor for emergency purposes can come in handy for offshore cruising sailboats. To keep the weight as close to the center of gravity as possible, the spare anchor should be securely fastened with a bolt, nut, and washer to a bulkhead, like this Delta anchor.

secondary than for your primary. For example, if your primary is a plow, concave-fluke, or roll-bar anchor, your secondary might be a claw anchor. If your boat is small enough to have a plate anchor as its primary, you'll probably want a plate anchor for the secondary as well. Regardless of your choice for a secondary, you could make it aluminum if a lighter anchor is a priority. (Some people *must* have lightweight anchors or they could not use their vessels. Our sixty-year-old friend Evi singlehands her 40-foot sloop and loves it—but she could not do so without her lightweight anchor.)

And finally, you'll want a third, lighter anchor to use as a fair-weather lunch hook, as an occasional stern anchor, as a kedge to hold the boat off a fuel dock while fueling, or to kedge the vessel afloat when it runs aground. This anchor is likely to be a plate anchor, since you're concerned above all with ease of handling on deck, ease of deployment in a dinghy, and high straight-line holding power. (Bear in mind, too, that a plate anchor may give better holding in soft mud than a claw, plow, or plow derivative, so if you anchor frequently in soft mud, you might want a plate anchor for your secondary.) If your secondary anchor is a plate anchor, you may not need this third anchor.

Beware of cheap imitations of anchors whose patents have expired. Numerous look-alikes of longtime favorites such as the CQR, the Bruce, and the Danforth abound, and some of these are badly manufactured from softer steel instead of high-test, quality steel. Some, too, have components—

The shaft of this cheaply manufactured copy of the classic original plow design was connected to the plow with a (useless) hinge. The soft steel plow broke off where the hole for the articulation joint was drilled.

particularly the shank—that are laminated from several thin layers of steel rather than being cast in one solid piece. Solid plate is far stronger than a laminate that is fused only at the welds around the edges. Pinholing in the weld joints allows moisture between the plates, with obvious consequences, and in the galvanizing process for steel anchors the pickling acid can get between the plates and create "bleeding" and other long-term problems. Solid plate can make an anchor more expensive because it is more difficult to work, but an anchor with solid-plate components is greatly superior in the long run.

Having chosen an anchor model, you have to choose an appropriate size. This in many ways is the hardest question of all. We'll return to that topic after we look in greater detail at how anchors set and how they hold.

35

A Lifetime of Anchor Testing
by Chuck Hawley

As a consequence of having worked for West Marine for the last twenty-five years, I have been fortunate to have participated in many anchor tests, including those sponsored by magazines such as *Practical Sailor* and *SAIL*, those sponsored by manufacturers such as Nav-X Corporation [now Fortress Marine Anchors], and those initiated by West Marine. I've also met and interviewed many of the pioneers in the science of anchoring yachts, including Robert Danforth Ogg, Peter Bruce, Gordon Lyall, Robert Smith, and others. I mention this in an attempt to anticipate accusations from readers that I have a vested interest in this subject: it's true, I have a very vested interest in the subject!

Few topics generate as many strongly held opinions as those related to anchoring: what type of anchor, what type of rode, how much scope, how to use two anchors, how large an anchor, etc. In the paragraphs that follow, I've attempted to distill what I have learned about anchors and anchoring, and to point out what I don't know (yet).

1. I believe that a boat's primary anchor should be a single-point anchor like the Delta (plow style) or the Spade/Rocna/Manson Supreme (concave-fluke and roll-bar styles). These anchors combine high holding power and stability with brute strength, all of which are important attributes of an anchor. I am purposely leaving the CQR off this list, despite its incredible reputation and widespread use, since I believe that more modern designs like those listed above have now proven superior. Fixed-shank single-fluke anchors do not suffer from the asymmetrical loading caused by different seabed densities and junk that lies beneath the surface to the same degree that Danforth-style anchors are impacted. This is especially true in sand littered with rocks or randomly strewn junk.

2. Danforth-type anchors with the traditional wide stock do appear to be more stable—i.e., less prone to rolling out of the bottom—than more recent copies in which the stock is arbitrarily shortened. This had long been the assertion of Bob Ogg, the inventor. When we

tested an otherwise great-performing European Danforth copy, we were surprised to see the entire anchor emerge from the bottom, stock vertical, after being thoroughly buried for several feet!

3. I have had mixed results with the Bruce anchor and its copies. In our local sand bottom, we obtain holding powers of just 320 pounds with an 11-pound Bruce, compared with 1,100 pounds with a 14-pound Delta. I believe that the favorable reputation that the Bruce enjoys comes from three of its properties: structural strength, quick bottom engagement, and reliable holding. What I think it lacks is absolute holding power, especially in mud. (I am also concerned about the quality of the Bruce copies for two reasons: some do not appear to be true to the original Bruce dimensions; and since the anchor is cast, the heat treating has to be done correctly.)

4. My experience confirms that many relatively new anchor designs—despite their national advertising, strong statements from their inventors, and great boat show sales pitches—do not work. They either:

    a. fail to engage the bottom

    b. distort under load

    c. are not stable when pulled for a period of time and "pop out"

    d. will foul if the boat swings

    Any of these failures can overwhelm a new anchor's attractive attributes (lightness, design concepts, low cost) and render it undesirable. Many new designs show great promise, however, and these include the Spade, Manson Supreme, Bulwagga, Rocna, HydroBubble, and others.

5. I have broken and bent many anchors during the course of our tests, but in fairness to the manufacturers, I won't mention them in print. I will say, however, that straight-line holding power achieved by large surface area, but without the requisite structural strength to ensure that the anchor remains in its intended shape, makes a

dangerous combination. Several anchors in our tests have held well initially but have failed when the tension has been increased modestly or when the anchor has been set and then pulled a second time.

Peter Bruce told me something in the late 1980s that has always stuck with me. He said, "Chuck, I would never want to be the defendant in a court of law in a case where my anchor is being blamed for the loss of a boat. Looking over at the plaintiff's table, there can be three situations: either they have no anchor, in which case I may win the trial; or they have an undamaged anchor, in which case I may win the trial; or they have a portion of an anchor, in which instance I will surely lose the trial."

6. I've tested many anchors that copy the designs of popular anchors but fail to replicate their performance. Recently we tested anchors that appeared to be identical to the 8-pound Danforth Standard anchor, including West Marine's popular Traditional 8 along with some Chinese and American copies that were sent to us for testing. The appearance of the Chinese and American copies was so similar to our Traditional 8 that, if not for the label on our anchor, we could have mixed them up. Testing, however, proved that the devil, as always, is in the details. The West Marine Traditional 8-pound anchor held twice to about 600 pounds of tension and twice to over 1,000 pounds. The anchor copies never held to more than 60 pounds of load—and even that, we suspect, was due more to the 20 feet of chain dragging on the sand bottom than to the anchors themselves. We tried to set all anchors four times: the "real" anchors set each time, but the copies never set. Upon further examination, we always found that the copies differed in some critical dimension that we had overlooked initially. That is exactly why Bob Ogg was such a stickler on the precision with which anchors have to be manufactured in order to work properly.

7. In a series of tests that were cosponsored by SAIL and Power & Motoryacht magazines, we were able to pull anchors in the 25- to 45-pound range at tensions up to 5,000 pounds using a large commercial vessel. This is a much greater load than we can achieve with West Marine's 26-foot lobster boat, and we learned a tremendous amount over the course of three days of testing. We were very pleased to see that several new, promising designs (generally fixed-shank plow-type anchors, including what Alain Poiraud calls concave-fluke and roll-bar anchors) had great holding power, strength, speed of setting, and other positive attributes. However, as in past tests, nagging problems persisted in our abilities to describe the results. For example:

- In the location we selected for the test, many popular anchors backed by extensive previous testing failed to set. The bottom was fine-grain gray sand, and previous tests had shown that most anchors could "get a grip." However, we had consistent problems with five anchors, which once again proves that a variety of anchor types is necessary to improve the odds of finding an anchor that works in the specific conditions you may encounter. It also proves that you cannot put too much faith in any one test, no matter how carefully it is concocted to be fair and conclusive.

- Unless you have a diver on the bottom who can communicate with those on the surface, it is very hard to understand what is actually happening underwater. Despite the use of GPS and shore-based ranges, we had a very hard time determining when the anchors were dragging and when they were stationary. (In this case, we had a diver for this purpose, but the water was so turbid it was nearly impossible to see the anchor!)

- Despite using a vessel displacing more than 50,000 pounds, we were unable to keep the rode from "surging" the vessel back and forth as power was applied. We experienced cyclical loads that varied by 1,000 pounds, and anchors that disengaged from the seabed did so during one of the tension "peaks." We had a hard time determining where on our tension graphs to pick the ultimate tension; we felt uncomfortable picking the highest peak, but we felt equally uncomfortable picking an arbitrarily lower value. It can be argued that the cyclical loads our test anchors were subjected to simulated how boats actually stress anchors, but it remained difficult to measure at what point an anchor drags or pops free.

- When an anchor successfully holds at 5,000 pounds, and you elect to terminate the pull, how do you compare this with an anchor that was either slightly dragging or released at 5,000 pounds? The tendency is to concentrate on the tension and not the failure mode.

- What's the best failure mode? I think that "false holding"—when an anchor appears to be set and yet releases without warning—is the most dangerous. What about an anchor that does not set at all? What about an anchor that drags slowly but never pops free from the bottom? What about an anchor that holds tenaciously to 4,000 pounds, yet distorts at that tension and cannot be used again?

- If an anchor holds extremely well at 5:1 scope, yet cannot set at 3:1 scope, how should this affect your choice of anchor? Are short-scope-capable anchors superior if you never anticipate using short scope?

As a result of these and other experiences, I recommend the following:

1. Have a variety of anchor types on board, including at least one fixed-shank plow (including concave-fluke and roll-bar derivatives) and one pivoting-fluke (Danforth) type.

2. Use rope-chain rode for most applications.

3. Larger anchors allow you to sleep better at night.

4. Proof-set your anchor by backing down on it with your engine using sufficient rpm [for more, see Chapter 6]. I suggest backing down at half-throttle.

5. Have an anchor available for immediate use as a kedge, even if it is smaller than your normal anchor.

6. The old adage that a boat length of chain provides adequate catenary is only an approximation but generally works well. Two boat lengths of chain is better.

Chuck Hawley is director of product development at West Marine, a leading U.S. distributor and manufacturer of marine products.

HOW ANCHORS SET

We can distinguish two means by which anchors set: static and dynamic.

Static Setting

Static setting depends on gravity—in other words, weight—to penetrate the seafloor. This setting mode is typical for monstrous ship anchors weighing anywhere from several hundred pounds to several tons, which are designed to sink into the seafloor from their sheer weight alone. It is also typical of the mushroom anchors used for permanent moorings (see Chapter 8), whose bowl-shaped flukes sink into soft mud over time.

All anchors employ static setting to some extent. Although anchors used on smaller vessels have nowhere near the weight of immense ship anchors, the principle remains the same. For example, most manufacturers do not offer plow anchors weighing less than

9 pounds (4 kg), simply because once immersed in water, anything lighter might not have the static setting capacity to penetrate the seafloor. Anchors that are not sufficiently heavy to penetrate a compact or weedy bottom offer no more than cursory holding on such a bottom, even though they might be highly effective in soft mud.

Correct Orientation

Static setting can't be effective unless one or more flukes are properly oriented so as to get a bite on the seafloor. The traditional means of achieving correct orientation was to incorporate a stock in the design, since early designers figured that anchors weren't likely to sit on the tip of a stock and would roll down to the correct fluke position when placed under load. This assumption is usually but not always correct. Many divers have observed stock anchors under tension doing acrobatic handstands on both stock and fluke, tumbling without setting.

When a single-fluke anchor drops to the seabed, it should lie initially on one side or the other of the fluke. A horizontal pull on the anchor rode should then set it via dynamic penetration (see next page). Even if by some fluke (no pun intended) it lands incorrectly, the horizontal tug of the rode should suffice to right it.

Without sufficient gravitational pressure on the fluke, however, the fluke may not embed and may instead skim the surface without setting. Since pressure is defined as force (in this case gravitational force) divided by surface area, we have two variables at play in static setting: the weight bearing on the fluke tip, and the surface area of the fluke's penetrating edge.

Anchor models such as the Delta and the Spade use tip ballasting to ensure proper orientation of the penetrating fluke and to maximize the downward bite on the sediment. The object is to facilitate static setting before dynamic setting can take place. The ballasted tip of the Delta contains 28% to 33% of its total weight in its fluke point, and the Spade carries 48% of its weight at this point.

Contrast this with older anchor designs that have unballasted fluke tips. The fluke tips of flat plate anchors, for example, comprise just 12% to 16% of total anchor weight, while the CQR carries 62% of its weight at the heavy hinge and only 18% in its tip.

As we have seen, some modern anchor designers believe that a roll bar is more effective than a dedicated lead ballast insert in the fluke tip for ensuring correct orientation. Thus the Bügel fluke tip carries only about 16% to 18% of the anchor's weight. Roll-bar anchor designers believe that their approach, pound for pound, permits a larger blade surface area for embedding.

Since downward pressure (gravitational force per unit of surface area) is helpful during the static and dynamic phases of an anchor's setting, most modern anchors have sharp fluke tips to reduce the surface area there. A narrow fluke tip maximizes setting pressure for a good first bite of the seafloor, but a knifelike fluke tip could prove hazardous or even deadly on a bow roller, so the designer seeks a good compromise.

Dynamic Setting

Dynamic setting complements static setting, using the load on the anchor rode and the resistance of the seafloor to embed the fluke or blade. Anchors that lie on their sides to set (such as the Bügel, Manson Supreme, Spade, Sword, and Rocna) generate torque once rode pull is applied, which twists the blade into the seabed.

Two parameters are critical to dynamic setting in virtually all seabeds: the proper setting angle, and the amount of downward force at the tip. Small earlike skids on the upper outside portion of the blade help maximize the torque to drive the fluke tip of a concave-fluke or roll-bar anchor into the seafloor. In addition, designers of concave-fluke anchors feel that a ballasted tip is very important for dynamic setting (as well as static setting), especially to generate the torque necessary to rotate

the anchor fully into a compact or weedy seafloor. Designers of roll-bar anchors feel that rode pull in combination with the geometry of the anchor is as effective or more effective.

Setting Angle

By *setting angle*, we mean the fluke's angle of attack on the seafloor.

We have all been guilty at one time or another of using a knife to tighten or loosen a screw, a fork to cut a chicken breast, or a metal spoon to scrape a Teflon pan clean, even though we all know these jobs are better done with another tool. We have therefore created a tool analogy to illustrate why some setting angles are more effective than others.

- **Putty-knife angle.** When we spread putty or caulking compound on a surface, we angle the knife at less than

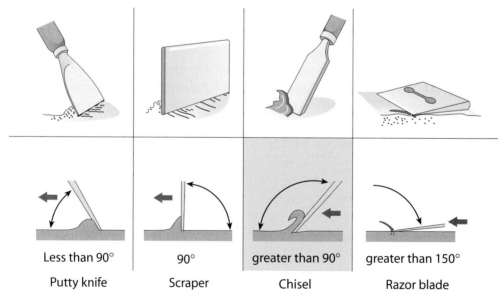

Less than 90°	90°	greater than 90°	greater than 150°
Putty knife	Scraper	Chisel	Razor blade

The operation of these tools helps illustrate a fluke's angle of attack on the seafloor.

90° to the surface and pull rather than push it. When a plow anchor falls upon the seafloor, it usually rests on one fluke edge or the other at an angle resembling a putty knife blade. Ideally, when the anchor is pulled by its rode, the tip will penetrate a mogul or soft spot, at which time the anchor pivots, presenting its active edge to the bottom at greater than 90°, like a chisel (or like a putty knife being pushed rather than pulled). This allows the anchor to embed itself. If the seafloor is hard or covered in weed, however, the plow may simply scrape along the surface without penetrating. The primary drawback of a plow—including new-generation plows like the Delta as well as more traditional models like the CQR—is that it falls to the seafloor with a putty knife angle of approximately 68°. This anchor therefore may not set well in very compact sand or weedy bottoms.

- **Scraper angle.** We usually use a scraper to strip and level a surface by angling the scraper edge perpendicular to the surface and pulling. No removable anchor is designed to meet the seafloor at a 90° angle, but any anchor designed with a bulky hind portion, such as the old-fashioned FOB models, may do a "handstand," alighting on its flukes. When this occurs, the flukes meet the seafloor almost perpendicularly, raking the surface without setting. Under heavy load this anchor type tends to

rise up on its flukes, acting like a rake upon the seafloor.

- **Razor-blade angle.** A razor blade "attacks" the surface with its sharp edge leading (like a chisel does) rather than trailing the rest of the blade (like a putty knife). But its angle as it attacks your early-morning stubble is greater than 150°—close enough to the horizontal, in fact, that it skims over your skin rather than cutting into it. That's exactly what we want from a razor, but not from an anchor that we want to set. The twin flukes of plate anchors (Danforth types) may in fact slide over the seafloor at a razor-blade angle, meaning that contact with a sand ripple or soft area is necessary for their fluke tips to pierce the surface; they then assume the chisel angle and set. On compact or weedy seafloors, these anchors may shave the bottom without ever taking hold.

- **Chisel angle.** Now we come to the Goldilocks angle of attack for an anchor fluke: not too small, not too great, but just right. We use a chisel's sharp beveled edge to cut and shape a surface, usually at an angle of 100° to 120° to the surface. This is an ideal attitude for an anchor fluke being pulled over the seafloor—one that neither shaves, levels, scrapes, nor spreads the seabed but rather digs in dynamically under load. There is no need for a sand dune or other unevenness to trip the fluke, and no need to pray for a soft area. Combined with a sharp-edged fluke (and, in our opinion, a weighted tip), this angle of attack offers the greatest assurance of penetration and setting. New-generation anchors are designed to assume a chisel angle under load.

HOW AN ANCHOR HOLDS

As we've seen, the weight of an anchor helps with static setting and with orienting the anchor properly for dynamic setting, especially when concentrated toward the tip of the fluke, but weight plays less of a role as dynamic setting proceeds. Once the anchor is firmly embedded, its weight is much less important than its surface area and geometry. Since the surface area of an aluminum anchor, for example, would be around three times greater than that of a steel anchor of the same design and weight, it's no surprise that aluminum anchors offer more holding power than steel ones of comparable or even significantly greater weight. The caveat, of course, is that the aluminum anchor must be sturdy enough not to distort or break under load, which is why we earlier recommended that your primary anchor be steel.

When analyzing how anchors hold under load, we make a distinction between unstable and roll-stable anchors (see Table 3-1). The former are prone to suddenly disengaging themselves from the seafloor under heavy load and then (hopefully) resetting themselves, while the latter, when their maximum holding power is exceeded, are more apt to drag slowly through the seafloor without disengaging. An unstable anchor may give highly satisfactory performance in the following situations: in fair weather; when the boat will not be left unattended; as a stern anchor, tandem anchor, or lateral anchor in port; or for kedging off after a grounding (in which case it will likely be set from a tender, as discussed in Chapter 7). But you want a roll-stable anchor as your primary anchor if at all possible.

The new generation of roll-stable anchors has shown consistent, superior holding power in comparison with their predecessors on all types of seafloors. Any boater with an interest in safety should invest in one of these anchors, especially if he or she expects to spend much time at anchor in bad weather as well as good.

Once set, roll-stable anchors tend to remain fully embedded. The harder they are pulled, the deeper they embed themselves, to the point of completely burying the anchor itself and the first several feet of chain. The holding power of a well-constructed roll-stable anchor is therefore limited mainly by the extent and shape of its fluke surfaces and by the seafloor in which it is implanted. (For the relative holding powers of various sediment types, refer back to Table 1-2.) Under high load, the anchor will slowly begin to drag when its maximum holding capacity is reached, but it is designed to remain embedded.

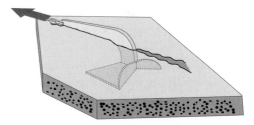

Roll-stable anchors remain embedded even when the pulling force exceeds their holding capacity.

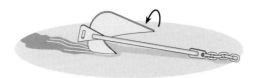

A Britany plate anchor without a stabilizing stock plows through the seafloor with the flukes in a vertical position and can break out abruptly.

In general, plate anchors without a stabilizing stock (e.g., an FOB) offer a relatively weak holding capacity. As soon as the force on the anchor increases, these anchors begin to rotate and disengage one fluke at a time.

Anchors with a stabilizing stock—such as the Danforth—are more stable up to a point, but the stock cannot prevent rotation once the bottom's holding capacity is exceeded, at which point these anchors too will tend to capsize and disengage. Once the anchor begins to pivot, it may assume a headstand-like, three-point attitude, balancing on the extremity of the shaft, the extremity of one fluke, and the end of one stock.

Holding Power in Changing Winds and Currents

Up to this point we've been considering how an anchor holds under a load from a single direction, but an anchor also needs the ability to remain embedded when the direction of the pulling force changes.

Winds and currents can reverse 180° or even make 360° loops. Most anchors disengage temporarily while pivoting, then reset in the new direction of the pulling force. An anchor with a very long stabilizing stock, such as the fisherman, Danforth, or Fortress, risks fouling its rode with the stock when the wind or current shifts. When this occurs, the anchor may dislodge immediately without resetting.

Among stockless anchors, the articulated shank of the CQR and its imitators was once considered a state-of-the-art defense against breakout in response to changing load directions. In addition to absorbing a modest sideways motion of the rode without requiring the anchor to turn, the hinge was also thought to permit the anchor to rotate horizontally with the pulling force while remaining embedded, keeping it set during shifts of wind and tide.

But when a CQR is lowered slowly onto a sand beach, the penetration angle of the plow worsens from the moment the plow touches the sand and the hinge starts to rotate until the fully lowered anchor comes to rest on its side. A fixed-shank Delta right next to the CQR will put much more weight on its penetrating edge because it does not rotate into this unfortunate position. The hinge actually prevents the CQR tip from penetrating a firm seafloor in static-setting mode before the rode begins to pull, and it then fails to transmit the necessary torque to embed the anchor blade with peak efficiency once a load is applied. In order to retain its tensile strength, the CQR's shank must be massive and heavy, concentrating undesirable weight in the shank and not enough in the plow tip.

Although articulating anchors are still widely used (just walk down any marina dock and observe), manufacturers and mariners have recognized the considerable advantages of a fixed shank. Anchors, unlike other boat equipment, don't often fall apart after a decade or two of use, and this may be the primary reason that earlier models still grace the bows of a good many boats in any given marina.

SELECTING YOUR ANCHOR

How Big Should Your Anchor Be?

Most people think a bigger anchor is better, and they equate bigger with heavier. The well-versed salesperson at your local marine store will ask for your boat's length, then recommend an anchor of the appropriate weight. But by now it should be obvious that it's not that simple. True, weight is correlated with size, and true, weight is far easier to quantify than any other indicator of size and remains the standard criterion for selection. But it's a good idea to consider an anchor's surface area and shape as well.

The larger the effective surface area embedded in the seafloor, the better an anchor's hold. Modern anchors manufactured from lighter metals offer a considerably larger surface area for the same weight or the same surface area with a much lighter weight. Further, the shape of the fluke surface is just as important as its size and weight. In a well-shaped fluke, almost all the surface area contributes to the anchor's grip; a poorly shaped fluke has more wasted surface area relative to its working surface.

A fully embedded Bruce anchor fluke is almost horizontal to the seafloor. Although the Bruce digs into most seafloors with great reliability, tests and experience suggest that its holding power is reduced due to its flukes' near-horizontal attitude, and it will tend to drag under relatively small loads.

And what of a plow anchor? The heavy blades of a farm plow are designed to break the soil—to cut a groove before planting—not to grip the soil. In the same way, plow anchors break through the seabed but are not ideally shaped to grip it under heavy load once embedded.

The flat shape of a plate anchor's flukes provides a higher proportion of working surface than a claw or plow. Indeed, a plate anchor's ratio of holding power to weight is unexcelled, and it is this attribute—as well as a plate anchor's ease of stowing on deck or in a locker—that makes it such a popular choice for a primary or secondary anchor on boats too small to stow an anchor on a bow roller. But still, as we've seen, a flat-plate anchor is prone to capsize or to slide right out of the seabed if the direction of the load changes.

Finally, we arrive at the concave-fluke surface employed by concave and roll-bar anchors (see Table 3-1). This shape, in our opinion, offers by far the strongest holding coefficient.

With these considerations in mind, we return to the question of weight. Here's the kind of query we hear frequently: "Our boat weights 5 tons, including water, fuel, and additional equipment, and is 32 feet long. We recently checked our anchor gear and found that the main anchor only weighs 25 pounds, with 150 feet of $5/16$-inch chain. We have not experienced any problems so far, but should we switch to a 33-pound model before we embark on the long cruise we're planning? We also carry a 22-pound plate anchor and a 12-pound fisherman as spare and kedge anchors, and I think we have an additional plow somewhere in the bilge for emergencies. What do you think? Are we too nervous about our main anchor?"

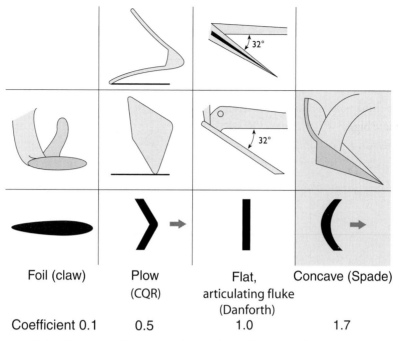

Foil (claw)	Plow (CQR)	Flat, articulating fluke (Danforth)	Concave (Spade)
Coefficient 0.1	0.5	1.0	1.7

Different shapes and their holding coefficients. The higher the coefficient, the better the holding capacity of a particular shape. Concave surfaces are the most efficient.

TABLE 3-2. ESTIMATED AVERAGE WIND LOADS ON AN ANCHORED BOAT (AND PEAK WIND LOADS ON A MOORED BOAT)[1]

LOA (ft./m)[2,3]	Beam (ft./m)[2,3]		Permanent Mooring (lb./daN)	Storm Anchor (lb./daN)	Working Anchor (lb./daN)
	Sailboat	Powerboat			
10/3	4/1.2	5/1.5	480/210	320/140	160/70
15/4.5	5/1.5	6/1.8	750/330	500/225	250/110
20/6	7/2.1	8/2.4	1,080/480	720/325	360/165
25/8	8/2.4	9/2.7	1,470/650	← 980/445 ←	490/225
30/9	9/2.7	11/3.4	2,100/930	1,400/635	700/320
35/11	10/3.0	13/4.0	2,700/1,200	1,800/820	900/410
40/12	11/3.4	14/4.3	3,600/1,600	2,400/1,100	1,200/550
50/15	13/4.0	16/4.9	4,800/2,140	3,200/1,450	1,600/730
60/18	15/4.6	18/5.5	6,000/2,670	4,000/1,800	2,000/910

[1]Though derived from wind loads, these values are conservative enough to include the effects of current and wave action as well, provided the boat is free to oscillate and there is moderate shelter from seas.
[2]When entering this table with your boat's overall length or beam, use whichever gives the higher load.
[3]For a boat with canvas enclosures or a large superstructure, use the load one category higher than that determined by using the powerboat column.
American Boat & Yacht Council

TABLE 3-3. SUGGESTED ANCHOR SIZES FOR WORKING AND STORM CONDITIONS (IN POUNDS)[1]

LOA (ft.)	Bruce	CQR		Danforth Standard		Delta		Fortress		Spade	Sword
	Storm (manufacturer's data)	Working (manufacturer's data)	Storm (derived)	Working (≤20 knots; manufacturer's data)	Storm (derived)	Working (manufacturer's data)	Storm (derived)	Working (manufacturer's data)	Storm (derived)	Storm (manufacturer's data)	Storm (manufacturer's data)
<20	11	—	—	9	14	9	14	4	7	13	—
20–30	16.5, 22	15	20	14	25	14	22	7	10	22	9
30–40	22, 33	36	45	25	43	22	35	10	21	33	18
40–50	44, 66	45	60	43, 70	70, 100	35	44	15, 21	32	44	26
50–60	66	60	75	100	100	44, 55	55, 88	32	47	66	35

[1]Due to lack of industry standards regarding what constitutes working conditions and how to group boat lengths, direct comparisons between brands are only approximate. Except for the Spade and Sword, recommended sizes for storm anchors are not based on manufacturers' data but are simply derived from recommended sizes for working conditions by moving up a size or two. All other things being equal, bigger is better.

Irish Luck's Pr?   Sec.

Does this situation sound familiar? Responsible skippers are forever questioning whether their onboard equipment is adequate for its purpose. Unfortunately it is not yet widely recognized that an anchor's weight is a relatively minor component of its holding power.

Why do manufacturers and marine standard-setters continue to equate weight with holding power? Perhaps this is due to the difficulty of quantifying size- and shape-holding coefficients, but most likely it's also a matter of custom, as in, "We've been doing this for years . . ." And it's true, as we've seen, that weight (as well as the concentration of that weight toward the anchor tip) can help a modern anchor penetrate the seafloor. Once you let out your anchor rode, however, your anchor's holding power depends more on its effective surface area than its weight.

Recommendations

We encourage anchor shoppers to learn as much as they can about each anchor model's setting performance and its ability to remain embedded while dragging. Having thereby narrowed your choices, review the manufacturers' data sheets, which should specify each anchor's holding capacity in a given seabed type, such as mud or sand. Then do your best to compare these holding capacities with the loads your boat is likely to generate at anchor.

Table 2-1 gives a means of estimating such loads, or you can use Table 3-2 (see page 45), which was also developed by the American Boat & Yacht Council (ABYC) and is closely akin to Table 2-1. Although developed for purposes of sizing the deck hardware to which the ground tackle will be made fast, Table 3-2 is equally useful for estimating the steady, straight-line loads due to wind to which an anchor will be subject under *working conditions* (same as 30 knots in Table 2-1) and *storm conditions* (same as 45 knots in Table 2-1).

Unfortunately, most anchor manufacturers continue to sell their models by weight (not by size, shape, or working surface area), and some manufacturers do not specify experimentally determined holding capacities for their anchors. Thus, although the ideal is to select and size your anchors according to their expected peak loads, this is not always possible. Even when it is, some boatowners prefer to have someone else do the calculations and present the resultant recommendations. Table 3-3 is our attempt to do just that. *Storm conditions* may be taken to mean winds of Force 9, 45 knots or more.

CHAPTER 4

Anchor Rode

So far we've discussed seafloors and anchor types, and we know the fundamental forces on the vessel. Now we have to attach the anchor to the vessel. This is the job of the anchor rode, and a demanding and technical job it is.

The rode should be durable to resist chafe, strong to withstand extremely heavy loads, flexible for manageability, and elastic to absorb shock and reduce shock loads. What rode material (or materials) can fulfill this wish list and how long should the rode be? These and other questions will be discussed in this chapter. For the mathematically inclined and the resolutely curious, the conclusions and suggestions we make in this chapter are further supported by the mathematical concepts set forth by Alain Fraysse in Appendix 1.

THE BEST ANCHOR RODE IS A COMBINATION OF CHAIN AND NYLON

We are aware that a number of you will read the above heading twice to make sure you understand it correctly. It is conventional wisdom in cruising circles that an all-chain rode is the best solution for connecting an anchor

to a boat—for it is tough, resistant to wear, and heavy enough to provide a favorable angle of pull on the anchor, even with short scope. But we hold strongly to our contrarian opinion. A *hybrid rode*, composed partly of nylon rope, which is stretchy enough to absorb peak loads, and partly of chain, which is virtually immune to chafe on the sea bottom, is the ideal combination. This type of rode works better than all-chain in the worst conditions and equally well in light to moderate conditions.

To see how we've arrived at this conclusion, let's look at the alternatives: all-rope and all-chain rodes.

Why Not an All-Rope (Nylon) Rode?

In contrast with chain, line is prone to chafing. One sharp rock, coral protuberance, or other sharp surface in contact with an anchor line from a pitching boat can set the boat adrift. And things aren't much better on deck. Critical chafing points, especially at the fairleads and the bow roller, can slowly or quickly abrade an anchor line to shreds. Protecting your rode from chafing both above and below the waterline is critical.

The principal advantage of line is its light weight, with a potential holding power equal to chain. What's more, nylon line is much more elastic than chain, dampening peak load jolts. However, the pulling angle of a nylon rode at the anchor shaft on the seafloor is relatively high, even in light to moderate winds, because of its light weight and lack of catenary. Alain Fraysse's appendix shows that, in practice, it is impossible to keep the anchor flat on the bottom with an all-nylon rode as soon as the wind exceeds a few knots.

We recognize that thousands of skippers on small craft set out with their lunch hook attached to an all-rope rode, which they set and retrieve by hand off a sandy beach for the afternoon. But this is a practice to be done with discretion and with one eye on the weather reports. What is perfectly acceptable on a fair afternoon with the skipper in close attendance is much less so on a stormy night with a lee shore nearby.

Why Not an All-Rope (Nylon) Rode with a Riding Weight?

Some skippers swear by using a frequently encountered yet controversial accessory, the *kellet* (also called an anchor angel, weight, chum, or sentinel). The principle behind this accessory is to improve the anchor holding by sliding the kellet more than halfway down the rode as close as possible to the anchor shaft in order to induce sag, or catenary. Proponents say this solution combines the advantages of an all-nylon rode with a lesser, more favorable pulling angle at the anchor. We agree that an all-nylon rode with a kellet placed close to the anchor can offer similar holding performance

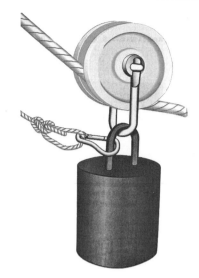

Kellet.

as an all-chain rode of the same length, with only half the total rode weight.

But although the idea is seductive, it is only moderately effective. The action of a kellet can easily be replaced by a chain leader of equal weight, which will provide the further benefits of resistance to chafe on the seafloor and easier handling in bad weather. (For a further theoretical and technical discussion of the kellet, see Appendix 1.)

Why Not an All-Chain Rode?

The short answer is that the drawbacks of an all-chain rode outweigh (no pun intended) its benefits. And what are those drawbacks?

The most obvious one is weight. When stored in a bow locker, chain adds a lot of weight in the last place you want it, at the forward extremity of the boat. One hundred feet of nylon rope weighs between 3 and 15 pounds, depending on the needed diameter, whereas 100 feet of chain for the same applications weighs anywhere from 50 to 170 pounds.

Second, an all-chain rode works well when it doesn't need to but doesn't work well when it should. In light winds, the catenary induced by the heavy chain provides a perfectly horizontal pull to the anchor and the very best holding, but in light winds *any* anchor rode will do just fine. In moderate winds, the weight and sag of an all-chain rode continue to provide a favorable angle of pull along with sufficient shock absorption, but in as little as 25 to 30 knots of wind the chain will straighten and become taut. Under heavy load the effective pulling angle will increase, and as a consequence the holding power of the anchor will decrease. At the same time, the rode is deprived of all ability to absorb shock loads as the straightened chain does not stretch and therefore has no elastic give. The net result is that a violent jerk from a pitching boat has a good chance of breaking out the anchor.

"Old salt" skippers who continue to insist on an all-chain rode should select the strongest deck gear possible and equip their first-aid kit for whiplash treatment. Even in light winds, if a swell develops in the anchorage, an all-chain rode can transmit serious jolts and tugs to the anchor and the deck hardware. When subject to these repeated loads, the ground tackle is likely to break at its weakest point, which might be the deck hardware, the chain, or a connecting shackle. The ideal anchor rode will absorb and mitigate such stress loads rather than transmit them undampened from boat to anchor.

Why Not an All-Chain Rode with a Nylon Snubber?

Some advocates of all-chain rodes insist that they can solve the problem of dynamic shock loads, discussed in Chapter 2, with a nylon snubber attached on deck. A *snubber* is simply a length of nylon line, one end of which is made fast to the samson post or foredeck cleat while the other end is fastened with a chain hook to a link of the anchor chain. Once tensioned enough to introduce slack in the segment of chain between the foredeck and chain hook, the snubber serves as a shock absorber in the rode.

We agree that a long snubber theoretically may offer the equivalent dynamic performance of a chain-rope hybrid rode, and we offer suggestions on creating and installing a snubber in Chapter 5 (see page 86). This snubber is also essential with a hybrid rode if you are anchoring in shallow water and with such a limited swinging radius that you don't reach the nylon portion of your rode.

However, we believe that a chain-rope hybrid rode is superior to an all-chain rode with nylon snubber for the following reasons:

- An all-chain rode adds considerable extra weight at the bow of the boat.

- You need a long snubber. This needs to be deployed during bad weather, which is not a fun or easy task.

- There is a distinct possibility of entangling the snubber with the chain when the vessel swings, making anchor retrieval a more daunting task.

All-chain advocates also argue that eliminating the transition from chain to nylon

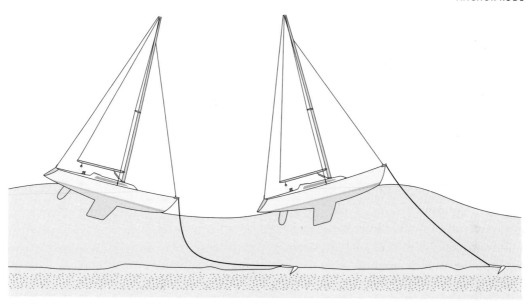

A sailboat's reaction to a swell shows how a rode will become taut on the wave peaks. A well-installed snubber or a nylon portion of your rode can provide the necessary elasticity.

rode simplifies retrieval of the anchor—especially if your windlass is not equipped with a combined chain-rope *gypsy* (a wheel with calibrated sprockets designed to accommodate a specified chain size for hauling up the chain and anchor). We will return to this question in the windlass discussion in Chapter 5. Suffice it to say for now that we do not view this as an important obstacle to a hybrid rode.

WHAT KIND OF CHAIN?

Anchor chain must be *marine grade*, which means it has been hot-dip galvanized in zinc to prepare it for the harshly corrosive marine environment. It must also conform to international (ISO—International Standards Organization), French (AFNOR—Association française de Normalisation), or German (DIN—Deutsches Institut für Normung) standards so that it fits flawlessly in a correspondingly sized windlass

gypsy. These standards ensure that the links have a consistent length, width, and diameter, with a manufacturer-supplied *safe working load* (the maximum load a chain can sustain without damage) and *breaking strength* (the load at which the chain will break). Unfortunately, anchor chain that has been subjected to loads in excess of the safe working load should

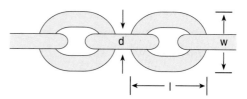

d = Link diameter
w = Link width
l = Link length

Measuring chain link sizes includes measuring link width, length, and diameter.

probably be replaced, because the chain has most likely suffered elongated links or other damage. See Table 4-1 for a summary.

Beware of the non-marine-grade "cow chain" on the market. It is much cheaper and can be identified by the lack of detailed specifications.

Proof-coil chain, made from low-grade carbon steel, is sufficient for light use on small boats and is the least expensive marine chain, but the two most popular chain types for the serious navigator are BBB and high test.

BBB (said "triple B") is the chain you will see most often aboard offshore cruising boats. It has shorter, stouter links than proof-coil chain and is better suited for windlasses; it is also less expensive than high test. BBB chain will endure many seasons if treated well and can be galvanized several times before the chain links finally wear down. It is important to rinse the chain well with seawater (or even better, fresh water) before stowing it, as fine sand and mud can abrade the galvanic layer

TABLE 4-1. WEIGHTS, SAFE WORKING LOADS, AND BREAKING STRENGTHS OF MARINE CHAIN

Chain Link Diameter (in.)	$1/4$	$5/16$	$3/8$	$1/2$	$5/8$
Proof-coil galvanized chain weight (lb./ft.)	0.63	1	1.4	2.6	3.8
Proof-coil galvanized chain safe working load (lb.)	1,250	1,900	2,650	4,500	6,900
Proof-coil galvanized chain breaking strength (lb.)	5,000	7,600	10,600	18,000	27,600
Proof-coil stainless steel chain (316) weight (lb./ft.)	0.60	0.88	1.4	—	—
Proof-coil stainless steel chain (316) safe working load (lb.)	1,570	2,400	3,750	—	—
Proof-coil stainless steel chain (316) breaking strength (lb.)	6,300	9,600	15,000	—	—
BBB weight (lb./ft.)	—	1.2	1.7	3.0	—
BBB safe working load (lb.)	—	1,900	2,650	4,500	—
BBB breaking strength (lb.)	—	7,600	11,000	18,000	—
High-test G40 weight (lb./ft.)	0.74	1.09	1.49	—	—
High-test G40 safe working load (lb.)	2,600	3,900	5,400	—	—
High-test G40 breaking strength (lb.)	7,750	11,600	16,200	—	—
High-test G70 weight (lb./ft.)	0.66	1.0	1.45	—	—
High-test G70 safe working load (lb.)	3,150	4,700	6,600	—	—
High-test G70 breaking strength (lb.)	9,450	14,100	19,800	—	—

Seduced by Shining Stainless? Stay with Gallant Galvanized!

Stainless steel chain is shiny and beautiful; it remains free of visible corrosion or wear and shows no insidious rust residue after only a few weeks of use. What's more, when stowed in its chain locker, it self-distributes and doesn't pile up in a cumbersome pyramid like galvanized chain does. There are so many advantages; if it were only less expensive!

But—and yes, there is a "but"—during the chain manufacturing process, whether galvanized or stainless, links are bent and then welded. When a galvanized steel chain's safe working load is reached or exceeded, the links elongate slightly, giving a kind of warning signal that it's time to replace the chain. Stainless steel chain does not have this built-in warning feature. In a saltwater environment, stainless steel chain tends to corrode almost invisibly over time—a well-known phenomenon, for example, with aged stainless steel shrouds and stays. Small, invisible cracks develop, especially at welded points of the chain links. Under heavy load, without warning, a stainless chain can shatter like glass. Our advice, therefore, is to avoid stainless steel in your anchor chain.

and retain moisture, causing the chain to rust prematurely.

Although more expensive, high-test chain (also known as G40 or G70) is made from high-tensile carbon steel and is therefore lighter and stronger than BBB, making it the best alternative for those concerned about weight in the bow.

Stud-link chain, used on megayachts and other vessels over 60 feet long, has bars across each link at its midlength perpendicular to the major axis to prevent it from deforming when overloaded.

WHAT KIND OF LINE?

Ancient Phoenician and Polynesian navigators set their anchors with ropes made of plant fibers and had to replace them every year or two. By contrast, today's synthetic fiber ropes offer high resistance to chemical and biological erosion and, when properly cared for, can last many years. Except for a few die-hard traditionalists, therefore, very few sailors employ traditional natural fibers for an anchor line. (And even traditionalists can order natural-looking natural fiber

imitations made of polypropylene.) This leaves us with several synthetic fibers to choose from (see Table 4-2 next page).

There really is no contest, however. Nylon, originally developed by DuPont, is the most commonly used material for anchor lines, and for good reason. It is strong, abrasion resistant, and not very sensitive to UV deterioration. Its main advantage, however, is its elasticity. It can stretch approximately 15% under safe working loads and to nearly 40% at loads close to its breaking strength. This elasticity provides the shock-absorption capacity you need in rough conditions. Nylon is heavier than water (it has a specific gravity of 1.14) and will not float. Its main drawback is that, when wet, it loses approximately 10% to 20% of its tensile strength—a factor that must be accounted for when selecting an appropriate diameter. It is also prone to internal heat accumulation from friction when subject to repeated peak loads that exceed its safe working load and approach its breaking strength. Under these conditions, nylon rope can even experience heat failure. But if you size your rode so that its safe working load

TABLE 4-2. SYNTHETIC ROPE FIBER CHARACTERISTICS

	Polyamide (nylon, Perlon, Enkalon)	Polyester (Dacron, Tergal, Diolen, Trevira)	Polypropylene	Polyethylene	Aramid
Breaking strength (daN/mm² – psi)	100–1,422	115–1,636	35–498	370–5,261	270–3,839
Approximate elongation (%; at safe working loads)	15	11	16	3.5	4
Strength loss when wet (%)	10–20	0	0	0	10
Resistance to abrasion	Very good	Good	Average	Good	Inferior
Rating as anchor rode	Excellent	Good	Poor to fair	Not suitable	Not suitable

limit is rarely exceeded, you won't need to worry about this, even in storm conditions.

Premium white three-strand nylon line exhibits 16% stretch at a load that is 15% of its breaking strength (i.e., at close to its safe working load). Thus, 100 feet of ⁵/₈-inch nylon line under a load of 1,830 pounds will elongate to 116 feet as shown in Table 4-3.

The choice of an anchor line does not end with the choice of material, however. Ropes made of nylon (and other synthetic fibers) are available in a variety of constructions, including three-strand twisted (also known as *laid*), plaited, single-braid, double-braid, ballasted,

and flexible webbing. Of these, three-strand and plaited are the most popular choices for anchor lines. (For information on unconventional rode choices such as webbing, see Appendix 2.)

Three-strand nylon is a soft-laid, elastic rope. The strands are normally twisted in a clockwise direction *(right-hand lay)* with the yarns in each strand twisted counterclockwise and the fibers in each yarn twisted clockwise; this alternating reversal of directions balances the rope. Three-strand is usually the most reasonably priced rope construction and is the easiest to splice. Its chief drawback is that

TABLE 4-3. WEIGHTS AND BREAKING STRENGTHS[1] OF PREMIUM WHITE THREE-STRAND NYLON LINE

Diameter (in./mm)	¹/₄/6	³/₈/9	⁷/₁₆/11	¹/₂/12	⁹/₁₆/14	⁵/₈/16	³/₄/18	⁷/₈/22	1/24
Weight (lb./100 ft.)	1.5	3.5	5.0	6.5	8.2	10.5	14.5	20.0	26.4
Breaking Strength (lb.)	2,000	4,400	5,900	7,500	9,400	12,200	16,700	23,500	29,400

[1]Rope manufacturers routinely list breaking strengths but hesitate to provide safe working loads because so many factors—including age, abrasion, knots, and conditions of use—affect the calculation. According to the Cordage Institute, the safe working load of a rope is simply its breaking strength divided by a safety factor that ranges from 5 to 15, depending on the application and conditions of use. For purposes of sizing anchor rode components, it is reasonable to assume that the safe working load is approximately 10% of the breaking strength.

Especially comfortable to handle, eight-strand braided nylon is easily spliced to a chain leader.

under extreme loads it can partially unravel and may impart a twist to the items it connects. If used under a heavy load that is subsequently released, it may form *hockles*, or small loops inside the lay of the rope. Hockles greatly reduce the rope's strength, and hockled sections must be replaced. Three-strand only coils in one direction, but when coiled properly, it is easy to store.

Eight-strand plaited line (sold under brand names such as Brait and Octoplait) is particularly well adapted to splicing, is very elastic, will absorb shock loads even better than three-strand, and will store in an anchor locker without kinking. It also exhibits fewer tendencies to form hockles than three-strand. It is a bit more costly and less widely available than three-strand, however.

Sixteen-strand braided line is rarely used as an anchor rode, since it offers little elasticity and is difficult to eye-splice around a thimble and even more difficult to splice into a chain leader.

SIZING THE CHAIN AND ROPE

Chain and rope of comparable safe working load limits (including the strength loss of the rope when wet!) should be combined to form an anchor rode. For example, you might use $^3/_4$-inch nylon line with a safe working load

(from Table 4-4) of 1,813 pounds (minus 20% when wet, equaling 1,451 pounds) to match a $^5/_{16}$-inch proof-coil galvanized chain leader with a safe working load of 1,900 pounds. Although the safe working load of the nylon line in this example is somewhat lower than that of the chain, the breaking strength of nylon exceeds its safe working load by a factor of 10 (compared with 3 or 4 for chain), so this seems acceptable. Check with the manufacturers for actual values. We do not recommend using a grossly oversized line diameter, because a gain in strength will mean a loss in elasticity, a factor that should not be underestimated in its importance for the cushioning of surge loads on both anchor and deck gear. Table 4-4 (next page) provides good guidance for matching rope to chain.

DETERMINING YOUR PRIMARY AND SECONDARY RODE LENGTHS

Modern anchors are designed to function with a pulling angle of less than 8° from the horizontal since the maximum holding is obtained with a horizontal pull. Any angle over 8° significantly decreases the anchor's efficiency of setting and holding. What's more, the greater the angle, the more likely the anchor is to dislodge even after it has set.

TABLE 4-4. SAFE WORKING LOAD LIMITS IN POUNDS (AND KILONEWTONS) FOR ANCHOR RODE COMPONENTS

Nominal Diameter (in./mm)	Nylon[1,2,3,4]		Galvanized Chain[1,4]			Shackles (weldless, drop-forged)
	Three- and eight-strand	Double-braid	BBB	Proof-coil	High-test	
1/4/6	186 (0.82)	208 (0.93)	1,300 (5.8)	1,300 (5.8)	2,600 (11.6)	1,000 (4.4)
5/16/8	287 (1.3)	326 (1.5)	1,900 (8.5)	1,900 (8.5)	3,900 (17.3)	1,500 (6.7)
3/8/10	405 (1.8)	463 (210)	2,650 (11.8)	2,650 (11.8)	5,400 (24)	2,000 (8.9)
7/16/11	557 (2.5)	624 (2.8)	—	—	—	3,000 (13.3)
1/2/12	709 (3.2)	816 (3.6)	4,500 (20)	4,500 (20)	9,200 (41)	4,000 (17.8)
9/16/14	888 (4.0)	1,020 (4.5)	5,875 (26.1)	—	—	—
5/8/16	1,114 (5.0)	1,275 (5.7)	6,900 (30.7)	6,900 (30.7)	11,500 (51.2)	6,500 (29)
3/4/18	1,598 (7.1)	1,813 (8.1)	10,600 (47.2)	10,600 (47.2)	16,200 (72)	9,500 (42.3)
7/8/22	2,160 (9.6)	2,063 (9.2)	—	12,800 (57)	—	12,000 (53.4)
1/24	2,795 (12.4)	3,153 (14)	—	13,950 (62)	—	15,000 (66.7)
1 1/4/30	4,345 (19.3)	4,838 (22)	—	—	—	23,000 (102.3)
1 1/2/36	6,075 (27)	6,875 (30.6)	—	—	—	—
2/48	10,575 (47)	12,363 (55)	—	—	—	—

[1]Only nylon rope is shown because of its elasticity and ability to absorb shock loads. Working loads for nylon rope are based on factors of safety, line strength loss due to knots and splices, and additional factors including abrasion and aging. Size your chain according to the manufacturer's working load ratings when possible.
[2]In eye splices, use only thimbles designated for use with the particular size of rope required.
[3]For three-strand twisted and eight-strand plaited rope, the breaking strength test figures used to determine working loads are "average." Minimum will be 10% below "average." A design (safety) factor of 8 was used for all rope types. These strengths are based on data supplied for new and unused rope in accordance with Cordage Institute standards.
[4]Strengths vary by manufacturer.
American Boat & Yacht Council

This is, after all, why we place ourselves directly above an anchor when retrieving it.

It is impossible to discuss optimal rode length without some discussion of *scope*, which is the ratio between the amount of rode you pay out and the vertical distance from your bow roller or bow chock to the seabed (i.e., the depth of the water plus your freeboard). In general, the higher the ratio, the more nearly horizontal the angle of pull will be on the anchor. The usual recommendation for anchoring with a hybrid chain-nylon rode is for a scope of 6:1, and we have found 5:1 to be a good starting point for us;

but in adverse conditions of wind and/or sea, you will need more (for a more detailed discussion of scope, see Chapter 6). We recommend an anchor rode long enough to reach a scope of 10:1 in the average anchorage of your desired cruising area. Thus, a skipper who intends to anchor frequently in 36 feet (11 m) of water should outfit himself with a primary rode that is 360 feet (110 m) long.

Advocates of all-chain rodes assert that less scope (say, 4:1 in normal conditions and up to 6:1 in storm conditions) is adequate with all-chain, but we disagree. We think the computations and graphs in Alain Fraysse's appendix build a strong case that an all-chain rode requires more rather than less scope than a hybrid rode to achieve equal performance under adverse conditions.

If you plan to anchor locally, your familiarity with local conditions may permit you to carry less rode. A boat remaining in the shallow waters of the Bahamas can get by with a shorter rode, while a boat outfitted for the deep anchorages of the Pacific islands should use a much longer rode.

In addition to the principal rode, you should consider carrying a secondary rode as an indispensable security measure. It will be pressed into service if your primary rode breaks or has to be abandoned, and it will also come in handy for anchoring maneuvers such as the V-form (forked mooring), Bahamian, or Mediterranean moors, which require more than one anchor (see Chapter 7). The secondary rode can be approximately 40% shorter than the primary. Skippers intending to anchor frequently should consider storing a third complete ground tackle in the bilge for emergencies and storm conditions.

We also recommend as a snubber an auxiliary 30- to 50-foot (9 m to 15 m) nylon rope, ending with a chain hook (see Chapter 5). This device gives the rode its needed shock-absorption capacity when the water height and/or wind conditions do not require paying out all of the chain section of the rode.

Calculating the Length of the Chain Leader

Having chosen a hybrid rode, and having settled on the overall rode length you need, your next question is how long to make the chain leader.

One popular rule of thumb is to incorporate 6 to 12 inches of chain length for each foot of boat length, but we prefer a determination based on estimated average anchoring depths. For example, during a recent eight-month cruise, Alain spent 129 days anchored in sixty-one different anchorages with a mean vertical height (distance between bow roller and seafloor) of approximately 21 feet (6.5 m). At an average scope of about 5:1, the average deployed length of anchor rode was about 98.5 feet (30 m), of which 77 feet (23.5 m) was lying on the bottom (see illustration next page). For his purposes, therefore, a chain leader length of about 82 feet (25 m) was about right, ensuring that the portion of the rode in contact with the bottom was chain.

Stated more generally, a chain leader of sufficient length will allow your boat to swing on chain (preferably with a nylon snubber) in shallow waters and calm weather. Should winds increase, pay out more scope until the rode reaches the nylon shock-absorbing portion, giving the rode even more overall stretch and shock-absorbing capacity. With the wind blowing harder, it is unlikely that the nylon will rest or chafe on the seafloor. Put another way, the length of the chain leader does not have to grow proportionately with the rode length to safely weather a storm.

Avoid using the chain-to-chain connecting gadgetry you see on sale at most ship chandleries, such as a riveted chain-to-chain link. The breaking strength of such hardware is far inferior to the chain links themselves. In fact, we recommend against connecting chain to chain at all; the chain leader should be comprised of a single length.

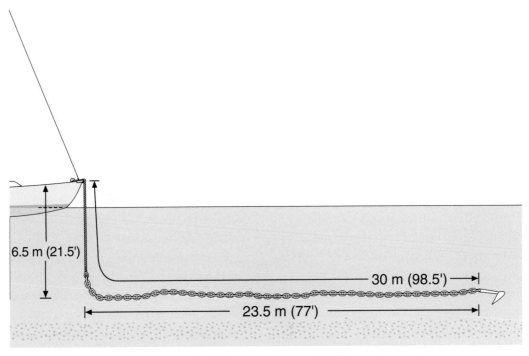

6.5 m (21.5')

30 m (98.5')

23.5 m (77')

Alain's 100-foot hybrid rode. The less-than-10% rope portion is critical for shock absorption.

Alternatively, you can calculate your chain length to achieve a desired proportion of your overall rode length. Depending on vessel size and cruising needs, you can choose any chain-nylon ratio within a wide range, say, from 40:60 to 80:20. For bluewater cruisers who plan on overnighting and gunkholing, we suggest a primary rode consisting of a 50:50 ratio of chain to nylon. If your average anchoring depths (including the height of the bow roller off the water's surface) will be 20 feet, you'll probably want your primary rode to be 200 feet long. If you want 50% chain, therefore, your chain leader will need to be 100 feet long. For smaller craft where weight is a critical concern, a 40:60 ratio would work, resulting in a shorter chain leader.

ANCHOR RODE CONNECTIONS

It makes no sense to carefully select the correct holding power of chain or rope if you do not also select each connecting element of the ground tackle with just as much care. After all, a chain is only as strong as its weakest link. Three points should be considered:

1. Connection of vessel to rode.

2. Connection of chain leader to anchor.

3. Connection of anchor line to chain leader.

We'll discuss each in turn.

Connection of Vessel to Rode

This is the easiest attachment problem to solve. The anchor rode should be attached to the boat at its *bitter end*, the shipboard end of the rode. This attachment should prevent the heartache of losing your entire ground tackle when the end slips unbidden through the foredeck crew's hands.

The anchor must always be prepared to drop in case of emergency, but some emergencies may force you to get free of your anchor as well. In this case, you may not have time to weigh anchor and will have to detach the bitter end to let it go. If possible in such a situation, try to attach a large fender or marker buoy to the upper extremity of the rode before releasing it. That will improve your chances of recovering your abandoned ground tackle once the emergency has passed.

Those who still insist on an all-chain rode—despite having read our arguments to the contrary—should make sure the connection point of the bitter end is easily accessible. Attach the last chain link with multiple long turns of lashing to an eyelet in the hull. If the bitter end is not easily accessible, at least this connecting line can be—provided you make the loops long enough to be reached effectively. Tie the bitter end with a knot that will come undone with a few tugs and consider keeping a sharp, well-greased knife next to the bitter end so that in the worst case you can cut the rode free.

If you use line at the deck extremity of your rode, as we recommend, make sure the bitter end—which may be attached to its hull eyelet with a soft splice or a shackle from a splice around a thimble—will fit through the deck pipe. If it won't, one solution is to

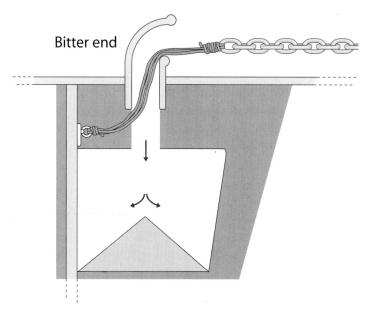

Bitter end

If you cannot be convinced to upgrade your all-chain rode to a hybrid rode, connect the end of the chain with a small rope that reaches outside of the chain locker so it can be cut from the outside in an emergency. A small pyramid directly underneath the chain pipe inside the locker can prevent the anchor chain from piling up and blocking the chain inlet.

substitute a spliced loop that uses only one strand of a three-strand rode. This solution is feasible because the loop needn't carry the entire anchor load; it is sufficient if the attachment can handle a load of 15% to 30% of the rode's breaking strength. Tying the bitter end to the hull eyelet with a bowline would accomplish the same thing. And again, keep a greased, sharp knife next to the eyelet.

Connection of Chain to Anchor

The simplest solution consists of one or two strong screw-pin shackles. These shackles should be stamped with their safe working loads, and those loads should at least match that of the chain. Shackles one size or more larger than the chain (e.g., a $^1\!/_2$-inch shackle for a $^3\!/_8$-inch chain—see Table 4-4) are preferable. If you choose screw-pin shackles, make sure to secure the shackle pin eyes with thin pieces of Monel seizing wire, which will prevent them from unscrewing on their own. This seizing wire must be regularly monitored and replaced as necessary; faulty seizing wire combined with a loose shackle has caused the loss of many anchors.

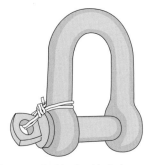

Monel wire secures this shackle bolt.

Galvanized steel chain should ideally be matched with galvanized steel connecting shackles of equal or greater safe working loads and breaking strengths.

However, the protruding head of a shackle pin can get stuck on the bow roller, and the likelihood of this occurring doubles when you use two. This problem can be solved by substituting a flathead threaded bolt for the shackle pin. Since you won't be able to seize the bolt with wire, you should apply a thread treatment such as Loctite, a hit of a hammer, and an extra twist of the screwdriver or Allen wrench to ensure that the bolt won't unscrew itself.

These two shackles connect a chain leader to the anchor stock.

Shackle with a flathead Allen screw; use an Allen wrench to tighten or loosen.

You will find shackles designed to link anchor to chain at ship chandleries. Use these with caution; the safe working load and the breaking strength *must* be indicated. If they aren't, suspect an inferior shackle. Even when specified, the load limits are valid only for in-line, not lateral, loads. If the anchor is blocked in its rotation axis (for example, stuck behind a rock while the vessel swings) the connector must withstand a lateral component of the load. Unless it is stout and well designed, the connector may break.

Another approach is to attach the anchor to the chain with a toggle, as shown in the photo at right. A toggle like this is easy to find in any rigging shop, and it will fit both the chain link and the anchor shank. It is strong and safe, avoiding any risk of a screw unthreading itself. This connection also facilitates the mounting and removal of the

Attaching an anchor to chain with a toggle. This is the setup used on Alain's boat, SY *Hylas*.

anchor. In contrast with stainless steel chain, there are no welds in a stainless steel toggle to constitute potential failure points. Galvanic corrosion with the attached link of a galvanized chain is a long-term possibility, but it is much less of an issue with anchor ground tackle than with a permanent mooring.

Should You Use a Swivel?

Although we do not recommend swivels, in some cases they may facilitate the anchor weighing maneuver. Especially in light winds, an anchored vessel tends to swing around its anchor. A swivel between the anchor and the chain should, in theory, prevent the chain from twisting and turning. But a swivel won't rotate under heavy loads unless manufactured with bearings. Further, you should look for precise manufacturer-supplied working-load specifications, because swivels can weaken your entire anchor rode, especially when they are undersized.

If your bow roller is equipped with a central groove to guide the chain during retrieval, the chain will untwist itself as it comes aboard (see Chapter 5). You can facilitate this by letting the anchor hang from the bow for a few moments after it rises from the seafloor, giving the chain time to untwist itself.

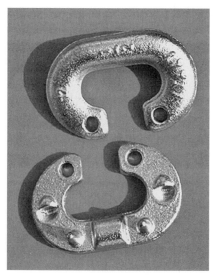

This riveted chain link is split laterally, significantly reducing its breaking strength.

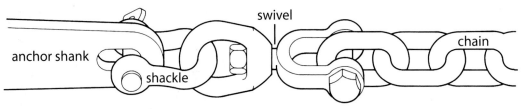

A swivel attached to the anchor shank with a shackle. (Jim Sollers)

If you feel you need a swivel—perhaps because you anchor frequently in areas of strong reversing tidal currents—verify these important points:

- It's better to use a swivel with bearings.
- Make sure the swivel strength matches or exceeds the safe working load and breaking strength of the chain.
- Make sure to mount the swivel in such a way that it can always align itself with the direction of the load.
- Follow the swivel manufacturer's instructions meticulously. If this is not done, the lateral load exerted on the swivel axis may bend and eventually break

A chain-to-anchor connector with a swivel. Verify the authorized maximum load in linear and lateral directions.

the swivel. Do not use a swivel that does not come with manufacturer-supplied working-load specifications and installation guidelines.

Connection of Anchor Line to Chain Leader

If your windlass is not equipped with a combined rope-chain gypsy, you should visibly mark the end of your chain leader to alert you that it is time to stop the windlass and execute the move from gypsy sprockets to windlass capstan for the anchor line.

Thimbled Eye Splice

A common and efficient way to attach rope to chain is to splice the rope around a thimble, then attach the thimbled eye splice to the chain with a shackle. There are several ways to make a thimbled eye splice, but here is our favorite way to splice three-strand line.

You will need:

- sharp knife
- hollow fid
- roll of adhesive tape
- tape measure
- spool of whipping twine
- thimble

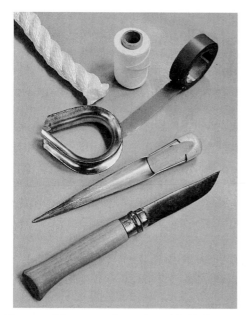

The materials you need to make a thimbled eye splice to connect rope to chain, using a shackle. Shown here is a stainless eyelet; we recommend galvanized.

Splicing a thimble into anchor rode, steps 1 through 4.

To make the eye splice:

1. Tie a seizing around the rope at a distance of ten times the rope diameter plus 2 inches from the end you want to splice (e.g., $10 \times \frac{1}{2}" + 2" = 7"$).

2. Unlay the three strands until you reach the seizing.

3. Attach several tight turns of adhesive tape around the very ends of each strand to keep the yarns from unlaying while you work.

The three-strand rope for the eye splice.

4. Place the end of the rope around the thimble and attach both parts at the throat of the thimble with seizings.

5. Feed strand end #1 underneath one of the three twisted strands in the standing part of the rope, selecting carefully so as to preserve the continuity of the lay and make the first tuck as smooth and snug as possible.

6. Turn the rope 90° to the left and feed strand end #2 over the standing-part strand you just tucked underneath the next twisted strand.

7. Turn the rope again and feed strand end #3 underneath the remaining of the three twisted strands in the standing part.

Splicing a thimble into anchor rode, step 5.

Splicing a thimble into anchor rode, step 7.

8. Pull the strand ends as tight as you can through the twisted strands and make sure they exit the standing part 120° apart from each other.

9. Continue the splice by feeding each strand end over one strand in the standing part and under the next,

working against the lay and pulling each tuck as tight as possible.

10. Three full rounds of tucks are sufficient; four or five are preferable for synthetic line; six rounds make a very strong and fair connection. When finished, cut the strand ends close to the standing part and secure them with a tight seizing around the standing part, at least a $1/2$ inch wide.

11. The splice is finished.

The disadvantage of a thimbled eye splice is that it doesn't always fit easily through a bow roller, a windlass's chain gypsy, or the deck pipe to the chain locker. In response to this, it is amazing how many mariners simply dispense with the thimble and splice anchor

Splicing a thimble into anchor rode, step 6.

The finished splice. Some suggest you should seize the thimble eye at the throat and the base to minimize it working out under load.

lines to chain leaders by feeding the strand ends through the last link of the chain, turning them 180°, then tucking them back into the standing part of the rope. This approach transmits the entire ground tackle loads, both static and dynamic, to three (or eight, if plaited rope is used) unlaid strands bent 180° around an abrasive chain link. The consequence is that the anchor rode loses up to 50% of its breaking strength. There is definitely a better way.

Three-Strand Splice onto Chain

Splicing the line directly to the chain with no 180° turns through the last chain link preserves nearly the full line strength while allowing a relatively seamless use of a combined rope-chain gypsy on the anchor windlass.

Since this splice is slightly more difficult to create in three-strand rope, we recommend using eight-strand plaited line (also known as *square line* and sold as Brait and Octoplait). Nevertheless, we'll show you the splice in both rope types. Until rope and chain manufacturers begin to collaborate on a well-designed, professionally spliced combination rode, we suggest doing this splice yourself.

You will need:

- permanent marker pen
- ruler
- electrical tape
- spool of nylon whipping twine
- knife
- soldering iron or cigarette lighter

To make the splice:

1. Count twelve strand turns back from the line end and mark the twelfth turn.

2. Lash a seizing around the line just after this mark and unbraid the line back to the seizing.

3. Insert the first strand end through the chain's end link from one side.

4. Insert the second strand end through the end link from the opposite side. Pull the end link up to the seizure.

Three-strand splice to chain, steps 1 and 2.

Three-strand splice to chain, steps 3, 4, and 5.

The completed splice.

5. Insert the third strand end through the second link.

6. Insert the first strand end through the second link from the opposite side.

7. Insert the second strand end through the third link.

8. Insert the third strand end through the third link from the opposite side.

9. Pull the strand ends tight at each turn, continuing in this manner until the ends are used up. Whip the extremity of each strand end and melt the yarn ends beyond the whipping with a hot soldering iron or a cigarette lighter.

Eight-Strand Splice onto Chain

In the eight-strand splice, also called the square line splice, you will be working with four strand pairs rather than eight individual strands. To make the splice:

1. Count twelve braid turns back from the line end and mark the twelfth turn.

2. Lash a seizing around the line just after this mark.

3. Unlay the line back to the seizing. Note that this eight-strand rope has four strands laid clockwise (we'll call these *Z* strands) and four laid counterclockwise (the *S* strands). As you unlay the ends, separate the S-strand ends from the

Three-strand splice to chain, steps 6, 7, and 8.

Square-line splice to chain, step 2. The twelfth turn is marked with whipping.

S-shaped strands.

Z-shaped strands.

Square-line splice to chain, steps 3, 4, 5, and 6.

Square-line splice to chain, step 7.

Z-strand ends. Divide each resulting four-strand clump into two pairs, and tape the end of each strand. Now insert a pair of S strands through the first link of the chain, and pull the chain up to the seizing.

4. Insert the second pair of S strands through the same link but from the opposite side, taking care to pass it between the strands of the opposing pair.

5. Insert the first pair of Z strands through the second link of the chain.

6. Insert the second pair of Z strands through the second link from the opposite side, once again taking care to pass it between the strands of the opposing pair. Pull the strands tight, making sure the chain stays snug against the seizing.

7. Proceed to the third link with the S strands, and continue in this manner until the strand pairs are used up.

8. Seize the end of each pair of strands with nylon whipping. Cut the strand ends approximately 0.2 inch (5 mm) beyond

Square-line splice to chain—reaching the last chain link.

The completed splice.

the whipping and seal the ends with a hot soldering iron or a lighter.

ANCHOR RODE INTERVAL MARKING

Having accepted the importance of letting out enough scope, how do you know how much you've deployed? There are expensive electronic gauges that indicate exactly how much chain has been released, but there are also much less expensive and perfectly reliable methods of marking the anchor rode. All of these involve color coding.

The choice of anchor gear is a touchy enough subject without getting into personal tastes regarding colors. Exercise the freedom of the seas, and choose a color scheme according to your preference. Here are two possibilities to get your imagination working.

First, the "national flag" method is easy to remember in countries with tri-colored flags. In the United States, where the red, white, and blue proudly waves, you could place a red mark at 2 fathoms (12 feet), a white mark at 4 fathoms (24 feet), a blue mark at 6 fathoms (36 feet), two red marks at 8 fathoms (48 feet), and so on. If anchoring where charted depths are in meters rather than feet or fathoms, you could place a red mark at 5 meters, a white mark at 10 meters, a blue mark at 15 meters, two red marks at 20 meters, and so on.

Alternatively, you can combine markers of different colors in a system like that shown in the illustration.

Marking an Anchor Chain

Paint

Painting the chain is a perfect off-season task. Paint is very visible, especially if you choose

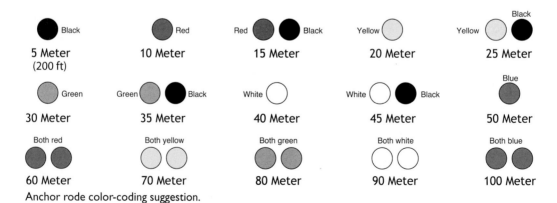

Anchor rode color-coding suggestion.

One way to mark a chain rode is to use stripes of highly visible and durable paint at intervals. For example, a single stripe for 50 feet, two for 100, three for 150 and four for 200. In this photo, the skipper chose to paint approximately thirteen links.

Colorful plastic cable ties mark intervals on an anchor chain.

bright or highly contrasting colors. Regrettably, no paint sticks to galvanized chain for long. If you anchor often, you will need to redo the marks every year.

Colored Cable Ties

Your local ship chandlery, or even your local hardware store or electrical appliance warehouse, sells colorful electrical cable ties, but you must take care to attach these correctly. Cable ties affixed to the sides of the chain links may get sliced off in the windlass chain gypsy or in the deck pipe. Worse, they can get stuck in the windlass and spoil your anchoring maneuver.

A better way to attach them is around the point of contact between adjacent chain links, with the cable tie circling both links. This confines the cable tie inside the chain, ensuring that the chain will still fit through the chain gypsy and the deck pipe without blocking or abrading. You may either cut off the cable tie's tail or leave it hanging. Choosing the latter improves the tie's visibility, but you

must make sure the tail points toward the anchor; otherwise it may get stuck in the deck pipe upon retrieval.

Marker Inserts or "Rainbow Markers"

In our opinion, these little plastic bits are the most elegant method for marking an anchor chain. They come in sets of eight and insert into the chain links. They are very visible,

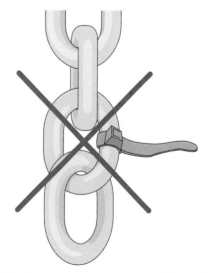

This is the incorrect way to mount cable ties. Ties affixed to the sides of the chain may get sliced off in the windlass chain gypsy or deck pipe.

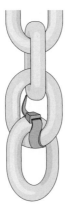

The correct way of mounting cable ties. This tie is attached between adjacent links, encircling both links.

Colored markers

Colored anchor markers are our preferred way of marking rode intervals.

Using a cable tie to mark an anchor line.

easy to implement, are practically indestructible, and in no way disturb setting or retrieving the chain.

Marking an Anchor Line

Unlike chain, synthetic fiber rope retains its paint markings very well, sometimes too well; if you ever need to splice or reduce the length of the anchor line, you're stuck with the old marks. It is also possible to introduce cable ties or small lengths of colored strips of spinnaker cloth between the strands.

ANCHOR GEAR MAINTENANCE

Preventing Chafe

Wherever an anchor rode bears against chocks, the boat's gunwale, deck hardware, the seabed, or adjacent rode components, it is subject to chafe. Chafe is an insidious enemy and must be guarded against with diligence.

Chain is mostly immune to chafe, and this is its greatest advantage. But even the strongest of synthetic ropes is vulnerable to chafe, and over time (and in choppy waters, this can be in less than an hour) the rode will fail if no antichafe measures are taken.

For the lower portions of the anchor rode, the best protection against chafe is an adequate length of chain, but other measures must be taken over the upper portions of a chain-rope rode. At the bow roller, deck pipe, or fairleads, chafe protection can be added by using sleeves made of thick leather, a solid rubber or plastic hose cut lengthwise, or a flexible fire hose (available commercially or, if you're lucky, from your local fire station's scrap heap). Considering how much the anchor line can surge in and out in bad weather, the protecting elements should be well lashed in place with wire ties, twine, or hose clamps. Make sure the sleeve is long enough to move slightly without exposing the critical chafe point. If the water is very choppy, any antichafe material will be moved within a few minutes if not adequately secured.

If the boat must be left unattended for a long period of time at anchor or on a mooring, create a customized anchor line protector, bridging the chafe-prone bow section of your anchor line with a length of chain. The chain piece should be long enough to reach from a deck cleat and through the bow roller (as shown in the illustration below) but not so long that the chain reaches the water's surface. This chain bridge should be fitted on both ends with a length of rope. You can achieve this either by using the rope-to-chain splice (see pages 65–68) or with a spliced eye thimble and shackle (see pages 62–65).

Attach this chain bridge to your rode at the waterline with a rolling hitch. Attach the upper portion of the chain bridge to a deck cleat. Be sure that the chain bridge, shackle, and attachment ropes have the same breaking strength as does the entire anchor gear. Then leave the chafe-prone anchor line section loosely fastened on deck.

For longer periods at anchor it makes sense to rig a short piece of chain fitted with rope at both ends in order to bridge the critical section at the gunwale to protect the anchor line from chafe at the bow roller.

Routine Inspection and Maintenance

Before every season, or before embarking on a bluewater cruise, do your routine inspection and maintenance on your anchor, chain, and line, as outlined below.

Anchor

Inspect the galvanization and regalvanize if necessary. Look for oxidation, deformation, or seized shackles.

Consider painting your anchor white or any other bright color, as this enhances its visibility in clear waters to verify proper setting.

Chain

Inspect the galvanization, and turn the entire chain end for end or newly galvanize it as needed. Abrasion is usually much more pronounced at the lower end of the chain leader, close to the anchor. End-for-ending the chain leader more evenly distributes abrasion over the entire chain length. This may permit you to postpone regalvanization a season or more.

Consider painting your anchor white for better visibility when it is submerged.

If you have an all-chain rode, do not neglect its bitter end. Some skippers never deploy enough rode to expose the bitter end, and if never moved around it can fuse itself into a hunk of rust in the chain locker.

In general, when inspecting chain, you should:

- Verify that no links are bent.
- Inspect for wear, especially around the contact points between links.
- Inspect for cracks or crevices in links.
- Inspect length markers and redo if necessary.

As stated before, the lower portion of your chain will be the most subject to chafing and corrosion and thus is the area where galvanization tends to wear out the quickest. One solution is end-for-ending the chain as mentioned, but after a while you may need to regalvanize your entire chain.

Before regalvanizing, you should confirm that the link diameter has not diminished excessively from wear or oxidation. A 10% loss of thickness is the maximum acceptable. Check with your galvanizing company to verify two important points:

1. Make sure the company uses an acid bath powerful enough to remove any length markers painted on the chain. If this is not the case, you must burn off the paint with a gas torch before you bring it in, otherwise these links will not receive proper treatment.

2. Make sure the company uses a vibrating drum during the cooling process, which inhibits the chain links from sticking

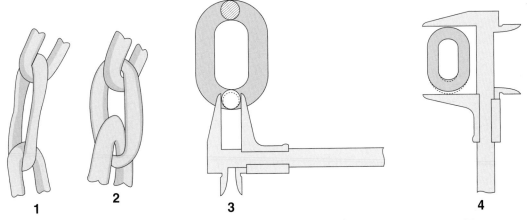

1   **2**   **3**   **4**

Galvanized steel chain is easier to examine for wear than stainless steel. If the links are elongated (1), or over-worked (2), the chain should be replaced. Check your chain annually with a vernier caliper. Make sure you know the original link thickness and length when new. Measure the thickness of the links, and if the chain thickness has decreased by over 10%, start shopping for a new chain (3). The same goes for a chain with links that have elongated more than 3% from the original length (4).

together. Otherwise, each link fuses with the next, rendering the chain unusable. You don't want to have to meticulously free each link one by one with a hammer; this is boring work without any guarantee of success, and it only damages the recent galvanization and requires an immediate repetition of the whole scenario.

Look at the difference between the rusty chain and freshly galvanized chain. Regalvanization can prolong the life of your anchor chain considerably.

Rust

Note the rust oozing from the anchor chamber. This can indicate that it might be too late to save the chain with a fresh coat of zinc.

73

Line

Routinely inspect the line portion of the anchor rode, looking for chafe, cut strands, and other possible deterioration. This can be done conveniently while anchoring in settled conditions, merely by letting the rope down slowly while examining it closely. If you discover severed strands, remove the defective part or replace the whole rope. If you find localized chafe, carefully inspect all the points where the rope bears on cleats, chocks, and bow rollers. Washing the rope in fresh water from time to time is a good idea, since fine sand, mud, and salt crystals cause abrasion. Inspect splices and cut and resplice as necessary.

Boaters are often advised to wash sheets, halyards, dock lines, and anchor rodes in a washing machine, preferably with fabric softener. Before you attempt this, however, be sure to ask permission from the washing machine's principal user. Most anchor lines are too thick to put inside a net, and they can damage the washing drum. It is safer to use a large basin or outside sink or trough for soaking in fresh water.

A PRACTICAL SUMMARY FOR SELECTING GROUND TACKLE

We hesitate to make quick-fix recommendations for outfitting a boat with ground tackle. Each vessel has its unique parameters, each skipper his or her needs, requirements, and budget. Instead, we hope the information and tables throughout this chapter and the preceding chapters will help guide you to the ideal combination for your boat. (You can also learn more about unconventional rode solutions in Appendix 2.) As you proceed, keep the following parameters in mind:

- What loads will your anchor and ground tackle be subjected to? Use Table 2-1 as a guide.

- Next, you need to select an anchor. Chapter 3 is not exhaustive, but it gives you an idea of what is available. Depending on your budget and needs, Tables 3-1, 3-2, and 3-3 will help you determine what model and size of anchor will work for you.

- Refer to Table 4-4 for sizing your chain, nylon rode, shackles, and connectors. Remember that all elements should offer comparable safe working loads, but that it can be disadvantageous to grossly oversize the nylon line diameter because of the consequent decrease in elasticity.

CHAPTER 5

Deck Equipment and Layout

Even the most luxurious megayachts must contend with the fact that usable deck space is as limited as the need and desire for specialized gear and equipment on deck is great. Careful organization, thoughtful design, precise placement, and methodical installation on deck are of primary importance in a properly functioning vessel and anchoring system.

In general, layout options for deck gear are somewhat less restricted for powerboats, since sailboat design must work around standing

Back in the days when boats were made of wood, the men had to be made of steel. Anchoring was a backbreaking job, requiring up to six able-bodied crewmembers.

rigging. However, whether for a powerboat or sailboat, anchoring deck gear must be chosen wisely and installed carefully—and then it must be painstakingly maintained.

Today's skippers have at their disposal a plethora of gizmos and gadgets to complete and complement their anchor gear. A boat could sink under the weight of all the items you just might need. As in all aspects of seamanship, strong opinions diametrically oppose each other and sometimes cancel each other out, even when they are based on fact and experience.

In this chapter we focus on the essential accessories your anchor and rode need to perform to their maximum potential. From fore to aft, we discuss the bow roller, mooring bitt, chain stopper and/or chain hook, deck pipe, chain locker, and windlass. Keep in mind that the need for this equipment will vary from vessel to vessel, depending on the size and weight of both the vessel and the skipper's wallet.

BOW ROLLERS

A bow roller (or anchor mount, bow fitting, or anchor roller) allows you to store your anchor in a position ready for launch and retrieval. It should keep your anchor some distance from your vessel's precious finish, yet the anchor should sit snugly and securely, presenting an elegant forward surface.

During passage, a well-designed bow roller should keep your anchor secure and stable, without rocking or shifting on its mount at the bow. During launch and retrieval, the anchor rode, whether chain or line, must run freely and securely through the bow roller.

This bow-roller setup offers little lateral support. Thin flanges can be bent by just the rode, let alone chain or any other object it may contact.

Finally, your bow roller should provide a dependable and sturdy point of contact for your rode when at anchor, especially in inclement weather.

Keep in mind that the forces and loads exerted on the rode are transferred directly to

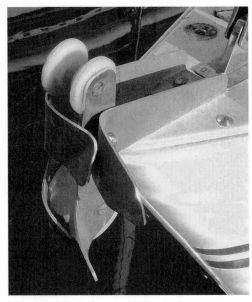

This is what happens if your flange plates are too thin; they buckle like an accordion.

the bow roller; it should therefore ideally be built of thick steel and bolted solidly through the deck, supported by reinforcement plates below.

Following are some specific points to keep in mind when choosing and using your bow roller:

- The bow roller should be crafted to cradle the anchor it supports, which should be permanently mounted there, ready for launching. Unless your bow roller was manufactured to specifically accommodate your particular anchor, this condition may not be met. Keep this in mind when you are perusing the market for anchors. You wouldn't buy a shoe without trying it on; see if one of your neighbors has your chosen model on his boat and ask him if you can borrow it for a trial run.

- The bow roller/mount must protrude sufficiently from the hull's sheerline to protect the hull from any banging from the chain and anchor. It must not, however, protrude too much; in a heavy swell, the trough must handle extreme loads of pressure, and the longer it extends, the heavier the torque.

- If you think your secured anchor might come in contact with the hull, consider attaching a small crescent fender under the bow roller (see top photo page 79). This can serve as a support system for the anchor and a safety buffer for the hull.

- It is wise to prepare your gear for heavy winds and seas. Your forward mount should be fitted with an immobilizing mechanism such as an anchor lock, removable bail, or keeper pin to prevent the anchor from skipping out of its trough in surges. The mechanism must be removable or changeable in case you have to decide to change storm tactics. This mechanism should not be a rod that penetrates the anchor (through a hole such as the trip line attachment point). Such rods can become jammed in the anchor when hit regularly by large masses of water.

- A pivoting bow roller (cantilevered mounting) facilitates the dropping and weighing of anchor gear remotely but can create problems with heavy loads. Pivoting bow rollers are not recommended for large boats.

- The wheel of a bow roller can be made out of metal (bronze) or plastic (e.g., Teflon or Delrin) and should adapt to both line and chain. If you use a chain leader, a rope groove with a chain slot in the center of the rolling wheel will encourage the chain to untwist and keep the rope centered on the bow roller upon retrieval.

- Dual rollers (i.e., one behind the other) offer the ideal setup. Failing that, the larger the diameter (within reason) of a single roller, the better behaved the anchor will be while moving over the assembly.

- The roller and its flanges should be wide enough to allow the anchor to come up on its side for some distance, as

Double-trough mounting with rounded flanges.

A custom-fitted bow roller for a roll-bar anchor with large, rounded flanges.

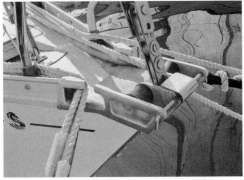

Production boats often have undersized bow rollers. It is doubtful that this roller can accommodate the shaft of most new-generation anchors. The smooth black plastic roller has a very small diameter and no groove in the center to guide the chain leader.

A CQR in a simple pivoting bow roller. The second bow roller offers nothing in terms of stability, no reinforcements, and no flanges.

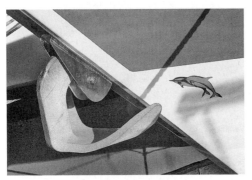

A custom-built bow roller is fine, but it may only accommodate one type of anchor. This bow roller is integrated in the hull to fit a claw anchor.

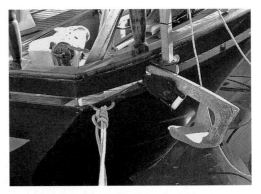

A stern anchor mount. The lateral white nylon wheels on the sides prevent line chafe.

This crescent-shaped bow fender helps avoid hull damage.

Neither of these two safety bolt systems actually prevent the anchors from unintentional launch. Note how the skipper needed to secure the crown of the articulating CQR to prevent it from flopping around.

We advise against using a bolt through the trip line hole for securing your anchor. This bolt could easily bend or get stuck at the wrong moment, making deployment impossible.

anchors do not always come home upright. Some poor anchor designs utilize a long shank design; these will jam in an assembly that is too narrow.

- At anchor, once the boat begins to heave and pitch, the anchor rode will put pressure on the flanges of the bow roller. Liberally flared trough cheeks offer an even, rounded surface for the chafe-prone fiber rope to run against. Consider adding additional chafe protection to your bow roller, including lateral antichafe rollers.

Bow Rollers on Multihulls

Catamaran bow rollers and ground tackle must be designed quite differently, since the anchor gear is usually located between the hulls, often close to the mast. Most agree that

anchoring can be more challenging on a catamaran, since the bow roller is usually located between the two hulls, but the anchor is usually stowed in one of the hulls. Few modern catamarans provide a structurally sound central foredeck for a bow roller. Under ideal weather conditions this doesn't pose much of a problem, since the rode can be belayed near the stem of one hull and the vessel made to lie at an angle to the wind.

We advise against central anchor rollers on catamarans, which are installed on the forward aluminum crossbar that supports the trampoline. Although this is a convenient design, it is only effective in stable weather conditions and has caused misfortune to many a multihull caught in a storm. The loads exerted on the middle of this relatively fragile crossbar are enough to override the mechanical resistance

Stowing Multiple Anchors

Some vessels have only one bow roller, but skippers nevertheless want to stow a second primary or secondary anchor on the foredeck or afterdeck. This anchor must be very well secured and should not encumber the operation of the vessel. Anchors poorly secured on deck may come loose during a rolly passage and cause damage to life and limb (which is not unheard of).

Extra weight at the boat's extremities may cause it to pitch more heavily in big waves. Remember the importance of reducing weight at the extremities of your boat. We recommend storing your spare anchors either in the chain locker, or even better, close to the vessel's center of gravity in the bilge, as close to the ballast as possible.

We often see boats equipped with two anchors on two separate rollers at the bow. Don't automatically assume the crews of these boats are experienced bluewater sailors who anchor frequently; this can also be a sign that the skipper doesn't trust his main anchor and tries

to compensate by doubling up with a second one (in which case he has no more confidence in his first anchor). Just because an anchor mount has two troughs doesn't mean it is meant to accommodate two anchors at all times.

Two anchors are not necessarily the sign of a serious offshore cruiser. This boat has unnecessary weight at the bow.

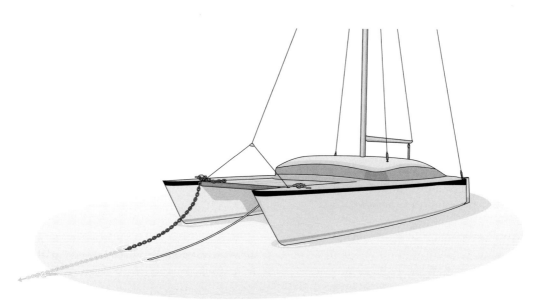

A catamaran at anchor with a bridle.

of the whole system and can even bring down the rig or capsize the boat. It is best is to distribute the load equally between the two hulls by using a bridle (for more on anchoring multihulls, see Chapter 6).

The configuration of bow roller and ground tackle on trimarans should be similar to that on monohulls, since they will have a similar anchor locker, bow roller, mooring bitt, and windlass located in the central hull.

BOW PLATFORMS AND BOWSPRITS

The bow platform can serve a variety of purposes. For the crew, it's a perfect spot for dolphin watching, keeping a lookout, or seafloor observation. For the rig, it may allow you to extend the roller furling or forestay for a genoa or spinnaker.

A bowsprit may also facilitate anchor storage, distancing the anchor from the hull and reducing risk of the two performing a damaging dance.

Platforms that have integrated bow rollers and bowsprits that have side-mounted rollers

One solution to having an anchor at the bowsprit is to place the bow roller on one side or the other of the bowsprit.

A bow platform with a heavy roll-bar anchor exacerbates pitching of the vessel in high seas.

present stowage problems for some anchors. The side flukes of the Bruce and other claw types can strike the underside of a platform or the bowsprit. Roll-bar anchors, such as the Bügel, may present similar stowage problems with a bowsprit.

If you plan on owning a sailboat with a bowsprit, or building a bowsprit with an anchor roller, be sure to accommodate the specific anchor(s) you wish to employ. Make sure that the anchor blade or roll bar doesn't get entangled with the bobstay during retrieval.

Also, consider the extreme loads the bowsprit must endure in bad weather. Front and side loads of bowsprits increase with their length. You must find a compromise between the necessity of building a solid, heavy-duty structure and the additional weight in an undesirable location (at the bow), forward of the vessel's center of gravity.

You must also have access to space in the forepeak for building solid reinforcements, which should absorb and distribute the vertical and horizontal loads on the hull and on the new forward structure.

Vessels equipped with a bobstay must face the common problem of their anchor rode rubbing against the stay, creating an annoying noise with the anchor chain and potentially chafing and shearing the anchor line. Some skippers choose to provide chafe protection for the rode for when it comes in contact with the bobstay while swaying at anchor, but this doesn't help with the noise. It is best to separate the bobstay from your rode, which can be done with a strong, sturdy chain hook attached to a nylon snubber.

Attach a line section at the water stay chainplate below the bobstay with a thimble and a shackle. At the other end of this line, which should be at least long enough to reach

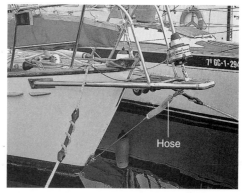

The hose at the bobstay—installed to prevent chafing of anchor tackle—suggests this bow platform causes friction and sleepless nights at anchor.

the deck, should be a single chain hook. Attach this end to the anchor chain on deck, and pay out chain until the entire load is on the snubber. The snubber will be held taut by

Bobstays are often problematic when anchoring, since the chain rode can grate against the stay, generating irritating noises.

the anchor chain's load at a forward position, below the water stay. When weighing anchor, the chain hook and line section can be retrieved and fastened on deck along with the anchor chain, ready for the next deployment.

The chain hook is also important for monohulls without a bowsprit, serving as a shock absorber or snubber. We recommend

The bobstay of this bowsprit might cause serious damage to an anchor line. See our solution with a snubber and chain hook attached at the bobstay chainplate.

This chain bobstay obstructs both anchors. Two full-chain rodes will probably cause sleepless nights due to the chain-on-chain grinding noise.

attaching a 20- to 25-foot (6 m to 8 m) portion of nylon line along the upper anchor chain portion to the mooring bitt. This shock-absorbing line should hook into an anchor chain link with a special single or double chain hook.

A double chain hook can connect two separate lines to the anchor chain and is therefore especially adapted to distribute the ground tackle load on two mooring bitts (discussed in the following section) situated on either side of the foredeck.

Double chain hook.

Single chain hook.

Double chain hooks are also an ideal solution on multihulls if you want to create a V-shaped bridle for the anchor rode attachment on both hulls.

SECURING AN ANCHOR AND GROUND TACKLE ON DECK

Riding at anchor for extended periods of time without a device to relieve the direct load from the windlass can place an unnecessarily heavy load on this precious piece of equipment.

A strong, elastic nylon snubber installed with the above-mentioned chain hook will greatly diminish this strain, and the best place to attach this snubber on deck is a *mooring bitt* (also called a samson post or bollard), the next indispensable piece of deck equipment.

Once the anchor is set, the mooring bitt allows you to protect the windlass from rode forces and swaying motion that will otherwise, with time, wear down and damage your windlass's gearbox and bearings. This sturdy pillar of strength should also serve as the attachment point between the bow roller and the windlass for the nylon portion of a hybrid rode. It also can come in handy if your vessel ever needs a tow due to an engine problem.

Some series-produced vessels do not offer a strong cleat or mooring bitt on the foredeck, so if you are currently boat shopping, check for this important feature.

In order to match and accommodate the breaking load of the entire ground tackle, check the mooring bitt for sturdiness and holding capacity. Positioning and size of the mooring bitt depends on the deck layout

A vertical windlass with a well-conceived mooring bitt.

and size of each particular vessel. The post needn't be so tall so as to dominate the foredeck; in fact, a shorter mooring post will be stronger and very effective. The mooring bitt must be installed using proper through-hull support fittings, and ideally they should extend belowdeck to distribute the load through a reinforced portion of the deck. A correctly mounted post should reinforce deck strength in the form of structural support.

Chain Stopper for a Hybrid Rode: A Necessity

A chain stopper adds additional security by preventing accidental free fall of the anchor while underway. This piece of equipment is also absolutely indispensable if your windlass gypsy does *not* accommodate both rope and chain, or if the windlass offers a separate capstan/gypsy configuration that requires you to change from one to the other, often under significant load.

The weight of anchor chain increases with its diameter. During strong winds or

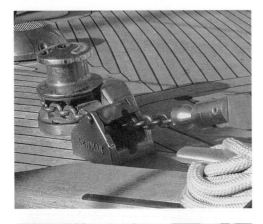

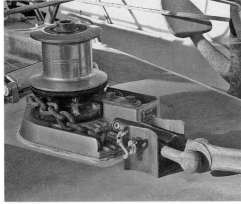

Chain stoppers.

There are several types of chain stoppers on the market. Most allow for quick release and quick relock, which can simplify the mooring process.

Skippers who feel uneasy about this challenging maneuver might choose to live with the disadvantage of additional weight in the forepeak and opt for a long or even full-chain anchor rode instead. But we still strongly recommend that those skippers have emergency anchor gear aboard with a chain-line combination rode to combat the heavy jolts brought on with the full-chain anchor gear in heavy-weather conditions.

Some recommend using a chain stopper to remove the load from the windlass when at anchor to protect your windlass. We disagree, since this device alone cannot provide elastic shock absorption. It is our opinion that a chain stopper should only hold the anchor chain directly during fair-weather conditions.

Snubber with a Chain Hook

An elastic line section, or snubber, should be added to every all-chain anchor rode in order to absorb shock load forces. We've discussed securing your chain rode on deck and demonstrated how a strong chain hook can be placed at any point of the anchor chain in order to connect an elastic line section to the deployed chain length. Beware of line damage due to friction at the bow roller and keep in mind that the shock-lessening effect of a snubber is proportional to its length and inversely proportional to its diameter.

waves, tricky maneuvers can turn into serious dangers. This considerable load becomes difficult to manage when the chain needs to be moved from the windlass chain gypsy to the rope drum during the anchor maneuver. It is *absolutely necessary* to secure the anchor chain with a chain stopper or the previously mentioned chain hook. Otherwise you can easily be pulled overboard by a heavy chain leader's weight load during the manual changeover from the chain gypsy to the rope drum.

Chain hooks.

Chain locker.

ANCHOR RODE STOWAGE

Chain Lockers

If your vessel is equipped with one or several all-chain or mostly chain rodes and at least two anchors, the forward weight can be in excess of several hundred pounds. This amount of weight placed near the bow can seriously alter the way a vessel maneuvers, particularly affecting its pitching behavior in heavy seas. However, the foredeck is indeed where we need our trusty chain. Some skippers attempt to tackle the problem by hacking up their chain into sections and putting a portion of it in the bilge, close to the keel. As we mentioned in Chapter 4,

we do not believe this is a good solution. The simplest and safest method is to leave the chain leader in one piece inside a chain locker.

A well-designed chain locker should be self-draining and both deep and narrow to minimize kinking. Ideally, the chain locker should be accessible from both below- and abovedeck.

Only second to the bilge, the chain locker will possibly be among the dirtier, smellier places on your boat. Although you will need to access its interior from below in case you have to untwist or flake the chain, you also need to be able to shut out its pungent odor and high humidity from your cabin, especially if your boat has a forward berth. No matter how much you scrub and scrape your chain upon retrieval, a certain amount of sand and mud—in addition to crustaceans—will be lifted over the bow roller and through the deck pipe and into this dark and dingy home. Many powerboats and luxury yachts are equipped with pressure hoses at the front to reduce the mess, but most of us are stuck with buckets and the unpopular job of intermittently cleaning and repainting the chain locker. Of course, a good time to do this work is when the chain is also getting a face-lift such as regalvanization.

Some yachts have their chain lockers located as close to the boat's center of gravity as possible, and this design has become standard with catamarans. Putting a lattice or grating at the bottom of the anchor chain locker creates a buffer between hull and chain, especially for a fiberglass hull. It also improves ventilation and drainage.

In order to ensure smooth anchor retrieval it is important to free the windlass gypsy from the running chain through the deck pipe. The weight force of the hanging anchor rode below the windlass should be sufficient to pull the rode inside the locker after it detaches from the turn around the windlass gypsy.

Keep in mind that anchor chain can pile up inside the chain locker below the deck pipe. If your chain locker is not deep enough, the piled-up chain can prevent your windlass from functioning properly by blocking the deck pipe or jamming the windlass. Having someone in the forepeak below distributing the chain upon retrieval can be helpful.

If you are stuck with a shallow or wide locker, there are a few do-it-yourself minor changes you can try. If there is space below, a

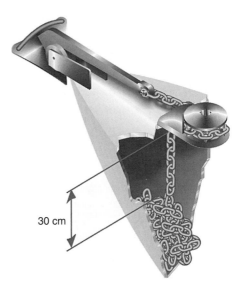

Chain fall. The minimum chain fall (the distance between the arrows) is 30 cm, or approximately 1 foot.

30 cm

A catamaran's chain locker, located close to the mast foot, close to the boat's center of gravity. (Courtesy Catana Catamarans)

Chain locker

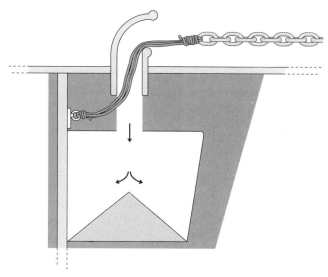

For those who insist on an all-chain rode, the lashing to the bitter end should be accessible from deck for quick cutting. A small pyramid built at the bottom of your chain locker will help prevent mass pileup of chain directly under the deck pipe.

chute made of sheet metal, narrow at the top and wide at the bottom, can help the chain flake optimally as it drops into the locker. Another design strategy to prevent chain pileup is to construct a small pyramid at the bottom of the chain locker.

Horizontal windlasses should allow at least 1 foot of space belowdeck for the chain to fall; vertical windlasses might need a bit more room (about 15 inches). Twisted three-strand anchor line is less flexible than braided line and needs even more space below the deck pipe.

If the anchor chamber is located below the waterline, you may not be able to place a drainage hole at the bottom, because it would fill with water every time you went to sea. If this is the case, make sure you have a solid plug for the deck pipe to keep water from coming in when you are offshore.

A chamber that is too deep may also be inaccessible by hand. If something is wrong down there, you can't easily manipulate the chain.

Line Stowage

Stowing line can be a real challenge. Even if you are planning to anchor in 30 feet of water, your rode should be at least 300 feet long, and that's one long rope. Coils can mesh together in an ugly knotty mess if they are not properly flaked. Plastic laundry bins can offer temporary storage for coiled rope. Use the kind that permits air circulation and prevents mildew. Square-line ropes store much more easily than three-strand ones.

Starting with the bitter end, neatly coil the anchor rope into your basket. As long as the coils are not moved during stowage, the rode should launch without difficulty.

WINDLASSES

A windlass, or an anchor winch, reduces the effort required to hoist and lower heavy ground tackle and might be the best labor-saving device you can add to your boat. Employing the power and mechanical advantage of an anchor windlass can make anchoring faster, easier, and safer. On small craft, where the anchor and anchor rode are less cumbersome, a windlass may be superfluous. This is not the case once the boat and its anchor gear increase in size and weight.

Having a windlass on board also opens up more opportunities for discovering a variety of cruising grounds. Without an anchor

Manual work with anchor line can be dangerous; this crewmember risks injury to hands and/or feet. Always wear gloves and closed-toe shoes when operating windlass equipment.

Do You Need a Windlass?

Boaters with small vessels may forgo a windlass, but this means choosing lighter ground tackle that can be weighed manually. This choice will certainly "limit the scope" of where and when these skippers can anchor. Shorter rodes cannot accommodate deeper anchorages, and lighter ground tackle may not withstand heavier weather.

If you don't have a windlass and are considering staying "windlassless," a good test is to first find out how much weight your legs and back can handle when manually pulling in ground tackle over the bow roller.

Go to a spot with deep water on a calm day and let out an anchor with chain over the bow. Stop *before* the pull becomes too much for you, then weigh (as in measure the weight of) the deployed overboard equipment. Don't forget to add a safety margin for bad weather conditions.

We are convinced this experiment will leave you wishing for an anchor windlass!

windlass, the size and weight of the ground tackle is limited to what the crew can handle, thus limiting the areas you can navigate in with any level of comfort. With the addition of a windlass, larger, heavier ground tackle can be added, expanding your ability to cruise new grounds.

Keep in mind, however, that more cumbersome ground tackle, including a windlass, offers new chances for injuring yourself—and badly. A windlass and chain are the cause of many serious injuries. A pair of heavy-duty gloves and sturdy shoes, or even boots, can protect your appendages and should be an integral part of any windlass equipment, along with the winch handle.

Windlasses are available with either a horizontal or vertical axis. Some windlasses can be operated only manually, while larger ones

Vertical windlass.

Horizontal windlass.

installation of a power-hungry electric windlass. If your vessel is equipped with a small outboard engine, or lacks a strong alternator to recharge your batteries, it might be a good idea for you to select a manual windlass for your foredeck.

A shorter lever will reduce the maximal force applied to the rode, and a low, non-ergonomic position of the lever will limit the leverage a person can apply. Manual windlasses must have a ratchet mechanism that allows the drum and gypsy to turn only in the retrieval direction, and a clutch or brake to help pay the anchor rode out smoothly. Manual windlasses come in single- and dual-speed models. Dual speeds offer fast, lower power for easy pull and a slower gear for breaking out a stubborn anchor or for rougher weather. We like double-action models in which both fore-and-aft strokes of the lever arm pull in more rode. Manual windlasses with a horizontal axis are usually equipped with this long double-action lever, which allows the operator

may be electric or hydraulic. All windlasses should have a manual option in case of electrical or hydraulic failure.

Manual Windlasses

Generally found on small to medium-sized boats (25 to 40 feet), manual windlasses operate through leverage, and gearing that amplifies human exertion with a crank.

Perhaps your small vessel's onboard electrical system is unable to accommodate the

A Lofrans horizontal manual winch. (Courtesy Imtra)

to stand upright and use both arms to weigh anchor. We feel that horizontal axis models are usually the better choice for manually operated windlasses for this reason.

Manual windlasses are available in both vertical and horizontal models, with the horizontal being the most common by far. Some small vertical models are operated with a standard winch handle by an operator, working on hands and knees on the foredeck.

The advantages of a manual windlass are:

- Relatively easy installation and maintenance.

- Low cost to purchase, install, and maintain.

- Few parts, which are usually accessible.

- Reliable, as it is not dependent on hydraulic or electrical systems.

  The disadvantages are:

- Hoisting your ground tackle with a manual windlass is a slow process and requires physical strength.

Electric Windlasses

If your vessel's main engine is equipped with a strong alternator and sufficient battery capacity, we think you will not regret the installation of an electric windlass if you hope to anchor frequently.

An electric windlass may be used both during launch and weighing of ground tackle. Although gravity does most of the work when dropping anchor, having the windlass control the speed at which the scope is paid out prevents a skipper from having to intervene at the bow. Electric windlasses are becoming

more popular with boaters simply because of the ease with which you can lower and retrieve the anchor. You press a button and watch the chain and anchor rise. This is an ideal solution for singlehanders. Thanks to remote-control installation, a skipper can remain in the cockpit while retrieving his ground tackle. If the anchor chain locker is well designed, it should be possible to motor forward while raising the anchor, all from the cockpit or command post.

Electric windlasses are commonly available in 12-volt and 24-volt models and range from units as small as 500 pounds of pull up to very large units of 10,000 pounds.

A common electric windlass is the vertical model with the rope drum mounted on top of the chain gypsy, although small horizontal models have been recently improved and are gaining popularity.

Whether horizontal or vertical, all electric windlasses share common design features.

- An energy source, be it a crank and lever for voluntary or emergency manual use or electrical/hydraulic power.

- A gearbox that converts the higher rotation speed of the windlass motor to the lower rpm of the warping drum or chain gypsy axle. Multiple-speed gearboxes provide several transmission ratios for slow reeling under heavy loads and high-speed reeling under low loads.

- A warping drum for winching in lines.

- A chain gypsy that consists of sprockets fitted with link pockets, which prevent the anchor chain from

Foot switches

Vertical electric windlass with foot switches.

slipping around the windlass axle and running amok. A combined chain-rope gypsy contains a deep V-shaped groove in the center of the sprocket to accommodate rope. These rippled grooves should also accommodate the chain-to-rope splices described earlier.

- A conical clutch that, when engaged, unites the shaft with the motor when under load. When disengaged, the chain gypsy is allowed to run freely with manual control of the anchor rode when dropping anchor. This clutch also may exist on some windlasses as a metal band over a cylindrical disk.

- The chain stripper, a minor element in a windlass, consists of a small finger centered in the sprocket, which forcibly separates the chain or line from the gypsy and leads it smoothly into the chain pipe.

The advantages of an electric windlass are:

- Exerts more pull than a manual windlass.

- Can raise and lower anchors by push button.

The disadvantages are:

- May require a substantial addition to the boat's electrical system; batteries may need to be beefed up.

- Additional wiring and circuit breakers may need to be added and maintained.

- Higher purchase, installation, and maintenance costs.

Hydraulic Windlasses

Megayachts and ships over 60 feet (18 m) require very large anchors with $\frac{1}{2}$-inch chain or even stronger. This is the world of hydraulic windlasses. These large vessels often cannot take advantage of hybrid anchor rodes and must go with all-chain rodes because manual intervention at the windlass becomes too dangerous due to the sheer weight of the equipment involved. Spare anchors must be installed at the bow, ready for deployment; they cannot be stored in the bilge because no one would be able to carry them to the foredeck without the help of a crane. Large hydraulic windlasses on big ships usually have custom-built outlet pipes that lead the chain almost vertically through deck and hull to increase the traction circumference of the chain around the gypsy.

Hydraulic windlasses are seldom seen on boats less than 60 feet long simply because of the expense and sophistication of the system. Usually, unless there is already a hydraulic system on board for other gear such as winches, it's not cost effective to install a hydraulic windlass on smaller vessels. Hydraulic windlasses are therefore available in models suitable for extremely large vessels.

The advantages of a hydraulic windlass are:

- Exerts more pull than any other type.
- Can raise and lower anchors by push button.
- Less fragile, lighter, and less sensitive to humidity than electric windlasses.

The disadvantages are:

- Very expensive; not cost effective unless a hydraulic system already exists on the boat.
- Higher purchase, installation, and maintenance costs.

SIZING YOUR WINDLASS

We rate windlass performance by how much weight it can lift and at what speed. Two considerations are the nominal pull and the maximum pull capacity. *Nominal line pull* is the force exerted continuously by the windlass during the retrieval of the anchor, while *maximum pull* (also called stall load) is the maximum force exerted by the windlass during a short period of time—for example, during the breakout of the anchor. The windlass can only support the maximum pull for a short time period since maximum pull is usually four times higher than the nominal pull.

When weighing anchor, a windlass passes through three stages:

1. Retrieving deployed rode

2. Dislodging the anchor

3. Lifting ground tackle to stowed position

The first phase is the longest and should require nominal pull with calm winds since the forward inertia of the vessel aids the windlass.

The second phase usually requires more than nominal pull, but doesn't necessarily overload the windlass with maximum pull. When a boat is anchored in a soft seafloor, the windlass pull increases just for a short time until the embedded anchor is dislodged and the final retrieval phase begins.

Windlasses should ideally be able to pull four times the weight of your entire main ground tackle (anchor, chain leader, and nylon section combined). So choose your anchor and rode, find out its weight, and multiply this value by four. This value should match the maximum pull of the windlass. Keep in mind that although your windlass may be able to do the job, we do not recommend dislodging anchors with the windlass under maximum pull (see the Anchor Retrieval section in Chapter 6).

Which Winch?

If you are shopping for a new windlass, advertising slogans such as "New Low Price" should be a hint that you will get what you pay for. Painted cast-aluminum housings will most likely start peeling quickly, revealing unprotected carbon steel components unsuitable for a saltwater environment. Some manufacturers attach electric windlass motors with hose clamps. A critical look at the windlass details in your local marine store can tell if a particular model has a chance of withstanding real-life conditions.

High rpm electric motors with low torque are often combined with several gears and shafts that need bearings, gaskets, and seals: this myriad of parts costs money and can fail.

Low rpm electric motors with high torque usually necessitate fewer components with a straightforward functionality. Unfortunately these positive features can result in a higher weight at the bow.

Take your time shopping and ask around. Compare the individual components of the various windlass models that would fit your boat. Most manufacturers supply sizing recommendations based on length overall in their catalogs (see Table 5-1 next page), but you should view these as guidelines only. Other factors for sizing your windlass include whether you plan weekend cruising or long-distance voyaging, your keel type, windage, and displacement.

Most anchor windlasses over 1,500 watts are equipped with hydraulic motors.

Chain Gypsies and Warping Drums

Rope-only windlasses include a capstan or warping drum around which the rope is wrapped, similar to the vertical sheet winch found on many sailboats. The rode must be hauled in by hand with the help of an electric motor, leaving a pile of rode that is stored once the anchor is fully retrieved.

TABLE 5-1. WINDLASS SELECTION

Vessel Length	Power (watts)	Maximum Pull	Nominal Line Pull	Speed
7.5–11.5 meters	500	300 kg	200 kg	20 m/min.
24.5–38 feet	1,100	660 lb.	440 lb.	65 ft./min.
7.5–13 meters	735	400 kg	275 kg	23 m/min.
24.5–42 feet	1,620	880 lb.	606 lb.	75 ft./min.
11.5–15 meters	1,000	600 kg	400 kg	25 m/min.
38–50 feet	2,200	1,320 lb.	880 lb.	82 ft./min.
13–16.5 meters	1,500	1,200 kg	500 kg	12 m/min.
42–54 feet	3,300	2,645 lb.	1,100 lb.	39 ft./min.
15–20 meters	Hydraulic	1,750 kg	1,000 kg	12 m/min.
50–65 feet	Hydraulic	3,860 lb.	2,200 lb.	39 ft./min.

By locking the chain into its gypsy sprockets, chain-only windlasses automatically tail, strip, and stow anchor chains. Aided by gravity and a chain stripper at the last pocket of the gypsy, chain rode should fall freely through the chain pipe into the locker belowdeck.

The windlass that accommodates our ideal hybrid rode offers a combined rope-chain gypsy with V-shaped grooves in the sprockets to self-tail and retrieve both types of anchor rode. For seamless retrieval of a hybrid rode, we recommend the chain-to-rope splice discussed in Chapter 4.

Just as we established that the ideal rode would consist of both chain and line, the ideal gypsy sprocket must be conceived to accommodate this combination. The next best thing is a windlass with separate warping drum for line rode and gypsy for chain, but with the heavy load at anchor it can be dangerous to your fingers and other body parts when moving the rode from the chain gypsy to the warping drum. It is essential to secure the chain leader with a chain

Gloves On

We (Achim and Erika) had just arrived at Cala Vadella on Ibiza after a three-day passage from southern France, and we were eager to throw the hook out and get some rest. It was the height of summer and the anchorage was very crowded. We were forced to anchor rather close to a rocky shoreline in about 40 feet of water.

This was our first anchor maneuver with our new sailboat, and our first time with a hybrid spliced rode. On the first try, the anchor set, but we felt we were too close to shore to get a proper night's sleep and decided to try again. The weather was good and the boat was not bouncing too much. Achim hauled in on the line portion of the rode and arrived at the pretty new splice just inches from the capstan, thinking, "Hmmm … it just needs to go down a few inches. How much could 120 feet of chain weigh on a gently rocking boat anyhow? If I could just hold the chain with my hands for a split second while there was a little slack moment, to just click those links down into that gypsy …"

Thankfully, Achim had gloves on, or he probably would have severed a thumb, instead of just leaving a bloody mess on the deck.

Erika wasn't much of an early fan of the hybrid rode once she saw Achim's mangled thumb. But we bought a handsome chain hook as soon as we arrived in Gibraltar, and since that lesson, making the transition hasn't been quite so threatening.

stopper or a chain hook during this tricky maneuver.

Chain gypsy sprockets should be size-matched to the chain links they drive. Even slight variations in the diameter, width, length, or shape of the chain link may make the system incompatible. Many windlass gypsies are designed for metric chain; they will not function correctly with chain that is imperial based. Checking with a sample of your chain in a chandlery may not be sufficient, since the difference is only a few millimeters (inches) that meter after meter (foot after foot) do add up and slip. It is best is to have actual documentation of the gypsy sprocket size before you purchase a windlass.

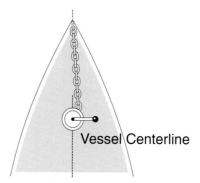

A vertical windlass works best on boats with a single bow roller on the centerline. As long as the gypsy is aligned vertically with the roller, the chain may approach from a skewed angle.

Vertical Orientation

Vertical windlasses are the most popular on medium-sized boats (27 to 45 feet). Resembling sheet winches on sailboats, vertical windlasses take up less space on the foredeck than horizontal windlasses. The gypsy and drum are stacked on top of a baseplate mounted to the deck, and electric vertical windlasses usually have the motor and gearbox belowdeck. Electric vertical windlasses may have a manual option, with the operator using a removable winch handle. The best use of a vertical windlass is on vessels with a single bow roller on the centerline.

In order to maximize the "grip" of the chain in the windlass gypsy, it is advantageous to have as many chain links touching the sprockets of the gypsy as possible. With a vertical windlass, the rode passes over deck from the bow roller to the windlass gypsy, where it wraps around 180° and feeds into the anchor chamber through a deck pipe. Horizontal windlasses have a clear disadvantage here, since their windlass gypsies cannot grab much more than 90° to 100° if the chain falls freely into the locker below.

Vertical windlass with combined rope-chain gypsy and warping drum.

We feel that the general advantage of 180° of rode traction around the chain gypsy circumference is significant, and we have therefore chosen vertical windlass models on our own boats. But if you do not have sufficient space belowdeck to accommodate the electric motor of a vertical windlass, you will likely choose a horizontal model instead.

The advantages of a vertical windlass are:

- Uses less deck space.

- The horizontal lead angle is not as critical, allowing you to warp from starboard or port on the rope drum.

- The motor and gearbox on electric units are located under deck, protected from the weather.

- Presents a lower profile and is therefore less likely to become tangled in sheets and lines than a windlass with a horizontal axis.

The disadvantages are:

- Often has a higher purchase and installation cost than horizontal models.

- Belowdeck parts are not easily accessed for maintenance.

- When using the manual option, you must kneel down on the foredeck to turn the winch handle of a vertical windlass in a rather uncomfortable position.

- Requires under-deck space in the forepeak where space may already be at a premium.

Horizontal Orientation

Horizontal windlasses are completely abovedeck systems with the gypsy and drum turning on a horizontal drive shaft. These are typically installed where space in the chain locker is limited and deck space is not restricted. A horizontal windlass is usually the most practical to install on boats with high bulwarks as the rode will lead fair from a position above or below the windlass. The rode must lead from the roller to center of the gypsy or drum on the athwartships plane, however. Boats with two bow rollers will often opt for a horizontal windlass, for these windlasses usually have port and starboard gypsies to deal with two anchor rodes on two bow rollers. Since most manual windlasses are also horizontal, smaller boats (under 30 feet) are often equipped with a horizontal windlass. Also, most larger yachts (over 55 feet) opt for the horizontal axis. The lateral alignment of horizontal windlass gypsies and the bow roller is important, since they cannot accept rodes leading from skewed

Horizontal windlass with chain-only gypsy and a separate warping drum. Beware! Keep your hands safe during the tricky shifting maneuver from the chain leader to the rode's line section.

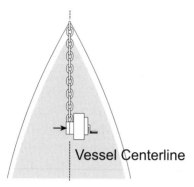

A horizontal windlass requires parallel alignment with the bow-roller axis.

angles. If you have a dual-rode setup, make sure that both bow rollers are in perfect alignment with their associated gypsy or warping drums on the windlass.

The advantages of a horizontal windlass are:

- All the parts are abovedeck for easier access and maintenance.
- Greater variety of gypsy configurations.
- Doesn't take up space in the forepeak.
- Better position for manual use (if this is an option).

The disadvantages are:

- The parts are exposed to the elements.
- The rode must lead to the center of the gypsy or drum, restricting the angle of pull.
- Takes up more deck space than a vertical windlass.

WINDLASS INSTALLATION

When installing an anchor windlass, keep in mind that it will be supporting extremely heavy loads. This is particularly important with windlasses that require a large opening in the foredeck in order to install the motor under the deck, as large cuts can substantially weaken your deck surface.

Proper anchor windlass installation incorporates metal beams under the deck to transfer windlass loads over a wide expanse of the deck and into the bulkheads and hull.

Fiberglass decks also need a wood base under the anchor windlass to prevent crushing the fiberglass composite. Wood decks need substantial under-deck reinforcement with metal plates or angles.

Positioning on Deck

With vertical windlasses, the horizontal placement (positioning toward port or starboard, fore or aft) of the warping drum is almost inconsequential, while the vertical placement must be aligned with the bow roller. Therefore, a vertical windlass may be installed in the center of the foredeck.

As far as vertical placement goes, if anchor line approaches the vertical warping drum from slightly below it is better to reel it in on a capstan. This avoids trapping the rope underneath itself on the drum when reeling it in. If a height disparity exists, elevate your vertical windlass with a wooden platform.

With horizontal windlasses, it is very important to perfectly align the warping drum and chain gypsy with the bow roller, meaning that the mechanical portion of the windlass will be slightly off-center on the foredeck. However, its vertical placement is inconsequential, and a horizontal windlass may, in theory and in practice, be installed inside the anchor chamber. However, make sure that the anchor chain remains in contact with at least a quarter of the chain gypsy's circumference and make sure there is enough space below for the chain to fall freely into the locker.

Positioning the Windlass

Vertical Windlass with Horizontal Motor

The mechanical power of this windlass type is transmitted from a horizontal motor shaft to the vertical gypsy shaft by a worm drive. This means that the gearbox automatically blocks if the motor stops, and the retrieved ground tackle won't unintentionally slip back in the water. Of course, this capacity shouldn't be abused as you could eventually strip the worm drive by putting too much load on it.

Upon retrieval, the chain leaves the gypsy and feeds through a deck pipe bent 90° into the chain locker. It is advantageous to allow the incoming chain extra free-fall distance (i.e., a deeper locker) to compensate for the friction in the chain pipe. When installing this configuration on the foredeck, it is crucial to allow for at least a 180° contact between chain and gypsy to assure that the links don't jump out of the gypsy sprockets under load.

These windlasses can be built relatively flush on deck, so genoa sheets are less apt to get caught underneath the windlass during a tacking maneuver. The horizontal motor under the deck is protected from the salt water on the foredeck and usually does not occupy too much space in the chain locker.

Vertical Windlass with Vertical Motor

These vertical windlasses have similar features abovedeck like their brothers with horizontal

Vertical windlass with vertical motor installed under the deck.

Gypsy

Deck pipe

Vertical windlass with horizontal motor installed under the deck.

motors. Since they do not have a self-blocking gearbox with worm drive, the operator must immediately engage a chain stopper in case the windlass stops unintentionally while weighing anchor. Otherwise the chain and anchor could be pulled overboard under heavy load. A vertically installed gearbox/motor assembly usually runs more efficiently than a horizontal one due to lower friction losses inside the gearbox. It depends on the individual chain locker design, but often an under-deck vertical motor is more cumbersome to install than a horizontal model.

Horizontal Windlass with Horizontal Motor Shaft Parallel to the Chain Gypsy

These windlasses can be quite efficient due to low friction losses in the gearbox. Like vertical windlasses with vertical gypsy shafts, they rely on the immediate use of a chain brake to prevent the chain from pulling out unintentionally with the weight of the ground tackle. They need a slightly shorter distance of

free-falling chain into the locker than vertical windlasses, but occupy more space on the foredeck, which is usually not problematic on powerboats.

Horizontal Windlass with Horizontal Motor Shaft Perpendicular to the Chain Gypsy

Like the horizontal windlasses with a parallel motor shaft, these models need a shorter distance of free-falling chain into the chain locker than vertical windlasses. On both horizontal types the anchor chain usually touches the chain gypsy for not much more than 90° to 100°. This can sometimes lead to the chain jumping and rattling over the gypsy under heavy load. These windlass models are often equipped with gypsies and warping drums on both, which can make them more suitable for handling two anchor rodes on two bow rollers, as opposed to other windlass designs.

They do not use much space inside the chain locker but can be cumbersome on the

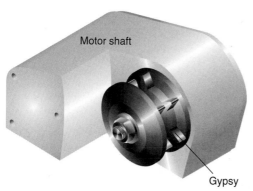

Horizontal windlass with horizontal motor shaft parallel to the chain gypsy.

Horizontal windlass with horizontal motor shaft perpendicular to the chain gypsy.

foredeck. Genoa sheets like to get stuck underneath the warping drums during a tack.

Wiring

Anchor windlasses are amp hogs, meaning they can consume a considerable amount of electricity when engaged; in some cases, over 400 amps at 12 volts when under maximum load. It is therefore necessary to install appropriately dimensioned wires between battery and windlass.

Using your main battery bank would simplify this installation, but you must then considerably increase the size of the wiring between battery and windlass, adding cost and weight throughout the boat.

Alternatively, you can put a separate battery near the windlass. This reduces the length of heavy wiring from the battery to the windlass. Also, since the charging circuit for a separate battery only needs to support the maximal current of the alternator or battery charger, you can decrease the wire diameter of this charging circuit. To minimize the negative effects of the additional forward weight, make sure the windlass battery is installed as low and as centered as possible.

The smaller the wiring diameter, the greater the drop in voltage, and the higher the loss of electrical energy in the circuit. The voltage drop equation is:

$$V = I \times L \times R/l$$

where

V = voltage drop

I = current, in amperes

L = length of the cable, in feet (accounting for both directions)

R/l = resistance per length unit (meters or feet), or ohm/length unit

In a 12-volt system, smaller windlasses draw around 35 amps of current under normal load, while larger ones draw from 85 to 125 amps under normal load. For example, on a 33-foot (10 m) boat, let's say we install a circuit from the main battery bank to the windlass and back to the main battery of approximately 50 feet (15 m). If we allow for 3% voltage loss at 70 amps consumption, the wire diameter must be no smaller than 50 mm² (0.03 Ω per 100 m – 328 feet). If we can live with a 10% loss, we can use a diameter half this size, or 25 mm² (0.07 Ω per 100 m – 328 feet).

Use Table 5-2 to select the appropriate wire diameter for a given maximal DC amperage load. The table makes the following assumptions:

1. **105°C insulation rating.** All anchor wire uses an 105°C insulation rating. Lower temperature insulation cannot handle as much current.

2. **AWG wire sizes, not SAE.** All anchor wire uses AWG (American Wire Gauge) wire sizes. SAE (Society of Automotive Engineers) wire sizes are 6% to 12% smaller, carry proportionally less current, and have greater resistance.

3. **Wires are not run in engine spaces.** Maximum current is 15% less in engine spaces, which are assumed to be 20°C

TABLE 5-2. AMERICAN WIRE GAUGE (AWG) WIRE SPECIFICATIONS

AWG Wire Size	Maximum Amperes	Outer Diameter (in.)	mm²	Circular Mil Area	Ohm per 1,000 Feet	Weight (lb.) per 1,000 Feet
10	60	7/32	5.3	10,500	0.98	44
8	80	5/16	8.4	16,800	0.62	86
6	120	11/32	13.3	26,800	0.4	108
4	160	13/32	21.2	42,000	0.24	178
2	210	15/32	33.6	66,500	0.157	277
1	245	17/32	44.2	83,690	0.127	350
1/0	285	9/16	53.5	105,600	0.1	437
2/0	330	5/8	67.4	133,000	0.077	549
3/0	385	11/16	85.0	167,800	0.062	675
4/0	445	13/16	107.2	211,600	0.05	837

hotter than non-engine-room spaces (50°C versus 30°C).

4. **Conductors are not bundled.** If three conductors are bundled, reduce maximum amperage by 30%. If four to six conductors are bundled, reduce maximum amperage by 40%. If seven to twenty-four conductors are bundled, reduce amperage by 50%.

Table 5-2 gives you information about the wire size you are using. For example, a 1/0 AWG wire will support a maximum of 285 amperes, will have a outer diameter of ⁹/₁₆, a cross section of 53.5 mm², and a resistance of 0.1 ohm per 100 feet.

According to the ABYC specifications, navigational lights, bilge ventilators, switchboard feeders, and electronic equipment require an electrical installation with maximal 3% voltage drop in the circuit. All other circuits for general lighting and electric motors are allowed to have a maximum of 10% voltage drop.

Use your windlass owner's manual to determine the wiring diameter you need to obtain the desired results.

If you want to save weight on your vessel because you have a racing yacht or a lightweight planing runabout, stick with the minimum wire size recommendations. On a cruising sailboat, saving electricity is usually more important than saving weight. Upgrading to a 24-volt supply voltage or using larger wire diameters than required will help you minimize the losses in your electrical wiring. Electrical losses in your onboard circuits can add up quickly, and you would lose a large portion of the precious electricity before it even gets to the battery. On *Pangaea*, we (Erika and Achim) chose larger-than-necessary wire diameters to connect the solar panels, the refrigerator, and other equipment that is used often (e.g., the 12-volt socket for the computer). Alain did the same thing on *Hylas*.

We did not apply the above logic to our windlass wiring, since we find it safer and

TABLE 5-3. ABYC CONDUCTOR SIZES FOR 3% VOLTAGE DROP IN A 12V CIRCUIT

Total Current on Circuit (amps)	Length of Conductor from Source of Current to Device and Back to Source (feet/meters)																		
	10 (3.0)	15 (4.6)	20 (6.0)	25 (7.6)	30 (9.1)	40 (12.2)	50 (15.2)	60 (18.3)	70 (21.3)	80 (24.0)	90 (27.4)	100 (30.5)	110 (33.5)	120 (36.5)	130 (39.6)	140 (42.6)	150 (45.7)	160 (48.1)	170 (51.8)
5	18	16	14	12	12	10	10	10	8	8	8	6	6	6	6	6	6	6	6
10	14	12	10	10	10	8	6	6	6	6	4	4	4	4	2	2	2	2	2
15	12	10	10	8	8	6	6	6	4	4	2	2	2	2	2	1	1	1	1
20	10	10	8	6	6	4	4	4	2	2	2	1	1	1	0	0	0	0	2/0
25	10	8	6	6	6	4	2	2	2	2	1	0	0	0	0	2/0	2/0	2/0	3/0
30	10	8	6	6	4	4	2	1	1	1	0	0	0	2/0	2/0	3/0	3/0	3/0	3/0
40	8	6	6	4	4	2	2	0	0	0	2/0	2/0	3/0	3/0	3/0	4/0	4/0	4/0	4/0
50	6	6	4	2	2	2	1	0	2/0	2/0	3/0	3/0	4/0	4/0	4/0				
60	6	4	4	2	2	1	0	2/0	3/0	3/0	4/0	4/0	4/0						
70	6	4	2	2	1	0	2/0	3/0	3/0	4/0	4/0								
80	6	4	2	2	0	0	3/0	3/0	4/0	4/0									
90	4	2	2	1	0	2/0	3/0	4/0	4/0										
100	4	2	2	1	0	2/0	3/0	4/0											

American Boat & Yacht Council

TABLE 5-4. ABYC CONDUCTOR SIZES FOR 10% VOLTAGE DROP IN A 12V CIRCUIT

Total Current on Circuit (amps)	Length of Conductor from Source of Current to Device and Back to Source (feet/meters)																		
	10 (3.0)	15 (4.6)	20 (6.0)	25 (7.6)	30 (9.1)	40 (12.2)	50 (15.2)	60 (18.3)	70 (21.3)	80 (24.0)	90 (27.4)	100 (30.5)	110 (33.5)	120 (36.5)	130 (39.6)	140 (42.6)	150 (45.7)	160 (48.1)	170 (51.8)
5	18	18	18	18	18	16	16	14	14	14	12	12	12	12	12	10	10	10	10
10	18	18	16	16	14	14	12	12	10	10	10	10	8	8	8	8	8	8	6
15	18	16	14	14	12	12	10	10	8	8	8	8	8	6	6	6	6	6	6
20	16	14	14	12	12	10	10	8	8	8	6	6	6	6	6	6	4	4	4
25	16	14	12	12	10	10	10	8	6	6	6	6	6	6	4	4	4	4	2
30	14	12	12	10	10	8	8	6	6	6	6	4	4	4	4	2	2	2	2
40	14	12	10	10	8	8	6	6	6	4	4	4	4	2	2	2	2	2	2
50	12	10	10	8	8	6	6	4	4	4	2	2	2	2	2	1	1	1	1
60	12	10	8	8	6	6	4	4	2	2	2	2	2	1	1	1	0	0	0
70	10	8	8	6	6	6	4	2	2	2	1	1	1	0	0	0	0	2/0	2/0
80	10	8	6	6	6	4	4	2	2	2	1	0	0	0	0	2/0	2/0	2/0	2/0
90	10	8	6	6	6	4	4	2	2	1	0	0	0	0	2/0	2/0	2/0	3/0	3/0
100	10	8	6	6	4	4	2	2	1	1	0	0	0	2/0	2/0	2/0	3/0	3/0	3/0

American Boat & Yacht Council

more convenient to run the main engine during our anchor maneuvers. We chose the recommended wire size for the windlass circuit and not a larger diameter, because we can live more easily with a little loss while the main engine alternator charges the batteries with 50 amps to 80 amps. If you have a very long wire from your battery to the windlass, it might be advantageous to upgrade the wire diameter for a different reason: your windlass loses power with a lower supply voltage. Check with the manufacturer regarding acceptable voltage levels for your windlass model.

The following list describes the individual components of an electric windlass circuit, as shown in the illustration:

- A circuit breaker protects the electrical circuit and avoids unintentional

deployment of the windlass at sea or in port.

- The circuit breaker should be specifically designed for use with windlasses, capable of handling high currents and protecting the windlass against overload.

- When tripped repeatedly, some thermal circuit breakers require a cooling down pause for a few minutes.

- A specific fuse protects the command circuit of the remote-control solenoid.

- For safety, install the two remote-control solenoids with push-button switches that operate the windlass only when the button is pressed.

- If you don't want remote-control wires, install a cordless remote control.

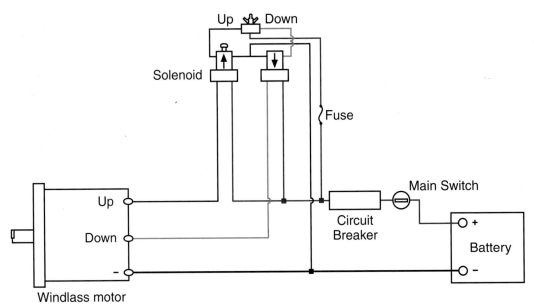

Circuit diagram of an electric windlass with a series-wound motor.

Singlehanded mariners will possibly appreciate a remote-control windlass installation that does not require manual intervention on the foredeck while setting or weighing anchor.

- Foot-operated push-button switches located on the foredeck permit control of the windlass while allowing the operator to observe his or her ground tackle's behavior.

- The windlass motor may be of either the *series-wound* type, meaning it has three electrical wire terminals, or the *permanent-magnet* type, which employs two wires for dropping and weighing, respectively.

- Always run the engine while operating the windlass. A separate charging system is not needed, but a dedicated

battery can be useful for reducing voltage drop and the wire length and diameter.

Vessels that require high-powered windlasses, such as larger yachts and fishing boats (for retrieving their nets), often choose hydraulic windlasses. They offer very high power without the need for large-diameter, heavy copper wiring or an upgrade from 12 volts to 24 volts or higher.

WINDLASS MAINTENANCE

The windlass is one of the more high-maintenance mechanisms aboard since it is situated in a humidity-prone area on the foredeck, subject to spray and waves. During the off-season, or when the vessel is not in use, protect it with a well-attached cover that allows humidity to escape and provides adequate ventilation.

Consistently protect and treat your windlass against corrosion, especially in areas where electrolysis is likely to occur, such as between the aluminum, bronze, and stainless steel parts. Check for leaks at the through-deck bolts of the windlass and the remote-control switches.

Windlasses must have the gearbox oil checked every year or two and supplemented with additional oil as needed. Do not use just any oil; refer to the manufacturer's instructions for the type of oil to use.

At least once a year, disassemble the warping drum and gypsy, clean them with diesel or petroleum, check all the springs and the clutch cone, and lubricate moving parts with saltwater-resistant grease.

Windlass Workout

On our (Erika and Achim's) first sailboat, we were particularly concerned about our installation budget and decided to save some money by installing an undersized circuit breaker we picked up at a flea market in the south of France. It worked fine, except when the windlass was working hard, the circuit breaker would trip too early. Since Erika was usually the one belowdecks in the forepeak monitoring the pyramid of chain, she was also the one who had to travel back to the chart table to untrip the fuse: click, run to the chart table, reset the fuse, run back to the forepeak berth for 20 seconds; click, run to the chart table; and so it went. If we had long scope out, the anchor maneuver was her aerobic exercise for the day.

If your windlass is electric, carefully check the entire electrical circuit, looking for corrosion and loose-connections. Make sure the starter solenoid and the remote-control device are functioning properly. If you use a separate battery for your windlass, check the battery charge and charge retention, check the charging circuit, and inspect the terminals for corrosion. If the windlass is not used often, allow it to run once a week or so to keep the components lubricated.

CHAPTER 6

Anchoring Techniques

You've stocked up and stowed all the supplies, you've studied some of the theory, and you've finally left port. Now comes the time for some action. All the reading and talking about anchoring is helpful, but there's nothing like the "gloves-on" experience. There will be times where the whole procedure feels almost self-evident, in which case the next two chapters may seem superfluous. The three most critical pieces of advice we can give you are: be prepared; take your time; and if at first you don't succeed, reanchor, reanchor, reanchor.

SELECTING AN ANCHORAGE

This aspect goes into the "be prepared" category. Just showing up at an anchorage you've heard about and hoping that you'll figure out the best place to anchor by following others is not the best strategy. Your friend's trusty advice or the little anchor marked on your nautical chart may offer great starting points, but only thorough research and careful observation combined with wise judgment will help you determine the actual spot where you decide to finally drop the hook.

You will want to study up on the location, preferably before you leave port, while you refresh your information underway. Cruising guides, magazine articles, chart kits, and sailing bulletins may contain helpful information about choosing a spot. Outdated guides might come your way for free—but they may also be worth what you paid for them. City streets are unlikely to change much, so old maps can still be useful. Anchorages, however, can change tremendously within only a few years, so using old charts can be risky. Tourism growth, natural disasters, environmental legislation, reports of burglaries or assaults, and military needs all contribute to these quick changes.

Where you anchor will also be determined by what you and your crew want to do while anchored. Do you want to zoom ashore to that famous tiki bar or fill up your stores or your diesel tank? You'll be picking a more populated anchorage. If you're looking for isolation, nature, and a quiet place to jump off the side of the boat, you'll choose a less crowded anchorage a few miles away.

Another consideration is whether or not you plan to stay only one day, one night, several nights, or longer. If you have a good weather forecast for the next 24 hours, you might risk selecting a spot that is open to one direction, but protected from the forecasted wind. If you are planning to stay for a week, the forecast may not be as precise or the wind direction may be forecasted to change; then your spot will no longer be protected. Whatever the case may be, it is important to have a plan B anchor spot in mind—and always prepare an escape route.

If you see a cluster of boats in one particular area, don't assume that just because boats have chosen that spot that this area is the best spot—especially in squally weather. It only takes one dragging boat to trigger a domino effect and pull the neighbors along for the ride. If the anchorage is overcrowded but you still want to stay, consider anchoring out farther from shore, away from the madding crowds. The few minutes of extra rowing time will be the price you'll pay for additional peace of mind.

An ideal anchorage offers shelter from wind and waves. An anchorage that is exposed to winds but protected from the open sea is acceptable, but an anchorage exposed to swell quickly becomes less than desirable. If the anchor doesn't drag, the anchor rode or deck gear might break. When heavy swell enters the anchorage, it is better to weigh anchor to find a better spot, or head for open waters until the swell subsides.

We have chosen three renditions of Port Genovés in Andalucia, Spain, as examples of the kinds of materials you'll be able to study before arriving at an anchorage and choosing your anchoring spot.

Port Genovés on the Andalusian coast (34°44′N, 2°07′W), as seen from the air.

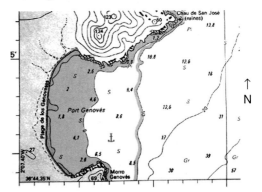

The chart shows enough water depth in the southern portion of the bay to anchor.

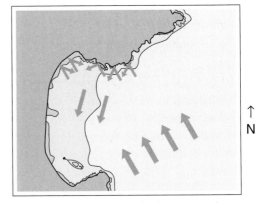

On this section of a retouched electronic chart, we've indicated that a skipper might want to take into account the backwash from wave action hitting the cliffs. Despite seemingly favorable conditions, the swell can be reflected at the rocky northern shoreline of the bay to create an uncomfortable chop in the entire anchorage.

The photo opposite, the likes of which are often found in guidebooks, may give you a general feel for the population of the area, the topography, and the vegetation you might expect to find in the area—and maybe provide a hint for finding a secret beach or some other place of interest. The photo and the navigational chart indicate that Port Genovés is well protected from north to south via the west but is open to winds from the northeast to southeast via the east. The navigational chart will show you water depths, potential hazards, forbidden areas, and designated anchoring areas.

Once you've selected an anchorage, observe the other anchored vessels. Why did they choose one side rather than the other? What are the characteristics of the terrain? Although a high cliff might seem to offer excellent protection, it may—on the contrary—act as a funnel to accelerate wind speeds. A beach extending out from a valley with high mountains on the sides might also act as a funnel for high winds.

Although a moderate surge poses little danger to holding, it can make life aboard just as bumpy as if you were in high seas, disturbing your sleep and tranquillity.

Near the shoreline, surge is greatly influenced and often magnified by the shallow seafloor. The waves may backwash, refracting and intensifying against the shore. As shown in the retouched electronic chart of Port Genovés, a vessel near the shoreline is protected from the primary wave but is subjected to the backwash reflected off the northern cliffs.

It is always prudent to slowly stake out the anchorage, observing the conditions and the other moored vessels. Once you have selected

what appears to be an acceptable anchorage, consider the details outlined below:

- **Prohibited areas in the anchorage.** Look for military zones, underwater cables, and throughway channels.

- **Water depth.** Observe the water depth. If depth visibility is good, a pair of eyes at the bow can help select the best spot. A bay may offer excellent shelter, but if the water is very shallow, only shallow-draft vessels such as catamarans may be able to access it. Or, on the contrary, if the water is too deep, your rode may not accommodate the absolute minimum 3:1 minimum scope.

- **Seafloor type.** What kind of seafloor does your chart show? Rocks and seaweed should be avoided when possible, and pebbles are also not recommended. In the chart of Port Genevés, the S signifies a sandy bottom, which is perfect. But watch out; the bottom is often covered with seaweed, which hopefully the sharp tip of your anchor can penetrate before it can set deep in the sand. Except in the tropics, sandy bottoms can be a rare find (review Chapter 1 for more on seabed characteristics).

- **Marked and unmarked dangers.** Are there any marked or unmarked dangers? Look for wrecks, large rocks, etc.

- **Crowding.** How crowded is the anchorage? In high season, an anchorage that is usually empty can be completely packed and therefore limited—especially anchorages that are known to be scenic and well protected. More and more excellent anchorages are also being overtaken by fish farms, which limit anchoring and sometimes make it impossible.

- **Escape route.** Always plan an escape route from an anchorage, and study it, especially if you may have to exit at night in case of a change in wind direction. If possible, have in mind your plan B. Take the few minutes

necessary to configure the waypoints to the next anchorage on your GPS.

- **Prevailing winds.** If prevailing winds are unpredictable or strong, consider anchoring farther from the shoreline. Your tender trip ashore may be slightly longer, but at least your conscience will be freer to enjoy people and places.

- **Swing room.** Keep in mind the swing room necessary in tidal zones where current might be present.

Pangaea's First Anchor Maneuver

We (Erika and Achim) had just bought *Pangaea*, a 43-foot steel ketch, on the French Riviera. Our maiden voyage was supposed to be a short passage across the Golf de Fos to the mouth of the Rhone River. Unfortunately we ended up demasting in a Force 11 mistral instead. The previous owner, at the last minute, had taken "a few personal items" off the boat—including all the nautical charts except the one to the Rhone inlet. The broken mast disabled our VHF, and the floating rigging caught our prop, disabling the engine. With no motor, no radio, no other local charts, and no sails, nothing was left to stop us from drifting toward Africa. (This was before GPS or charting software became affordable.)

In the dead of night on Christmas Eve, Achim activated our EPIRB and launched our CQR, letting out every bit of chain we had. The anchor held with 300 feet (100 m) of all-chain rode. Once it held, with the heavy winds and wave action, the chain at the bow of the boat thundered with every swell. Afraid that the bitter end might tear out of the locker, Achim shoved a heavy screwdriver into the last link of chain below the deck pipe inside the chain locker. I was so seasick that, for hours, I couldn't raise my hand high enough to remove the "dinner bell" above my head, which loudly clanged in rhythm with the screwdriver bashing against the steel hull.

A helicopter arrived at daybreak, evidently responding to the EPIRB distress beacon. Achim signaled that he wanted a tow, to my dismay, since all I wanted was an airlift off this nightmare of a boat and to never set foot on a sailboat ever again! We waited "at anchor" until the rescue ship came, and I watched from the gangway as a 70-foot French customs vessel approached us from windward . . . and then smashed directly into our bow. The old minesweeper was made of wood and *Pangaea* was made of steel; wood chips flew when our bow fell back from the gaping triangular hole in the front section of the customs cruiser. Our rescuers were frantically trying to reverse when they caught the heavy nylon towrope in both of their propellers. Both vessels were now hanging on *Pangaea's* anchor. Achim pulled out a huge bolt cutter and sent the chain and CQR to the bottom of the Golf de Fos. French Customs had to dispatch two more rescue boats to tow us both, now drifting side by side.

The next morning, over his espresso, the man who had sold us our boat read about the fiasco in the local paper *Le Provencal*.

I swore that I would never go sailing again. But three months later, we got married and this episode at sea became the maiden voyage of a sixteen-year extended voyage—with visits to anchorages between the Mediterranean and the South Seas—that has not yet come to an end. We still keep one of the wooden minesweeper chips as a souvenir, along with the bent-in-half screwdriver.

COMMUNICATION BETWEEN HELM AND FOREDECK

Unless the skipper is singlehanding the maneuver, there is usually one person on the foredeck, ready at the windlass, and one at the helm. We have identified three possible means by which the two can communicate: talking/screaming, hand signals, and walkie-talkies. No one way is always the right way.

We don't use hand signals, preferring to shout out the few words necessary and maybe use the occasional thumbs-up when all goes hunky-dory. The advantage to this method is that you don't have to learn any hand signals or buy equipment! We have not yet run into a situation where this didn't work for us; perhaps it would be less comfortable if we were shyer types, or weren't used to screaming at each other in the first place! It is also probable that we subconsciously do in fact use a certain amount of hand signals for the basic commands along with the occasional, "No, reverse, schmuck!"

Many boating folks swear by their hand signals and claim that once you get the hang of it, signaling can decrease the stress of having to scream and perhaps misunderstand each other.

Hand Signals

We've studied a variety of hand signals and think these might work best for a bowperson who needs to communicate with the helmsperson.

Direction: arm and hand extended, pointing in the desired direction

Increase throttle/speed: fist with thumb upward, extended arm pointing in desired direction

Decrease throttle/speed: fist with thumb down, extended arm pointing in desired direction

Engine in neutral: fist

Stop boat's movement: hand held flat, palm down, and moving side to side

What is depth?: hand flat, open, with palm up

Dropping anchor: index finger pointing down

Anchor set and holding: OK symbol with thumb and index finger

Raising rode: index finger pointing up

Anchor broken free, raising anchor: index finger pointing up making small circles

Anchor up, free to maneuver boat: one thumbs-up (eye contact if possible), then point the up-thumb in the general direction to move

The following hand signals can be used by a helmsperson who needs to communicate with a bowperson (special thanks to Dennis Clarke of the Aloha Owner's Sailing Club).

Depth of water/number of feet: raise the correct number of fingers; or, if the depth is more than 10 feet, flash ten fingers, make a fist, then flash the additional number of feet until you reach the total

Drop anchor now: index finger pointing down

Anchor set and holding: OK symbol with thumb and index finger

Walkie-Talkie Headsets

We are becoming more and more wired for communications these days—or shall we say wireless. Walkie-talkies reduce the stress of having to scream over the motor and waves. They can also be useful for other maintenance work on the boat, especially if a crewmember has to go up the mast or in situations where a wiring or deck hardware repair needs hands both inside and outside the hull.

Perhaps the biggest problem is remembering to have the headsets ready, charged and waiting when the moment arrives to anchor.

ANCHORING UNDER POWER

A popular, safe, and comfortable way to anchor is under main engine power. Once you have selected your designated anchoring area with care, slowly approach with the engine at low rpm. Your sails should be down but ready to be hoisted if necessary.

Engage the main power switch for the anchor windlass and confirm that the anchor in the bow-roller fitting is prepared for launching. If your windlass is manual, make sure to have a winch handle or crank handy.

In general, the rule is that a just-arrived vessel must adapt to the vessels already anchored; observe these other boats, watch how they

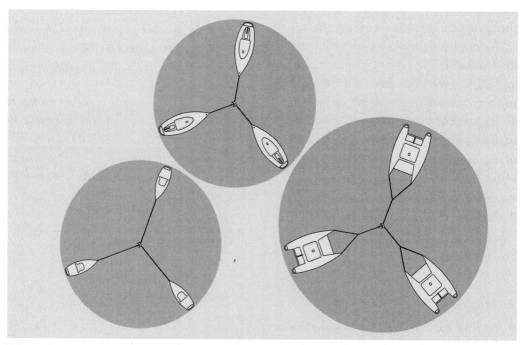

When setting your anchor under power, first circle your chosen spot and approximate your anticipated swinging radius. Be aware that other skippers will usually pay out more rode once the wind gets stronger.

swing and whether or not they swing in unison or apart. Try to ascertain where they have set their anchor or anchors. If it's especially crowded, try to determine whether or not you could be in their line of swinging, keeping in mind that a modern shallow-draft yacht or a sailing catamaran might swing much more readily in response to wind shifts than a heavy, long-keeled ketch. Indeed, there is no sure way to know whether a neighboring boat will swing about exactly as your vessel will. Keep in mind that boats on moorings are likely on much shorter scope, and watch for some boats lying on more than one anchor.

Draw an imaginary line just behind the transoms of the boats in front of you and launch your anchor just behind that line. Once your anchor is securely set, look to the boats astern of yours. They should lie behind the line that runs across your transom.

Wind direction and currents will affect how vessels lie relative to their anchors. And again, there is no certainty that a neighboring boat will swing about exactly as you do. If wind and/or current change direction, try to determine your swinging radius in terms of boat lengths. On a 28-foot boat with 70 feet of rode out in 10 feet of water, your anchor will lie approximately two boat lengths forward of your bow.

Now you've found your spot. Slowly point your bow into the wind. If you encounter strong current, compromise between wind and current. Drop your anchor, along with a scope of one-and-a-half to two times the depth while simultaneously giving some reverse with the engine or using the force of the wind to push your vessel backward. Once

you feel the boat begin to move in reverse, slowly let out more rode by carefully trimming the windlass clutch while using chain, or by adjusting the anchor rope tension looped around the windlass drum, until you've reached the desired scope.

Immediately secure the rode on deck with a chain stopper, or fasten it to the mooring bitt, before the ground tackle comes under load. New-generation anchors set quickly and are less prone to dragging, so there is a risk that the anchor chain might slip off the windlass gypsy, damaging the gypsy sprockets and chain.

Once the rode is successfully secured on deck it is safe to begin motoring backward to set the anchor. The best way to make sure your anchor will embed is by pulling on it hard. Often skippers put the boat in reverse for just a few seconds. But to be sure the anchor is set you must put a reasonable strain on the rode for a reasonable length of time. If anchoring a sailboat, don't hesitate to run your engine at full speed in reverse to assure proper setting. Even with the highest possible rpm, most modern sailboat engines offer about the equivalent load of 25 to 30 knots of wind. However, when setting anchor with a powerboat, do not use full throttle backward if you have super-high-horsepower engines. You probably can imagine why. It's better to use your reverse gear with modest power for a longer amount of time, rather than full power for a few seconds followed by none. Your boat should surge forward when you back off the power, indicating that you have put some strain on the rode to test the anchor set.

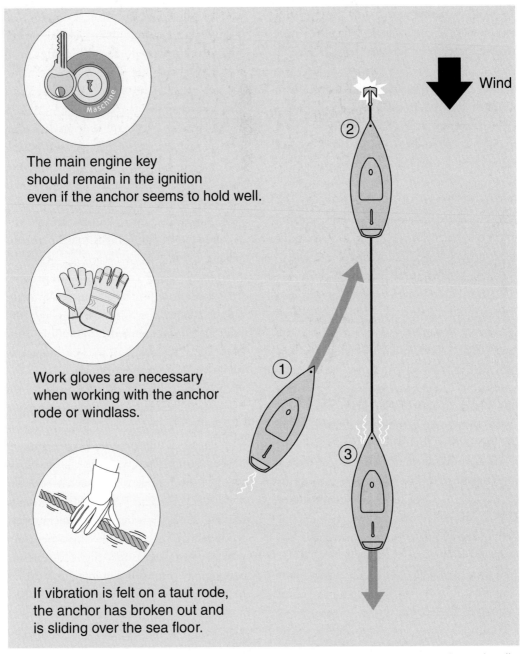

The main engine key
should remain in the ignition
even if the anchor seems to hold well.

Work gloves are necessary
when working with the anchor
rode or windlass.

If vibration is felt on a taut rode,
the anchor has broken out and
is sliding over the sea floor.

Wind

Anchoring maneuvers under power. When backing down on your anchor, touching the taut anchor rode will tell you if the anchor is holding or dragging across the seafloor. Remember that manual work with an anchor rode and windlass requires protective gloves. The engine key should stay in the ignition, even if the anchor seems to be holding well, in case you need to reset the anchor quickly.

Verify that your anchor is holding by closely surveying bearings to fixed landmarks. Another way to determine if your anchor is dragging is to hold your hand or foot firmly on the chain or line as you reverse under motor. With an anchor dragging on chain only, you should feel the rumbling vibrations of the anchor dragging on the seafloor. These vibrations will be less pronounced if you are touching the nylon section of the rode. If your anchor drags while in full reverse, it did not set sufficiently and you should try again at a different spot.

As long as someone is aboard, the engine key should remain in the ignition in case you need to suddenly weigh anchor.

ANCHORING UNDER SAIL

When anchoring under power, things can go wrong: a stalled engine or a fouled propeller are only two of the many Murphy's Law scenarios that can occur. Your best protection is to familiarize yourself with the beautiful art of anchoring under sail.

The actual maneuvers are quite similar to anchoring under power. Lower your foresail, but leave it so it remains ready to hoist. With a lowered headsail, you will have improved visibility over the bow. Turn the rudder and head the bow into the wind with all sheets loose and sails luffing. The boat will continue to drift; estimate the inertia of your vessel so that it stops at your designated spot and you can launch your anchor. Drop the anchor with a scope of around one-and-a-half times the water depth (plus freeboard). Once your boat begins to drift backward, slowly let out the rode (see illustration next page).

Once the anchor starts setting, the boat will swing with its nose into the wind. This is a good time to secure the rode and back the mainsail to embed the anchor as deeply as possible. If you are uncomfortable with setting under sail alone, consider a snorkeling trip to confirm that the anchor has embedded. Once you are certain that the anchor has set deeply and there's enough distance between you and the other boats, lower and stow the mainsail.

ANCHORING MULTIHULLS

Catamarans have become very popular in the last decade thanks not only to their speed and large outside living space, but also to the many advantages catamarans offer over monohulls once the anchor is set.

For one thing, catamarans are more stable; they don't roll as much as monohulls do in a swell. Many sailors feel they can live aboard far more comfortably because of this stability. However, shallow-displacement multihulls can produce significant loads at anchor due to windage. These vessels, lacking deep, steadying keels and hefty ballast, are much more animated at anchor than comparable monohulls. At anchor in light winds, the lack of the ballasted keel can actually lead to motion discomfort sooner than on a monohull.

No one can deny the luxury provided by a cat's spacious cockpit and outside space. Especially in tropical latitudes, cruisers enjoy their time at anchor lounging about their beamy deck space under the protection of a bimini.

Also, since the main saloon of a catamaran is not as deeply set as in a monohull, the crew doesn't go "below" but "inside" when they

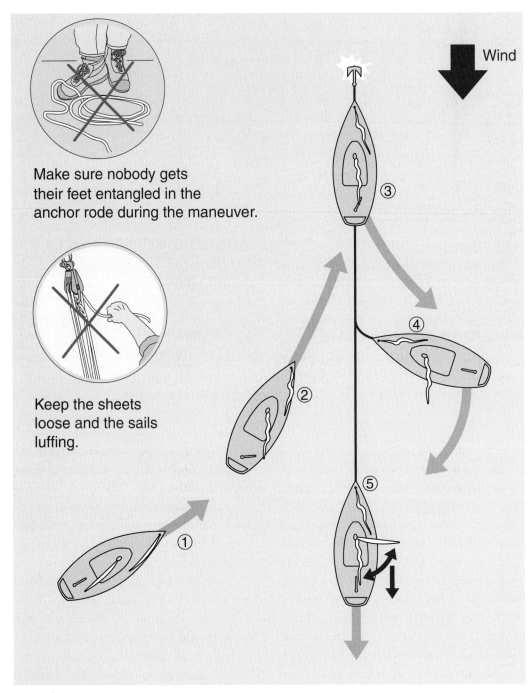

Wind

Make sure nobody gets their feet entangled in the anchor rode during the maneuver.

Keep the sheets loose and the sails luffing.

Anchoring maneuvers under sail.

In a swell, catamarans don't roll as much at anchor as monohulls. However, they can create significant loads at anchor due to windage. Anchors, rode, and deck gear need to be selected accordingly.

enter the cabin. This creates a comfort factor so that, for instance, you can stay warm and dry on night watch from the inside and still have panoramic vision.

Marinas today are crowded and expensive for a monohull, let along a multihull. Some marinas charge twice the price for multihulls, while others may not have slips that are beamy enough. Therefore, anchoring is often the only option for the voyaging cat or tri.

Because multihulls incur more windage than monohulls, we recommend selecting an anchor and accompanying rode that is one size bigger, compared to a monohull of similar length.

When anchoring a catamaran, we recommend a full-width bridle attached to the extreme outboard tips of the hulls on solid cleats or mooring bitts, affording maximum leverage and security when it comes to keeping the yacht facing squarely into the wind.

The bridle also reduces horsing—the back-and-forth veering characteristic of multihulls at anchor—since it shares the heavy anchor load between the two hulls (see illustrations next page). If you insist on using all-chain rode, consider a double chain hook (see page 84). If using a rode with a nylon upper section, use a rolling hitch to attach the bridle.

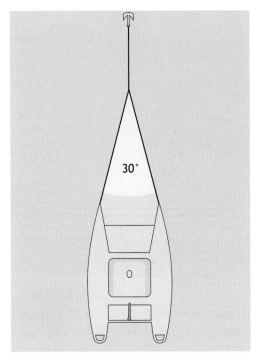

The angle of the bridle on a cat should be at least 30°.

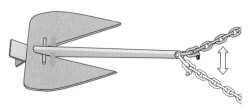

Due to the increased horsing of catamarans, the anchor should be able to withstand high tensile strain at the shaft.

ANCHORING TENDERS AND SMALL CRAFT

Imagine that you've left your boat at anchor and have gone ashore to check for messages at the nearest Internet café. By the time you return to your tender, it's evening and the offshore wind has picked up to 25 to 30 knots. You start the outboard and about midway back, the

motor dies. You yank on the starter cord and fiddle with the choke for several minutes with no luck. Now you feel yourself drifting away, so you grab your stashed-away oars to counter the rapid drift toward the open ocean. After 15 minutes of steady rowing, you've almost reached the spot where the engine originally stopped—and then you hear a loud crack. The left oar has broken right where the wood was getting darker. (Next time, better not leave it in the bilge where rainwater collects.) Only 1,100 nautical miles left until you reach Hawaii!

Now is the time to deploy your tender anchor with sufficient scope. Luck is on your side. The anchor finds holding ground not too far away from your vessel, and just in time. A few minutes later and the howling winds would have blown you where the water is too deep to anchor. A friendly neighboring boat in the anchorage finally hears your calls for help and gives you a tow back. You're finally back aboard to sleep.

This is a situation we've heard about and experienced one way or another ourselves. An anchor on a small craft can be used as a stern anchor to keep the tender clear from damage at rusty and crowded dinghy-dock bars, but the tender anchor's primary purpose is for such emergency situations. Folding grapnel anchors with a relatively short anchor line would perform well at the dock. But a miniature version of the main anchor gear would be much safer to tackle the unexpected.

THE IMPORTANCE OF SCOPE

By this point you have a good anchor, a strong and elastic anchor rode, and strong connecting hardware between these elements. You also

Anchoring on a Slope

Some anchor grounds are sloped significantly, and significant seafloor slope should be reflected in your scope calculation.

The anchorage in front of St. Pierre in Martinique, which is west of a tall volcano, is one good example. The beach slopes quickly there, leaving vessels only a slim band of seafloor in which to set their anchors.

A nautical chart of a particular anchorage should give you a good idea of how steep the slope might be. Find out if your designated spot is next to a submerged cliff, where your anchor and rode would simply dangle vertically in the water if you dragged for a while in the wrong direction.

You can also obtain a good idea of slope angle by surveying the chosen anchorage area while taking continuous measurements with your depth sounder. If it helps, jot down the soundings around your chosen spot on a piece of paper. If you have time, draw a sketch to scale to help visualize how much and in which direction the slope of the seafloor actually rises.

Use the deepest spot in the swaying circle around the designated spot in your scope calculation. Will your vessel go aground if the wind blows from a particular direction? If yes, set two anchors in a Bahamian moor (see pages 140–41) on the same depth along the sloped seafloor to reduce the swaying circle of your vessel and prevent grounding. If t he wind blows offshore, setting two anchors in a Bahamian moor parallel to a steep slope will also force both anchors to drag along the sloped seafloor in a favorable direction.

know how to select an anchorage and set your anchor. Your next question is likely to be, "How much rode should I let out?"

As Alain Fraysse demonstrates in Appendix 1, in general, shallow anchorages need relatively large scopes, while deep anchorages make the best of moderate scopes.

In calm conditions, when the pressure of the wind on the boat is negligible, the mere weight and friction of the chain on the seafloor will suffice to hold the boat. If the anchorage is crowded and the crew does not intend to leave the vessel unattended, a scope of 3:1 is probably sufficient under such circumstances (see Table 6-1). But the moment the vessel faces less favorable weather conditions, increase your scope; you should plan on needing a scope of as much as 7:1 to 10:1 in an exposed anchorage. Practically speaking, when you go beyond a scope of 10:1, the additional rode offers little improvement in the anchor's holding capacity.

Waves also require greater scopes. Since they lift the bow up, they increase the effective height you need to consider when deciding the rode length to pay out. For example, if the waves cause 3 feet (1 m) of pitching at the bow and the scope for a calm sea is 6:1, adding 18 feet (5.5 m) of rode would be safe.

TABLE 6-1. ESTIMATED PERCENT OF MAXIMUM HOLDING POWER AS A FUNCTION OF SCOPE[1]

Scope Ratio	2:1	4:1	6:1	8:1	10:1	> 10:1
Percentage of Maximum Holding Power	10	55	70	80	85	> 85

[1]Expressed as a ratio with vertical distance from bow roller to seafloor.

The first step when anchoring in an unfamiliar location is therefore to determine the anchorage's water depth. This is not always easy, especially when anchoring in an extreme tidal zone. Tidal ranges of 30 feet (9 m) and greater are not unusual in parts of the English Channel and the Canadian Maritimes, for example, and scope should be based on the expected water depths at high tide.

If you know the local times and heights of low water and high water, you can estimate the height of the tide when you anchor by using the Rule of Twelfths (see the sidebar on estimating water level in a tidal range opposite). The rule assumes, given a 6-hour tidal range, that the tide rises or falls by one-twelfth of its overall range in the first hour, two-twelfths in the second hour, three-twelfths each in the third and fourth hours, two-twelfths in the fifth hour, and one-twelfth in the sixth and final hour.

When you add the estimated height of the tide to the charted low-water depth, the result should come reasonably close to matching what your depth sounder is telling you. Before calculating the needed scope, you should add to the present depth the further increase expected at high water and the vertical distance from your bow roller or bow chock to the water surface.

Note that simply reading the depth from a depth sounder display may lead to a calculation error, with consequences that are literally a drag. This reading usually represents the distance between the transducer and the seafloor. Modern depth sounders can be calibrated to show the distance between the seafloor and either the bottom of the keel, the transducer (the default value), the water surface, or the bow roller—but they must be explicitly programmed to do so. Otherwise the resultant error, if unaccounted for, can be substantial in shallow water.

As an extreme example, let's say we are anchoring a boat in water that is 6 feet (1.8 m) deep according to the depth sounder. The weather is favorable and the anchorage is crowded, so we decide to pay out a scope of three times the water depth (3:1) according to the depth sounder, or 18 feet (5.5 m) of rode. In our example, the depth sounder's transducer is mounted inside the bilge and is calibrated to show the distance between the bottom of the keel and the seafloor, and our boat has a draft of 5 feet 4 inches and freeboard (from the water surface to the bow roller) of 3 feet 6 inches.

In reality, the depth we should have calculated is the 6 feet (1.8 m) from the depth sounder, plus the draft of 5 feet 4 inches, plus the freeboard of 3 feet 6 inches for a total of 15 feet (4.6 m). Multiplied by 3 for a 3:1 scope, we should have paid out 45 feet (13.7 m) instead of 18 feet (5.5 m). Instead of the intended 3:1 ratio, we have only paid out a ratio of 1.2:1! With such a short rode, our anchor is unlikely even to set.

Admittedly that is an extreme example. After all, how often do we anchor with only 6 inches of water under the keel? So let's take the same boat and anchor in deeper water. This time we read 45 feet (13.7 m) on the depth sounder. Making the same error, we release 135 feet (41 m) of rode. The depth we should have calculated is 45 feet from the

How to Estimate the Water Level in a Tidal Area

Known as the Rule of Twelfths, the following instructions can help skippers predict the actual water level for a given time after high water (HW) or a given time after low water (LW).

First, it is important to determine the height of the falling tide (FT) for the time after high water and the height of the rising tide (RT) after low water; then we divide the time of the entire tidal cycle into 1-hour sections.

As shown in the illustration, the water level roughly follows a pattern that is quite easy to remember. The water level:

- Falls during the first and the sixth hour after HW for about $1/12$ of FT.

- Falls during the second and the fifth hour after HW for about $2/12$ of FT.

- Falls during the third and the fourth hour after HW for about $3/12$ of FT.

- Rises during the first and the sixth hour after LW for about $1/12$ of RT.

- Rises during the second and the fifth hour after LW for about $2/12$ of RT.

- Rises during the third and the fourth hour after LW for about $3/12$ of RT.

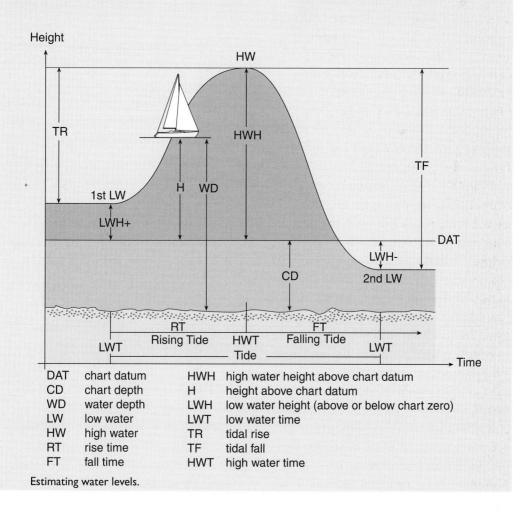

DAT	chart datum	HWH	high water height above chart datum
CD	chart depth	H	height above chart datum
WD	water depth	LWH	low water height (above or below chart zero)
LW	low water	LWT	low water time
HW	high water	TR	tidal rise
RT	rise time	TF	tidal fall
FT	fall time	HWT	high water time

Estimating water levels.

depth sounder, plus 5 feet 4 inches of draft, plus 3 feet 6 inches of freeboard for a total of 54 feet (16.4 m). We should have paid out 162 feet (49.4 m) instead of 135 feet (41 m). Instead of 3:1, we have paid out a ratio of 2.5:1. This time, with a little luck, our anchor will manage to set and hold provided the weather remains perfectly calm. But the holding power attained on such short scope is only approximately 25% of the anchor's maximum holding capacity. Even if we're using the best anchor on the market, chances are good that the anchor will drag if the wind increases.

MAKING SURE THE ANCHOR HOLDS

Once you've anchored your boat, there are several methods you can use to make certain that your anchor is not dragging. During daylight hours, you can take bearings on several landmarks with your compass and observe if the bearings change over time. Observing the angle between one close landmark and one landmark farther away can indicate quite clearly if your vessel is dragging or not. At night, try using light sources on the shoreline to take bearings. But make sure you are not looking at the moving headlights of a car, as this will definitely lead you to false conclusions!

Setting a depth sounder's low- and high-water alarms is another helpful indicator. The accuracy of modern GPS receivers combined with the zone-alarm feature inside the device is equally helpful. Large powerboats with sufficient electricity on board or smaller boats equipped with low-power LCD radar can additionally run the alarm features of this useful instrument to prevent against unintentional drift.

Of course it also never hurts to dive down and check to see if the hook is properly buried.

Anchor Watch

If the weather turns bad, it's best and sometimes necessary to have a person on anchor watch. Some mariners feel comfortable with an alarm on their GPS to do the work, but machines can fail in dire consequences so we have included a duty list for your anchor watchperson:

1. Use visual bearings to ensure the boat is not dragging. If your angle to other boats or to the land has markedly changed, you are likely dragging. It's up to you to decide if you need to immediately weigh anchor or observe a bit longer.

2. Reduce windage as needed. Make sure all sails are well stowed.

3. The key should be in the ignition and ready to start. Consider starting the engine to keep your batteries fully charged.

4. Plan an escape route, preferably with GPS waypoints, to the next safe anchorage.

5. Have your air horn ready. Turn on the VHF and the GPS (with area alarms set, if your GPS has this function).

6. Electronics such as a depth sounder with both shallow and deep alarms, wind instruments, and boat speed indicators are helpful.

7. Dock lines and fenders should be out and ready for use.

8. Your frequent eyeball checks on neighboring vessels and landmarks will help determine if you or other boats are dragging. If you think a neighboring boat is dragging, try to ascertain its potential drag track and, if needed, try to alert the skipper with the air horn.

9. If you have deployed a hybrid or all-line rode, check for and protect against chafe.

10. Be prepared to pay out more scope, and if possible, prepare a second ground tackle in case it will be needed.

The Art of Dragging

In Chapter 3, we learned that excellent ground tackle, once subject to loads above and beyond what it is designed to handle, will slowly drag but remain embedded. Even when a skipper does all he can to prevent this, it can happen to the best anchoring systems; the vessel may be subject to dragging.

More often than not, dragging is due to a combination of poor holding ground (e.g., a thin layer of sand over flat rock, soft mud, hard sand, weed, or boulders), an inefficient anchor, and/or insufficient scope.

Nearly all anchors hold well with light winds, most of the time relying only on the weight of the chain to stay put. Some anchors seem to hold when set, but if the wind increases, they break out suddenly. Strong winds, heavy side current, and wave action also play a role in whether or how anchored vessels drag.

If you realize your boat is dragging, make sure your VHF is on and start your engine. Analyze the situation. Where are other boats in relation to yours? Is there any danger in the direction in which you are dragging?

A skipper has several possibilities, depending on the particular situation:

- **Increase scope.** The easiest method is to pay out more rode to increase the scope and to ascertain whether the anchor will reset. Perhaps better holding grounds are just a few feet away. This solution is only workable if your vessel has plenty of space to drag and no other boats or obstructions are on a collision course with yours. If the anchor resets, you should maintain a vigilant anchor watch—at least until the unfavorable weather conditions subside.

- **Use your engine.** The second option is to relieve the heavy anchor load with your main engine intermittently engaged in the direction of the anchor. This might be a sufficient tactic to weather out a temporary tropical squall, but you must find another strategy if you are facing many hours or days of bad weather.

- **Use a second anchor.** If there is enough space in the anchorage, the next option is to set a second anchor in the forked mooring (see pages 138–39).

- **Reanchor.** The fourth option is to weigh anchor and reanchor elsewhere. If you are dragging fast toward a danger zone, we don't suggest paying out rode and praying. The most prudent course is to assume that reset is unlikely. Try for a different area if there's space available.

- **Head for open water.** The last option is to leave the anchorage for the open sea if the anchorage is no longer secure. This has more than once been the wise choice of many prudent mariners, especially in crowded anchorages where the risk is great that other vessels will drag and pull you with them.

If a neighboring boat drags and slides on top of you with the skipper aboard, try to stay friendly and start your main engine. (Quickly hand him a copy of this book over the railing; not everyone knows what to do in this situation and we've seen many a panicked dragger.) Put out all fenders immediately to avoid hull damage. Unless your judgment tells you that the other vessel is of inconsequential displacement, do not raft up and hang both boats on your one anchor as this will very likely cause both vessels to drag, even if your anchor is holding well. If the other skipper isn't going to weigh his dragging anchor, consider weighing yours, or at least reel in enough rode to move your vessel forward of his and let him drag by. Observe both your rodes and try to make sure they don't foul each other. If no one is aboard, don't try to save the other vessel at the expense of yours. Free yourself from the dragging vessel and use your VHF to warn the other vessels in the anchorage.

ANCHORING ETIQUETTE AND CUSTOMS

Birds of a feather all think they know a safe, comfy nest when they see one. The most desirable anchorages, when overcrowded, can become marine battlefields unless anchoring etiquette is followed and respected.

The first rule of thumb is simple: Vessels already at anchor have priority, and those arriving later must adapt to the conditions at hand. A subsequently arriving skipper must choose his space from what is available.

In a crowded anchorage, it's up to you to find your own space.

While staking out a spot, a skipper must take into consideration the estimated swinging radius of the already anchored boats, as well as his own. Keep in mind that the wind could change direction. There is no way to know a boat's scope, but you have no choice but to make a safe guess, or ask. There is nothing wrong with a friendly, "Ahoy! How much rode length did you pay out?" Observe the neighboring boats' behavior while there's daylight to guard against unexpected position shifts at night.

If the wind shifts at 3 A.M. and boats begin to swing dangerously close to each other, the crew that arrived last has to pull up anchor and move. A skipper loses his spot whether his anchor drifts or he weighs anchor intentionally, and he must start at zero, readapting himself to the new arrival hierarchy.

Setting anchor near other boats can sometimes feel like setting up a tent in someone else's garden. When you're anchoring in a crowded anchorage it is not unusual to hear a nearby crew comment: "I don't think this is gonna work." Respect others people's rights and privacy. If you're the boat that was there first, don't gawk at the new arrivals. A smile and wave is always a welcome gesture, but let the newcomer start any dialogue if something needs to be said. Even if the new crew strikes up conversation, don't start telling your life story until the new neighbors are completely finished with their anchor maneuver.

Just as you would in a campground, keep your noisemaking to a minimum. Noise travels very well across the water. Playing music or charging batteries with a loud generator should be daytime activities. Consider securing

When rafting up with other boats, be considerate of your neighbors.

any banging halyards, which can drive neighbors crazy.

Picking up a vacant mooring without asking permission shows not only bad manners but can be embarrassing if the owner returns unexpectedly. Also, when you do this you are only guessing at the holding power of the mooring. Mooring policies vary from place to place; educate yourself by reading the cruising guide or websites, or ask a local fisherman.

If you want to avoid making enemies in crowded anchorages, don't hog the whole place by letting out more scope than is actually necessary. The more scope, the larger your swing radius will be if winds or currents shift. We remember especially well a large, rusty steel ketch in Las Palmas, Canary Islands, that hogged the center of the busy main anchorage for many months if not years with a super long rode and loud requests to respect his scope.

Anchor Signage, Lighting, and Sounding

Part of Rule 30, Anchored Vessels and Vessels Aground, of the *Navigation Rules, International–Inland*, states:

(a) A vessel at anchor shall exhibit where it can best be seen:

    (i) in the fore part, an all-round white light or one ball;

    (ii) at or near the stern and at a lower level than the light prescribed in subparagraph (i), an all-round white light.

(b) A vessel of less than 50 meters in length may exhibit an all-round white light where it can best be seen instead of the lights prescribed in paragraph (a) of this Rule.

Principles of Anchoring Etiquette

The following list of anchoring etiquette principles is taken from the guidelines of the Southwest Florida Regional Harbor Board Standards for Anchoring (www.flseagrant.org/program_areas/waterfront/anchorage/local_restrictions/index.htm#umbrella), and represent the basic management approach for anchoring in Florida. No third party has any rights or cause of action based upon failure to enforce any of these standards.

1. All federal and state laws continue to apply to all vessels, including laws concerning overboard discharge of petroleum products, waste, garbage, and litter. Local laws regarding nuisance, noise, etc., would continue to apply to all persons, including those at anchor.

2. Vessels may not anchor in a manner that:

    a. jeopardizes other vessels at anchor or underway;

    b. might cause damage to other property or persons;

    c. impedes access to docks, slips, or public or private property.

3. Areas of seagrass, living coral, or rock outcroppings as identified by Florida Sea Grant (FSG) or the Department of Environmental Protection (FDEP) cannot be used for anchoring. Special care must be taken to avoid anchoring impacts in aquatic preserves.

4. Vessels must be capable of navigating under their own sail or power, or have ground tackle capable of holding the vessel until winds are fair or a tow or repairs can be arranged. A reasonable amount of time must be allowed for such situations.

5. In emergencies, the safety of the crew and the vessel will be of paramount importance until the emergency is past or the vessel has been moved to safety. Each mariner remains responsible for damages caused by his vessel or its wake.

Hylas, Alain Poiraud's ketch, at anchor with an anchor ball on the inner forestay.

Thus, during the day, you should hoist an anchor ball at the forepart of the vessel to let other mariners know that you are at anchor. At night, you should display a white light, visible from all quadrants, from 30 minutes before sunset to 30 minutes after dawn.

The light can be at the top of the mast, or just above deck level. A light at the top of the mast is easily seen from a distance and doesn't disturb your sleeping crew or neighbors. If folks are still on deck, then a lower light serves simultaneously as illumination and an anchor light. What's more, it enables other vessels to see your whole vessel once inside the anchorage.

For the most part, states have uniform anchor lighting requirements for boats. As of this writing, only Indiana and Maryland do not require anchor lights. Additionally, eleven states do not specify which vessels must have

anchor lights. The U.S. Coast Guard recommends that anchor lights be visible at a distance of 2 miles. Some states exempt vessels from displaying anchor lights when in special anchorage areas.

Anchor balls and anchor lights are only helpful when other boats can see them, of course; when engulfed in thick fog, an anchored boat must use its ship's bell.

ANCHOR RETRIEVAL

Under Power

Your vessel is once again ready for the high seas. The wineglasses are stowed, sails (if you have them) are ready for hoisting, and the engine is purring. First, motor slowly against the wind toward your anchor. Ideally, one crewmember will be at the bow observing the rode, operating the windlass, and giving directions to the helm.

Before hauling in the anchor rode, it is always prudent to verify that the windlass is ready and waiting to do its hard work with an engaged clutch. Press the main power switch for the windlass to start hauling the anchor rode.

If you have deployed a hybrid rode and your windlass is not equipped with a combined rope-chain gypsy, you must stop the windlass shortly before you reach the connecting splice between chain and rope. Without this pause, the anchor line may slither away uncontrollably around the windlass's chain gypsy like a runaway python.

Remember that chain can pile up in the chain locker, blocking the incoming rode from passing through the deck pipe and jamming the windlass, so keep on eye on the locker to make sure the chain is flaking properly as you retrieve the rode.

Monitor your windlass and listen to its sound, which will indicate whether the load is creating duress. If it sounds and looks like the winch is under undue stress, stop for a few moments and then try again. Once the chain is hanging vertically over your anchor, the anchor should disengage on its own from the seafloor—especially if the anchor is now only partially embedded. Then you can finish the retrieval maneuver without pause, until the anchor sits snugly in the bow roller.

If your anchor is still deeply lodged, don't persist and overload your windlass. Just maintain your position above the anchor with a vertically pulling rode and attach the rode with a snubber to a cleat or mooring bitt.

Bahamian Anchor Retrieval

This technique facilitates the retrieval of ground tackle if the vessel is not equipped with a windlass, and is best suited for small or medium-sized anchor gear. This procedure can also serve as a backup plan in case your windlass fails.

Attach a large 20- to 24-inch-diameter (50 cm to 60 cm) fender or buoy to a large-diameter ring with a 3-foot length of $^3/_8$-inch to $^1/_2$-inch (10 mm to 12 mm) line and a carabiner hook. These rings are usually stainless or galvanized steel and can be found in most chandleries.

To weigh anchor, slide the anchor line into the large-diameter ring through the opening and close the ring with the carabiner hook, attaching the buoy at the same time.

Put your main engine into forward gear and steer a course of 30° to 45° away from your anchor's position. As your boat pulls forward, the buoy will submerge until the large ring with the submerging buoy reaches the anchor shaft, pulling your anchor out of the seafloor and to the surface with its buoyancy.

This might sound like a seaman's yarn at first, but it worked for us. Try it out for yourself.

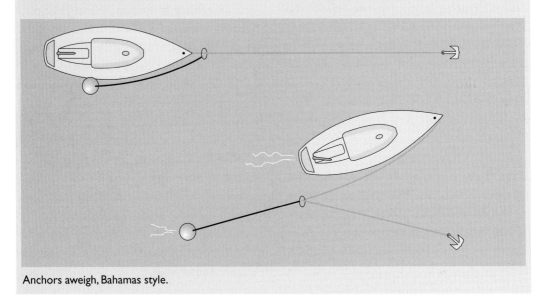

Anchors aweigh, Bahamas style.

Wait a few minutes to allow the movement of the ship and the vertical load to loosen the anchor's grip and rotate it toward the surface. If necessary, a sharp, quick reverse of the engine should help dislodge the anchor.

Once the anchor frees itself from the seafloor, retrieve the rode and anchor entirely. If you encounter strong winds or current during retrieval in a small or crowded anchorage, it is best to have the helmsman keep the boat in position with the engine until the anchor is safely retrieved. If the seafloor is particularly muddy and slimy, you can motor forward a bit with the anchor hanging to clean it off before completing retrieval. Consider having a brush and a bucket or deck hose for cleaning ground tackle.

Mount the anchor in its correct position on the bow roller; even if it ascends upside down, it should flip over with gravity alone. If this doesn't happen naturally, don't try to turn the anchor manually; release the rode somewhat and give the anchor a chance to flip into correct position. You can also try motoring slightly backward with the anchor barely in the water to help flip it over.

With the anchor correctly positioned, secure it on the bow roller. Some bow rollers have bolts or pins to prevent the anchor from falling overboard inadvertently. A short lashing line through a chain link will also do the trick. Release the chain leader load from the windlass with a chain stopper or chain hook and snubber to prevent overloading. Once the anchor maneuver is complete, don't forget to shut off the power to the windlass at the main switch.

Under Sail

In light winds, it's fairly easy to weigh anchor under sail. Start pulling in the anchor rode. Have your foresail ready to run on the lee side and hoist the main, allowing plenty of slack on the mainsheet. Retrieve the remainder of rode and anchor as quickly as possible as the boat swings into the wind. Once your anchor is weighed and the bow falls off the wind, hoist or unfurl the jib as quickly as possible to get underway. The less your sails flop around, the better; the goal is to minimize that "no-man's land" between drifting and sailing. Pay attention to which way your boat falls off, especially if you are surrounded by neighbors. Don't leave to providence which direction you will take; figure out the best tactics for your course. If there are sandbars, reefs, or other vessels to negotiate, keep your sail load manageable while completing your exit strategy.

It is especially important to anticipate your vessel's swinging and drifting behavior if the wind is strong while you reel in your rode with a hoisted main. The boat will very likely drift and gain speed quickly once the anchor comes loose, and you have to be prepared to gain control over your vessel at the helm immediately—sometimes even before the anchor is completely stowed at the bow roller. Letting the anchor clean off some collected mud while it is dangling in the water just below the surface and your vessel is gaining speed under sail can look quite elegant to any spectators. But don't get the anchor stuck in other people's lines while you are trying so hard to demonstrate your cool and exceptional seamanship.

CHAPTER 7

Advanced Anchoring Techniques

There are times when anchoring isn't as cut and dried as just arriving at your chosen spot, setting, snubbing, verifying, and going snorkeling or fishing. Anchorages are more crowded than ever before, and when anchoring, boaters increasingly need to contend with vast mooring fields. Space at a dock is often limited, and you may be forced to squeeze yourself in if you want your share of a landline. If crowding isn't the problem, a skipper may face uncomfortable swells, strong tidal currents, or inclement weather.

Contending with the above situations requires a deeper grasp of anchoring principles and methods. With practice, your skills will improve. Make sure you bring along your secondary anchor and rode and be prepared to use them.

ANCHORING WITH A STERN ANCHOR (MED MOORING)

A stern anchor system can be very helpful, especially for skippers who intend to visit crowded harbors. If you are docking alongside a crowded seawall, you can set a stern anchor off the seawall and secure your bow on a bollard or ring ashore. Setting an anchor

from the stern can also be useful for single-handed mariners who have a relatively small stern cockpit and no electric windlass. (We also discuss using a stern anchor as a secondary anchor in the section on setting a fore-and-aft mooring below.)

Select stern anchor gear using the same principles as for the bow anchor system.

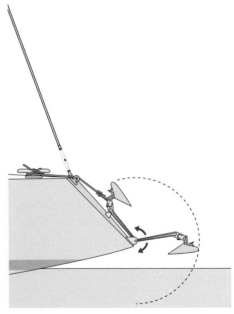

This stern-anchor mounting bracket helps prevent gelcoat scratches.

A rail-mount anchor bracket.

reached the bottom, the speed of the running anchor line on deck will slow to equal the speed of the boat. The speed should be slow enough to allow you to bring the remaining anchor line on deck around a solid cleat, at which point you should gently slow the vessel's speed down to a halt while your anchor sets in the bottom. After the vessel has come to a complete stop, the anchor line can be secured at the stern or brought forward to the bow roller, providing the wind is not too strong.

Mediterranean Mooring

The Mediterranean mooring derives its name from the manner in which vessels have been tying up in harbors in that part of the world for centuries. Since quay space is limited and the number of vessels numerous, mooring perpendicularly—the Med moor—rather than alongside, allows more vessels to access the quay.

Choppy waves bouncing off the seawall, powerful currents, or crosswinds can turn this maneuver, however, into a real hair-raiser. It's understandable to feel apprehensive about negotiating a tight squeeze between two pricey yachts with a crowd watching. Med mooring can occur under many eyes; some are unwilling to help and—even worse—some are all too eager to offer rude comments or bark out bad commands as to how to approach. If ever there's a situation where communication between helm and foredeck is crucial, this is it.

In many countries, the wharf is the "looky-loo" center for tourists and locals alike. Many motorboats choose to moor

A second properly located windlass may be useful on very large vessels. Without a second windlass, a new-generation, lightweight aluminum anchor will be valuable.

Prepare the anchor for launch at the stern, lay out the rode carefully in long loops on deck so it cannot cause problems during the deployment. Secure the bitter end of the anchor line on a solid cleat at the stern. Approach the anchorage very slowly under power, or with reduced sails following the wind direction. Put the engine in neutral or take down all sails once you reach the desired anchoring spot and deploy the anchor over the stern. Make sure to stay clear of the running line on deck. Once the anchor has stern-to, perhaps to show off their beautiful interiors. This maneuver is easier for powerboats, which move relatively predictably in reverse, but this is not always the case for every craft. Long-keeled cruising sailboats can be difficult to maneuver in reverse. If you do decide to moor stern-to, take care to protect your fragile windvane or other gear at the stern from collisions with the concrete quay.

Unless you enjoy having your cockpit and center cabin under public scrutiny, tying up bow-to may provide some privacy. Although it may be easier to embark and disembark from the stern, it is also prudent to keep the bow in the shallower waters near the quay—where everything from shopping carts to scrap metal gathers—and leave your fragile rudder in deeper water, away from such dangers.

If you know you will have to perform a Med moor in a potentially crowded space, we suggest arriving early in the afternoon so you will have a little more space to maneuver and more places to choose from; you will likely also be busy helping the neighbors who come in after you.

Secure your fenders on both starboard and port sides, even if the neighboring boat is not close to you, to protect you from later arrivals. If you moor stern-to, it's good practice to cushion the stern of your vessel facing the quay as well.

Slowly approach the area where you wish to moor, perpendicular to the quay. How far from the seawall you wish to drop anchor may depend on how many other boats are also Med moored, since you may opt to launch your anchor farther out than your neighbors to avoid fouling.

If there is a strong crosswind, position yourself upwind before launching. Try to launch your anchor directly in front of your targeted space at the quay. You risk fouling in your neighbor's anchor line with any sideways deviation. Before dropping anchor, we suggest maintaining approximately 1 knot of speed toward the quay, so as to not drift out of position and to maintain some setting tension.

As soon as the anchor is dropped, start paying out rode. Part of the art of this maneuver is to put the right amount of tension on the launched anchor rode. With too little tension, the anchor cannot dig in deeply, but too much tension may slow your boat speed down too much, causing undesired sideways drift.

If you are planning to sit stern-to the quay, remember that most sailboats will veer to either port or starboard in reverse. If you know your boat's tendency, try to compensate with steering and short, stronger bursts of power. Practice will improve these skills. Remember that the seafloor close to a busy quay is a sanctuary for debris of all sorts; consider disengaging the propeller for the last few feet toward the quay.

Continue until either a crewmember can secure a line to the quay, or someone on the quay can take one of your lines. Make sure to secure the windward quarter dock line first. As soon as the bow lines are secured, snub the stern anchor. Once all adjustments are made to the bow lines, pull the stern anchor line tight to keep the bow off the quay.

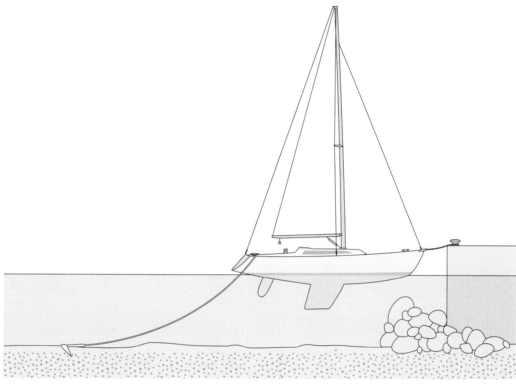

A stern anchor can help keep your bow away from a pier.

LATERAL ANCHORS

In high season, when pickings are slim, a skipper takes the anchoring space he can get and must be satisfied to find a spot at all. If you must anchor against a wharf with an onshore breeze or a surge pushing your boat against the seawall, a *lateral anchor* can be very useful (see illustrations page 136 and page 137, top). You can deploy a lateral anchor from your boat or from your tender.

Deployment

To set a lateral anchor from your vessel, place your boat parallel to the quay but leave plenty of distance from the quay. Allow your boat to come to a stop slightly in front of the space you wish to occupy. Drop your lateral anchor and allow the wind to push your hull sideways towards the quay, using plenty of fenders. Use short spurts from your engine in forward or reverse to maneuver into your desired position. Once the lines are securely warped to shore, snub the lateral anchor tightly to keep your hull a safe distance from the quay. You may also set the lateral anchor once the boat is in its place using your tender (see below). In most cases, it is useful to attach a lateral anchor amidships.

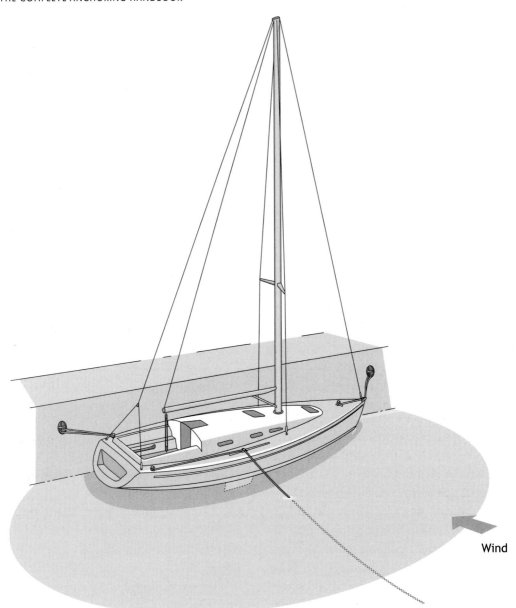

Wind

A lateral anchor can keep your boat off a seawall if there is a surge or an onshore breeze.

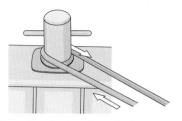

Bring shore lines back and attach them to your vessel so you can adjust their length from the vessel, or to set up for a quick departure.

Deployment from the Tender

In practice, launching an anchor from your tender can be challenging, especially if the weather conditions are not favorable or your tender is dwarfed by the size of your anchor gear. An 80-pound plow anchor with 200 feet of $^3/_8$-inch chain is no match for a small two-person tender. You will have a good chance of capsizing and sinking in the harbor in front of a cheering crowd of spectators.

To minimize the difficulties, you can tie the anchor to your tender's bow cleat and let it hang in the water. The tender may lean sideways on your way out from the weight, but when you get to your drop point, it is easy and safe to untie or cut the rode free and let it drop.

For some it's impossible, impractical, or undesirable to have their hefty anchor hanging outside their tender. If that's the case, place the anchor carefully in the tender's stern, slowly warping the chain leader and the anchor line behind. Make sure the line and chain leader do not get entangled. Secure the other end of the anchor line at a cleat amidships on your primary vessel. Now you should be ready to board your tender and row (or motor, if you have an outboard) slowly away in a lateral direction.

The anchor rode should slowly pull over the stern of your tender loop by loop as you pull away. Make sure the gunwale of your tender does not get damaged once the chain leader starts to pull overboard behind the anchor line. Rowing will get harder and harder the farther away you get from your vessel, especially once the chain leader starts to hang in the water. Once you reach the end, launch your anchor in the opposite direction of the chain pull. The flukes have a better chance of staying clear and not getting caught in their own rode.

Now you are almost done setting your lateral anchor. After the cheering from the crowd on the quay subsides, row back to your vessel and pull in the slack on your lateral anchor line. Make sure the anchor has set well by tightening the line; you can do this with a sheet winch. Hopefully your anchor holds. If not, drop your anchor again at a different spot or choose a different type.

Seeing your boldness for tying up where you did, another boat may want to raft up to you in a pack. Tying a piece of red cloth or a fender near your hull on your lateral anchor rode will alert a newcomer that you are holding with a lateral anchor.

Mark your lateral anchor line with a red cloth to warn new arrivals.

Using a Lateral Hitch

If you want to point your vessel in a particular angle in relation to the wind in order to take an uncomfortable swell from the bow, you can attach a second line with a rolling hitch or a chain hook at your anchor rode and bring it to the stern. You can adjust the angle of your vessel toward the wind now by trimming the additional line at the stern.

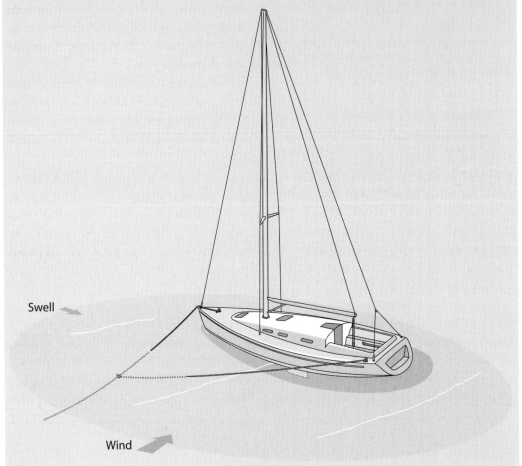

Swell

Wind

You can use a lateral hitch and an additional bridle at anchor to adjust the angle of your boat relative to a swell.

ANCHORING WITH TWO ANCHORS
Forked Mooring

In bad weather, it can be comforting and outright indispensable to prepare a second ground tackle in case the first one drags or breaks. If the weather worsens, you can drop your second anchor in the following manner: Motor in the direction of your first anchor until you are almost above it but to one side of it (see A in the illustration opposite), enough so that once you drop the second anchor, the anchor rodes should fork with an angle of about 60° under load (see B in the illustration). Snub the second anchor and see if that feels more stable. Both anchors deployed from the bow should ideally share the load, but in reality the load shifts from one anchor to the other. You might consider this technique where the consequences of dragging are particularly dire and you hanker for the extra comfort of having two instead of one.

When you do this, however, you gain holding power at the expense of a degree of mobility; two anchors may complicate things if you have to quickly weigh anchors and go. The weighing process is the same as with one anchor, but can take twice as long.

Hammerlock Moor

When winds and wave action become more aggressive in an anchorage, a vessel has the tendency to horse—swing back and forth on its radius. Hoisting a riding sail or countering with the rudder can help. But when excessive loads threaten the anchor gear and things become uncomfortable on board, consider setting a *hammerlock moor*, which reduces the tacking motion, taking some of the load off the primary anchor.

Motor forward in the direction of your ground tackle. After only a few feet, drop a second anchor and pay out a short amount of scope (approximately 2:1). This second anchor will drag over the seafloor and reduce the boat's swinging motion, even if it does not penetrate the seafloor.

Here is a case where you can permit an anchor to drag! If the anchor holds, that's fine too. If the winds change direction, the hammerlock mooring will most likely pivot and

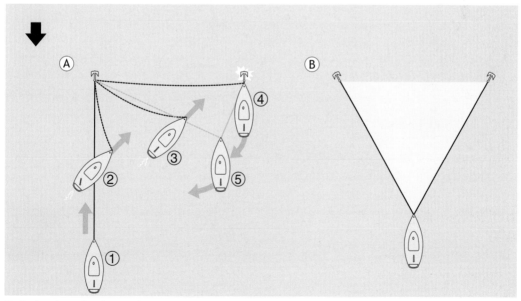

Forked anchors. It is best to have your anchors and your vessel form an equilateral triangle.

continue to provide some relief from the back-and-forth sheering movement while the main load is still taken up by the primary anchor. The hammerlock mooring is also useful for avoiding an undesirable or hazardous area close to a quadrant of your swinging radius.

Since your bow anchor will bear the wind loads and the hammerlock mooring will pacify violent swinging, this second ground tackle may be a smaller anchor than the first. However, if the second anchor is the same size as the first, it serves yet another added benefit: if your principal anchor begins to drag, your second anchor is ready for action once

you pay out enough line to reach a sufficient scope.

Bahamian Moor

A strong, reversing current running through an anchorage is not unusual. Every vessel responds somewhat differently to a combination of wind, current, and swell. In an anchorage with reversing currents, it is not unusual to see boats anchored near each other, all facing different directions, swinging willy-nilly. Hulls may collide under such conditions if their swinging radii overlap slightly.

Reversing currents are not a problem if your swinging radius is unconstrained.

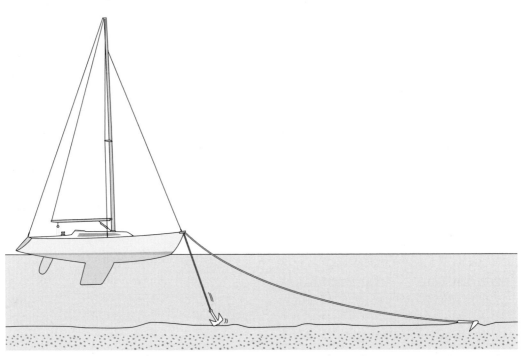

A hammerlock mooring minimizes the swaying motion of a vessel at anchor. The secondary anchor is ready to become the primary anchor if the first anchor drags.

However, there are instances where you may be required to restrain your vessel's swinging radius, such as in a narrow creek, between shoals or islands, or in a crowded anchorage. In a mooring field, where boats are lying on extremely short scopes, the Bahamian moor can also be useful.

The Bahamian moor entails two anchors both set from the bow, one upcurrent and the other downcurrent, 180° apart. The vessel pulls on either or both anchor rodes, and is immobilized within a tight radius regardless of wind direction or current flow (see A in the illustration next page).

Because this technique allows either rode to be partially or wholly under the keel, it helps to have a chain leader so that the catenary sag keeps the rode away from keel, rudder, and propeller.

The most conventional way to set a Bahamian moor is to first anchor against the existing current, then pay out twice as much scope as required, letting the boat drift downcurrent. Then launch the stern anchor and pull on your first rode until the two lengths are nearly equal.

Crosswinds may complicate this technique, however. Another possibility is to launch the secondary or leeward anchor first. This can be done off the bow while the vessel is still motoring upcurrent, but some prefer dropping this anchor from the stern to avoid catching the rode in the propeller or around the hull as the vessel motors forward to windward. When the boat has reached the point of double scope, secure the rode either forward or on a stern cleat, depending on if you launched it forward or

aft, and power forward slowly to set the anchor. Now pay out more scope, motoring to windward, where you will launch the primary or windward anchor. Once the windward anchor is launched, let the boat settle back downcurrent while hauling in the slack from the leeward rode, making sure it doesn't get caught in the propeller or wound around the keel.

Pay out the desired scope for the forward anchor and set as usual, using reverse to help set the anchor. During this portion of the maneuver, make sure the leeward rode does not become fouled on the prop, rudder, or keel. Once you've set the windward anchor, position the boat halfway between your two anchors, then bring your leeward rode forward to the bow if you dropped it from the stern. The boat should now pivot freely between the two moors.

Another possibility is to use your tender to launch the aft anchor once the main anchor is set, especially if you use one that is lightweight aluminum. (See above for more on dropping an anchor using a tender.)

To weigh anchor, pay out rode from the windward anchor while hauling in from the leeward anchor so that the vessel drifts backward. Once this anchor is dislodged, hauled, and stowed, the vessel can motor up to haul in the windward one.

Fore-and-Aft Mooring

The forked, Bahamian, and hammerlock moorings use the bow roller as the entry point for both rodes to their attachment points on deck.

In contrast, the fore-and-aft (bow-and-stern) technique has an anchor set off the bow

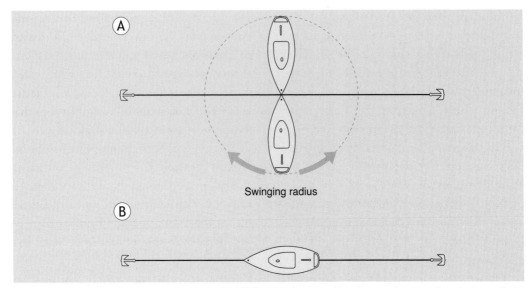

In the Bahamian moor (A), two anchors are set 180° apart, dramatically reducing the vessel's swinging radius. The fore-and-aft mooring (B) prevents the vessel from swinging in either direction.

and one set off the stern, restraining a boat's swinging and virtually immobilizing it between two points (see B in the illustration above). This can be handy to align the vessel to winds, current, and wave action. Since there is no slack rode below the hull, this method alleviates the problem of the rode scraping along the hull or getting caught on the rudder or prop.

This technique can be accomplished the same way as the Bahamian moor, except that you either bring the aft rode to the stern once launched from the bow, or leave it at the stern if launched from there.

Once both anchors are set, haul in the slack on both rodes to limit swing or align the vessel in the desired direction.

Keep in mind that vessels, especially sailboats or boats with considerable windage, do not react positively to being kept from swinging bow into the wind. Deployed in moderate to strong winds or strong currents, a stern anchor can exert considerably higher loads on ground tackle, vessel, and deck hardware than if it were secured off the bow.

Tandem Anchoring

We do not recommend attaching two anchors to one rode, known as *tandem anchoring*. This approach attaches a second anchor with around 15 feet of chain in front of the first anchor. In his early sailing days, Alain almost lost his boat trying out this idea. At the time, his first anchor dragged. He added a smaller anchor in front of the large, traditional model. This worsened the holding power instead of doubling it, and he drifted swiftly on the smaller anchor while the larger one couldn't grip at all.

Alain practiced tandem anchoring in the clear waters of the Mediterranean; he dropped anchor this way approximately seventy times, diving on nearly all of them. In 62% of the cases, only one anchor was set. During bad weather, performing a dive check on your settings is almost impossible; you can only "trust" your anchors—and this is tantamount to Russian roulette.

It might seem logical that two anchors would hold better than one. This is only true, however, when both anchors can set perfectly. Whatever anchoring technique you use, there's never a guarantee that both anchors are going to set well. On the contrary, once the first anchor is set in the seafloor, it will hinder the other anchor from setting also.

The first dragging anchor plows a trench behind it, leaving a path of loose disturbed

sand. These areas, still visible after several tides, explain why more popular anchorages are crisscrossed with patches of poor holding. If the anchor closest to the vessel drags even a few feet as it sets, chances are good that the second anchor behind it will drop into this loose bottom with poor holding.

There are those mariners who swear by tandem anchoring, and there probably isn't much we can say to convince them otherwise. For those who *insist* on using two anchors on one rode, we believe that the following suggestions will improve your chance of success at this risky maneuver:

• Only use two anchors of the same size and model. Although it is rare to have

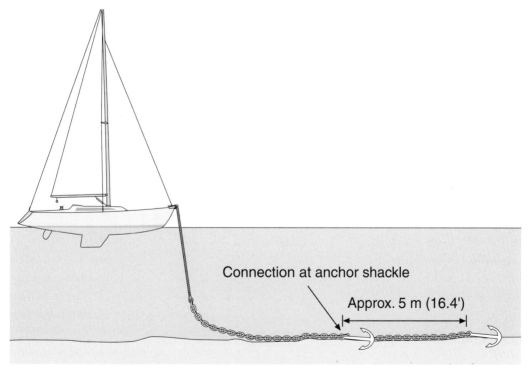

Connection at anchor shackle

Approx. 5 m (16.4')

We advise against tandem anchoring. If you insist on tandem anchors, only use two of the same kind of anchor, and attach the second one to the chain or shackle of the first, not directly to the crown of the first.

two of the same anchors, we feel this is the lesser of evils when doubling up on a rode.

- Each anchor should be capable of accommodating the load of your boat on its own, without the second one.

- Separate the two anchors with a 10- to 16-foot (3 m to 5 m) length of chain.

- Never attach the chain from the second anchor directly to the first anchor; instead, attach it to the connector of the first anchor (see illustration page 143).

- Finally, remember that new-generation anchors have far superior holding power than older models, and they do not suddenly disengage from the seafloor. Instead, they slowly drift, remaining embedded. We are convinced that a single new-generation anchor with high holding power is safer and more reliable than linking two traditional anchors in tandem.

SPECIAL ANCHORING TECHNIQUES

Anchoring and Securing Your Boat on a Rocky Shoreline

What can you do if you do *not* want to avoid rocks because you want to moor your boat in a beautiful secluded bay on a lake or in a breathtaking inlet with a rocky shore? What if this is your only option? We can't cover every aspect of the idea, but hope to give you an idea of what attaching your boat to a rocky coast might entail.

First, equip your boat with the necessary gear to get your vessel well secured and centered inside the "obstacle course." You'll need several shorter chain lengths (that can be placed around solid rock formations), additional shackles, and at least four 12-foot dock lines equipped with thimbles and eye splices at one end.

Marine equipment distributors usually carry land anchors and rock fasteners. Some mountaineering stores also carry rock-climbing gear with safe working load and breaking strength certificates, which can be useful to secure a land line in a rocky spot. Ask about the gear's corrosion resistance and make sure you get the products that will do the trick in a saltwater environment. Don't forget to bring your hammer for the anchor maneuver, and check with local authorities if possible to ensure that such "defacing" of the coastline is permitted.

Select your spot with care; if possible, evaluate the local conditions with an exploratory dinghy trip before you approach with your vessel. Of course, carefully study wind direction, water depth and any currents or whirlpools. It won't hurt to have all your fenders out as a precaution. Consider first immobilizing the boat to windward to avoid any extraneous movement while the rest of your attachments are being prepared. Deploying a stern anchor (see pages 132–33) might be useful during your departure maneuver, especially if weather conditions become less favorable. Use a trip line with your anchor on a rocky ground to prevent fouling. Approach very slowly with the main engine; fiberglass hulls are no match for pointy rocks or sharp oyster shells. Someone should stay at the helm, ready to reposition the boat if it starts

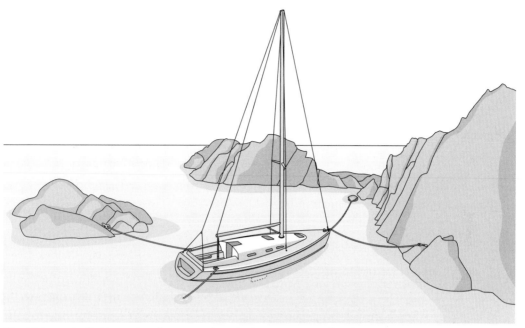

Combining rock climbing and anchoring can be risky, but sometimes it's well worth it.

Small rocky islands quite often come without trees. If you bring an additional piece of chain, you can put it around a rock to attach your line. Add chafe protection to the line wherever it touches the rock directly.

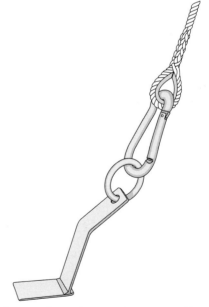

Anchor gear for rocky coastal areas resembles mountaineering equipment. Bring the right tool to attach your rock fasteners.

to drift. Bring out the tender and have one crewmember row ashore to secure one line after another until your vessel lies safely at the desired spot. Protect the lines from chafe with rubber hoses.

Anchoring in Environmentally Sensitive Areas

Mother Earth's oceans belong to all of us. At anchor, we especially appreciate the beauty of clear waters, pristine coral reefs, and teeming sea life. It is our responsibility to preserve these areas in their most pristine state. Already—from Hawaii to Turkey to Chile—many of the world's most beautiful spots are off-limits for anchoring.

As mentioned earlier, we feel that anchors designed for easy retrieval on coral reefs imply that anchoring directly on coral reefs is acceptable behavior. We respectfully disagree and suggest that we all make a strong effort to aim for the sandy spots between the coral instead. It is not difficult to imagine what even a perfect "reef anchor" would do to a fragile coral garden.

The areas that are still accessible must be preserved or they too will become off-limits or destroyed. The best-organized environmentally sensitive areas ban anchoring and instead install moorings, which minimize destruction of the surrounding ecosystem. If you sail or motor into areas with installed mooring buoys, use the provided buoys and keep your anchor at the bow roller.

If you do anchor, realize that when an anchor sets, it usually drags for a distance, leaving a mark on the seafloor that can take a long time to disappear. Anchors can rake over

seedlings and regrowth can be slow. Fast- and deep-setting models do relatively little damage to the seafloor.

Ground tackle can irreparably destroy coral heads that took generations to develop, with anchor chain abrading everything in its path on the seafloor. Using a shorter chain leader coupled with a fender float as a pneumatic shock absorber will reduce seafloor damage from chain (see illustration page 148).

If you are lucky enough to have found your dream anchor spot in sand surrounded by pristine coral reefs, you can use the "fender-float" tactic to prevent your anchor chain from destroying the environment around you while protecting your line from chafe damage.

First, use the largest fender you have to buoy your anchor rode at the chain-rope connection. This offers several advantages:

- It lifts the abrasion-prone rope-to-chain splice of the rode off the seafloor. This is especially convenient with highly abrasive rocky or coral seafloors.

- When the load on the rode increases, it stretches; but in order to stretch, it must pull the fender underwater. Then, once the load lightens, the fender pops up to the surface again. Depending on its buoyancy, this can work as a shock absorber in a nasty swell.

- The fender works as a kind of warning marker to other boats that otherwise would have anchored directly in front of your boat's bow.

- An extra advantage is that you don't need to buy extra equipment! Simply use your largest fender.

A mooring is ideal for anchorages in ecologically sensitive areas.

Unfortunately, the fender's buoyancy neutralizes some of the chain's weight and might affect the pulling angle at the anchor shaft. Overall, however, we think the fender float can be a valuable tactic to keep in mind for a special time in a special place.

As a final environmental caution, once you've weighed anchor, always wash off your ground tackle as best you can to avoid dispersing foreign elements into new environments (for example, poisonous algae).

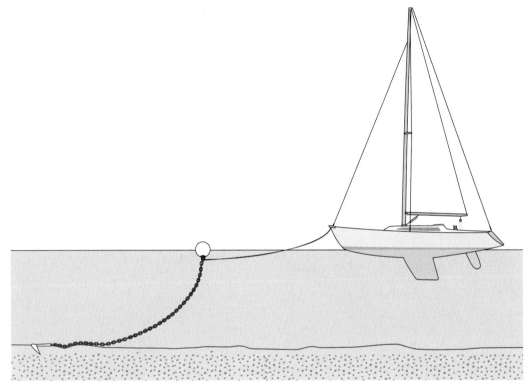

Pneumatic shock absorber.

WHEN THINGS GO WRONG

Fouled Anchor

Thankfully, your anchor doesn't get fouled every day. But when it does, there are few more frustrating situations. Following are some retrieval tips.

Trip Line

If your anchor gets fouled, using a *trip line*—a line attached to the crown of the anchor—can help break your anchor loose. Most navigators don't use trip lines all the time. Of course, this can lead to a Murphy's Law situation, as the few times you don't use the trip line are the times you would really need one. In

particular, harbors and ports near urban areas may have been used as a dumping ground for decades, complete with old cars, appliances, and hefty junk. Here a trip line is good insurance since these are not your most pristine waters for diving on your fouled anchor.

Most modern anchors have a dedicated eye at the crown for installing a trip line. Because of its inelastic, abrasion-resistant properties, polyester is the ideal material for a trip line.

What to do with the bitter end? Trip lines are often run from the crown of the anchor to a float. But installing a buoy marker at the trip line's bitter end can be hazardous, especially if there is a chance someone might mistake it for a mooring. Also, the buoy can be a nuisance to passing boats when it wanders away from the anchor at low tide. A sinker directly below the buoy helps hold it vertically and adjust for tidal changes in water depth, but the buoy can still wander off—especially if there's current. If you must use a buoy, try to mark it with large letters or stick a flag with an anchor on the buoy to indicate where your anchor is.

If the anchorage is crowded and there's a good chance a speedboat would chop a buoyed trip line in two, try attaching your trip line to the anchor rode and launch both simultaneously. Pay out about 2:1 scope. You will need to place your trip line at a point on the chain so that when you weigh anchor later, the end of the trip line will arrive on

deck before your vessel is directly above the anchor; don't forget to factor in tidal differences. Put a brake on the chain and tie off the trip line's end to the chain with a rolling hitch or a shackle. Then continue letting out your rode. If you need to use the trip line, it's already rigged for you. Just brace the chain and pull on the trip line until your anchor pulls free.

If you've been anchoring in mud, your trip line can offer you the opportunity to give your ground tackle a good cleaning if it's not too heavy. Weigh anchor by pulling on the trip line only. Attach the trip line to a deck cleat so that the anchor will still be just under the water, retrieve the excess chain until the muddy section appears, and then motor slowly forward until the ground tackle is clean.

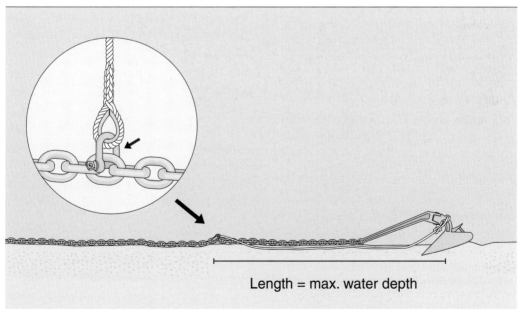

Length = max. water depth

Instead of using a float, the loose end of the trip line can be connected to the chain leader with a shackle. Make the trip line at least 10% longer than the chain portion to which it is attached.

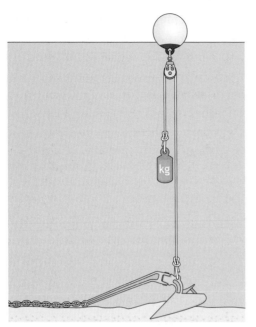

A trip line with a pulley and kellet to compensate for different water levels.

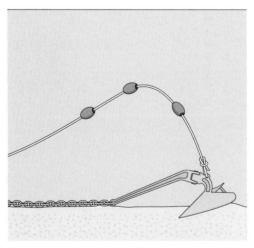

A trip line with small floats (the type that are also used for fishing nets). These floats prevent the trip line from tangling with the rode but keep the trip line at a low-enough profile so as not interfere with surface marine traffic (rudders, propellers of passing vessels).

When your anchor is fouled, try to figure out what is stuck and why. Knowing the cause of your misfortune can be half the solution. Sometimes, it is not the anchor at all but the chain that is fouled around a rock or some kind of debris. In this case, your trip line won't help at all. You can try advancing the boat slightly forward toward the anchor to help liberate the chain. Of course, it helps to have good water visibility in these cases, but unfortunately debris under your keel often comes with "chocolate" water and only a few inches of visibility. If you didn't install a trip line, try a little lateral motoring, to port and starboard of the rode, giving each position several minutes to dislodge. Remember, nudging is OK, but don't pull too hard; some anchor shafts are not designed to withstand strong lateral tension and they bend or break easily.

Still no success, and you don't have diving equipment? Here are a few more tricks. Attach a large heavy ring, a loop of chain, or an extra-large shackle to the end of your trip line. It must be big enough to fit over the anchor shaft. Slide this ring or shackle down the anchor rode with the goal of sliding it over the anchor shaft. This may be easier to accomplish from a tender, but once you feel the loop or shackle has gone over the anchor shaft, return with the trip line to the main vessel. Now free the bitter end of your main rode from the vessel, attach it to a large fender, and throw the whole ensemble overboard. While keeping the load on the trip line, allow the engine to pull the trip line in the opposite direction of the original anchor load in order to move the anchor backward, away from the submerged obstacle.

Other Retrieval Tips

If your anchor or chain is fouled under the chain of a enormous yacht whose skipper "politely" dropped his ground tackle on top of yours, you can probably pull up both rodes at once with your manual or electric windlass. However, it is almost certain that the other boat's chain will get wrapped around your anchor on the way up. Here's the moment

you'll be happy you brought that folding grapnel anchor aboard! Attach a trip line, along with its regular rode, to the grapnel. Pull your anchor rode tight and allow the grapnel to rake through the seafloor and catch the yacht's chain with one of the flukes. Pull the grapnel's anchor line taut and attach it on deck; the grapnel should now lift the other anchor chain from the seafloor. Now loosen

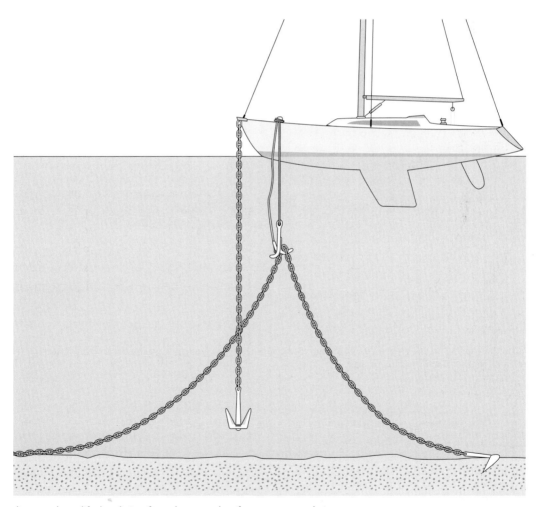

A grapnel can lift the chain of another vessel to free your own chain.

THE COMPLETE ANCHORING HANDBOOK

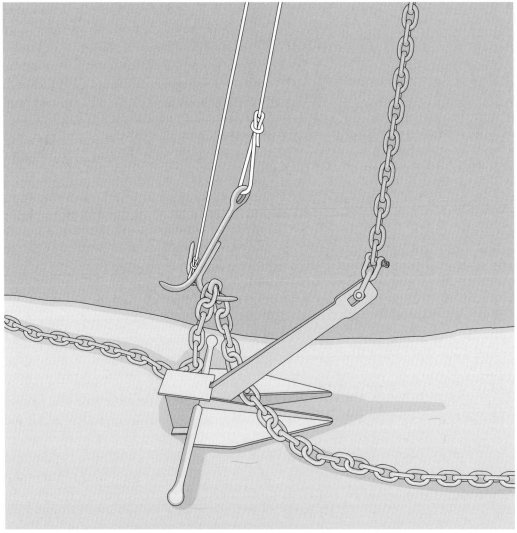

Note the trip line on the grapnel, which allows you to disengage the grapnel from the obstructing anchor chain once your anchor has been freed.

your own anchor rode; your anchor should come free from the other chain. Your vessel should now hold with the grapnel on the yacht's chain and anchor, which will very likely give you the necessary time to clear, raise, and secure your own ground tackle on deck. To let go of their chain, simply transfer the load onto the grapnel's trip line, and let go of the grapnel anchor line, releasing the other chain.

Dire Straits near the Strait of Gibraltar

One of the most challenging spots we (Erika and Achim) have fouled an anchor was in Gibraltar harbor. Although the Mediterranean Sea offers pristine boating waters, its industrial harbors couple rich history with generations of sunken debris, wrecks, and relics.

In our case our anchor got stuck under an old chain. In some harbors they lay this chain on purpose to reduce the danger of dragging. The water near the seawall was so chocolate-muddy that Achim felt like he was diving in a swamp. Even with his diving mask, he could see nothing underwater and had to perform "Braille reading" to free our ground tackle. While diving 20 feet might be a piece of cake in a secluded, less populated anchorage, diving even half that depth in an industrial harbor can be daunting.

You may save yourself time and frustration by deploying a trip line when anchoring in any industrial waters.

Grounding

Whoops, you meant starboard! Too late. Due to a navigational or steering error, you have just involuntarily turned your keel into an anchor. Consider calling the Coast Guard or other local authority to inform them of your grounding, even if you do not need assistance.

If possible, use your tender to take soundings and bottom samples from around your vessel. If you can see that the boat has alighted on a hard shoal, it may be better not to attempt to immediately refloat your vessel. First, check that the hull is not damaged and that you are not taking on water. Try to figure out where you are on the chart and the direction you arrived from. See if you can ascertain where the deeper water lies, and confirm where you are in the tidal cycle at that moment.

Perhaps you are lucky enough that the tide is rising, and increased depths will be sufficient to float you off the shoal. Even if it's speedier to be pulled off by another vessel, allowing increased depth to float you off is less traumatic for the crew and your hull.

If weather could push your vessel farther onto the shoal, it may be necessary to set an anchor in the direction of the wind and swell. Bring your (larger) anchor out in deep water, preferably with a chain leader and a long line. If you are only slightly ashoal, you may be able to wedge yourself free without assistance. Lighten the vessel by hanging all your spare anchor chain overboard and—if necessary or possible—empty your water tanks. Try to set your anchor in the direction you wish the vessel to move. Carry the anchor out by dinghy if possible, although it's not unheard of to "swim" an anchor out on floating life vests or closed-cell-foam cushions. Use your anchor windlass or a genoa sheet winch to haul in the anchor line.

Someone in the water pushing the boat sideways in both directions may be just the extra force you need to get it "over the hump." Of course, this depends on the size of your vessel, which may preclude any such attempts.

First try to motor in reverse, keeping a close eye on your movements and making sure the engine doesn't overheat. Monitor your temperature gauges carefully. Shut down your engine immediately if you notice a rapid rise in temperature. If the vessel doesn't free itself immediately, stop and take a moment to reassess your predicament. If you've run

A strong side current caught us dreaming at the helm in the narrow channel between Bell Island and Cambridge Key in the Exumas. We were lucky to have good anchor gear on board. To hide our embarrassment in front of a crowd of spectators, we pretended that this "haulout" maneuver was planned well in advance.

aground on a soft seafloor, such as mud or sand, the experience will likely be one only of inconvenience and memorable adventure— taking time and tide, wind and wave action to free you. Consider this one of your "off" days. Inspect your keel, and take advantage of a half-exposed hull to start scraping barnacles or cleaning the bottom.

If you've run hard aground, however, damage, leaks, and injury can result. If your vessel was traveling at a speed higher than a few knots, it could even result in total loss of the vessel. Do not abandon ship immediately, however. Have everyone put on life jackets and use your VHF to call for help. If your hull has sustained serious damage and you are taking on water, try to stop any leaks you can find. If possible, it's better to stay put on your shoal and wait for help.

If you run aground on a falling tide and/or in agitated waters, you should act quickly.

There is little chance of refloating your vessel if the tide is falling. Unless you are utterly certain that you have encountered just a small shallow area and deeper water is ahead, we strongly discourage you from trying to plow your way across with main engine power as you risk pushing yourself deeper aground. What's more, full throttle in reverse may cause the prop to stir up all sorts of seafloor muck, including weed and mud, which can easily infiltrate your cooling water circuit and cause the engine to overheat just at the wrong moment.

When *Pangaea* ran aground in the Intracoastal Waterway near Beaufort, North Carolina, we used the wake of a passing barge to lift us off a tricky shoal. We made sure that our engine ran full speed when the waves hit the hull to lift our keel for just a moment. This was enough to make our heavy steel ketch perform a triple jump back into the deep channel.

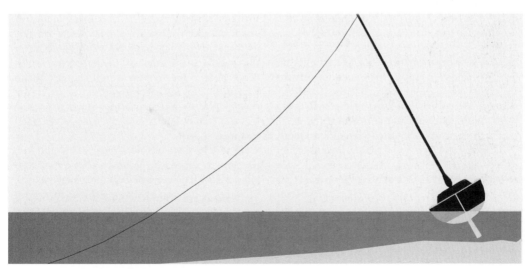

Use a lateral anchor to "heel the keel" so you can slide into deeper water.

If the skipper of another vessel is willing and able to help out, he can first try zooming back and forth to make as large a wake as possible. Of course, this method should only be tried if the bottom is soft and your hull is strong enough to sustain at least one triple jump.

If that doesn't work, and the other boat is willing to pull you off, attach a line to a strong cleat and let the boat pull you in the desired direction. Both boats must have solid deck hardware to endure the strain; this is another situation where your mooring bitt will come in handy. Not every vessel is outfitted for such a serious tow job. Watch out that the helping boat doesn't run aground alongside you. When pulling, all crew should be kept away from the straining towline. The towline can part and snap back, causing serious crew injuries.

When You *Want* to Run Aground

There are times when you may want to intentionally place your boat on the beach. Multihulls and boats with twin or retractable keels have the advantage of being able to manage little or even no water under them for repairs and maintenance, or when you simply want to be close to land. Flat-bottomed monohulls and some large powerboats might be able to beach safely and stay upright if their propellers and rudders are well protected. Deep-keeled monohulls may also deliberately fall dry with the help of crutch stands—although this art would deserve its own chapter and has more to do with maintenance on a dime than anchoring.

If you have a boat that is suited for beaching, observe your beaching area at low tide, scouting for boulders hidden in sand or mud. Look for the flattest, most homogeneous patch. Beaches usually slope gently toward the water, and multihulls ought to beach perpendicular to this slope. Of course, an ideal beaching area is protected from surf and surge.

Carefully calculate tidal highs and lows. Beaching on a rising tide is relatively useless, unless you want to beach your vessel over and over again every few minutes. If the water level is falling rapidly, better pick the right spot on the first try because you will likely not be able to get off before the next flood comes a few hours later. At high tide with minimal drop in water level you might have a second chance by going into reverse and trying it again at a different location. Don't forget that in a 12-hour tidal cycle, the major height variation is during the third and fourth hours, while the lowest disparity is in the beginning or end of the cycle (see the section on estimating water level in a tidal area on page 123).

Once you've chosen the optimal maneuvering time, drop your kedge or stern anchor as far out as possible with a short chain leader and a long line. With reasonable speed, approach the beach at a perpendicular angle. Unless your boat has a twin keel, don't forget to cut the motor before the cooling water inlet can suck up any sand or debris.

Keep in mind that with only a few inches of water beneath your keel, a sudden surge can violently smack the hull onto the seafloor. To avoid this, approach the beach slowly but steadily, with centerboards up and crew weight aft, making the landing in one fell swoop without stopping or reversing. Once beached, bring your bow anchor forward or tie a line ashore to a fixed object, such as a tree.

Especially if the waters are perfectly calm, it is possible to approach the beach with a deployed stern anchor. You can wait with a minimum amount of water under the keel at a shallow spot until the tide falls instead of driving your vessel onto the beach under motor. When the flood returns and the water level is sufficiently high, you are ready to launch again, winching in your stern anchor as quickly as possible to reach deeper water.

If your boat is a keelboat with a mast, and you have powerful winches—and muscles, you can try the following technique. Once the principal anchor is set, bring a second anchor out to the side, attach one or more halyards to the anchor rode from the masthead, and heave in the line from the deck. This second anchor will have the task of heeling your hull either to port or starboard, thereby reducing your vessel's draft. You can literally keelhaul your vessel—just like sailors did in the good old days of yore, careening their schooners by leading the line through a block on deck and hauling it with a powerful winch. Once the keel gently moves in the mud, the vessel should be able to slide into deeper water, especially if you can use the main anchor to assist in the process. But watch out that all your rigging components are strong enough to survive such a risky maneuver.

If you have waited through a full tide cycle and you are hopelessly stuck, a commercial towboat may be your only option, and that can cost a pretty penny. Hard grounding may even be considered a "salvage" operation and might cost considerably more than getting a tow off a soft shoal.

HEAVY-WEATHER ANCHORING

Let's talk for a moment about extreme weather conditions in an anchorage. Of course, your decisions will depend on the specific conditions that you expect during an upcoming blow. Try to imagine all possible scenarios in advance and develop a plan of action regarding what you would do if a particular weather factor changes.

If you are anchored in a relatively shallow anchorage next to a steep slope, expect to face high waves or even breakers in case the swell rises.

Prepare yourself and your vessel to leave the anchorage unless you are facing hurricane conditions. (The sidebar next page best expresses the process for hurricane preparation.) In some severe cases it might even be advisable to leave your vessel and seek shelter on land. Some owners intentionally submerge their vessel at a controlled spot before the waves can smash the hull to small pieces. We will not go into this procedure, but a water-sogged interior is preferable to a total hull loss.

If you decide to stay at anchor we cannot overemphasize the importance of two aspects: chafe protection, and shock absorption with a hybrid rode and/or snubber (both chafe and shock absorption are covered in Chapter 4).

If you're not in a hurricane hole, have sufficient space around your vessel to increase line scope to a ratio of 10:1. Check for chafe as often as possible, especially at the bow roller, the cleats, and the hawsepipe. If you are riding on chain only, make every effort to build a snubber. If winds increase to, say, over 50 knots and a swell builds, you may need to abandon your rode and anchor—especially if the wave shocks are stressing your ground tackle. Consider having a large, shackled float or fender prepared in case the bitter end must be let go, which could be attached toward the front of the chain at the bow before letting go of the bitter end. In reality, if it is a real emergency, you likely will have no time to fiddle with such things. You should always have a metal saw blade or serrated knife available to cut a nylon line. Bolt cutters come in handy if you are facing a piece of chain that needs to go (Erika and Achim needed theirs during *Pangaea*'s first anchoring maneuver—see the sidebar on page 112). Remember, these are *not* everyday conditions and if you are lucky you may never encounter them; but others have had to contend with these conditions and it's a good idea to be prepared.

Hurricane Plan for Boaters
by Mark Amaral, University of Rhode Island Coastal Resources Center/Sea Grant

If your boat is moored, docked, or stored in a recreational harbor on the East Coast, the threat of hurricanes is a very real concern. Even the least severe Category 1 hurricane can have devastating effects in today's crowded harbors. These high-density areas can be disasters waiting to happen because of the close proximity of vessels to one another, faulty mooring maintenance, and lack of hurricane preparedness.

Although the harbor manager, harbormaster, or port director tries to ensure that boats in their harbor are safe, the final responsibility falls upon the boatowner. Owners are ultimately responsible for their vessel. In order to protect personal property and the vessels around them, owners must: (1) know their boats and their own skills; (2) know the surrounding area; and (3) have a plan.

Creating a plan and being ready for a hurricane starts well in advance of the boating season. When vessel owners prepare their vessels for the boating season, they should also prepare a hurricane plan. This plan should review all the options available. Prior to the hurricane season, decisions should be made as to where the safest place for the vessel would be, the adequacy of the present mooring or dock, and what type of equipment is necessary to have on board.

The following are options for safeguarding recreational boats. Only the vessel owner can decide which is best.

OPTION 1: GET OUT OF THE WATER
If the vessel is small and trailers easily, it should be taken out of the water and moved to higher ground.

This is the safest means of protecting a vessel. Getting a vessel out of the water, however, does not automatically mean that it is safe. It is only protected from the storm surge and wave action—rain and wind must still be considered. The best solution is to store these vessels in a covered area, such as a garage. If this is impossible, then all equipment, including oil and gas cans, personal flotation devices, oars, paddles, and other loose gear, should be removed and stored indoors. The trailer frame should be placed on blocks so that the frame will carry the boat's weight instead of the axle and springs.

The drain plug should be installed, and the boat should be partially filled with water if the hull is strong enough to withstand flooding (as are most fiberglass hulls).

If the hull is not strong enough to hold water (plywood- or wooden-planked hulls), use multiple anchor tie-downs to hold the boat and trailer in position, and remove the plug. Consider large tent pegs (2 feet) or house trailer tie-downs for this anchoring system.

OPTION 2: STAY IN THE WATER
Staying in the water assumes that the vessel will either: (1) stay on the mooring or dock; (2) go to a hurricane hole to anchor; or (3) head out to sea. Each of these options should be considered and accurate information collected well in advance of the hurricane season.

Dock
The decision to remain in port will probably depend on the intensity of the storm, the protection afforded by the harbor, and the condition of the dock or mooring. If the decision is made to stay at the dock, then precautions need to be taken.

Ensure that all lines are doubled and that chafing protection is in place where dock lines pass through fairleads and chocks or over the side of the vessel. The best chafing protection is to cover lines with a rubber hose of the same diameter as your line, then tightly wind it with heavy fabric and fasten with a heavy commercial tape. A vessel tied to a dock should have ample fenders to provide protection to the hull. Dock lines should be attached to the high end of the pilings, rather than to the cleats or other fastenings on the dock. As flooding and the storm surge raises the water level, dock lines will move up the pilings.

Mooring

Staying at the mooring may be the best option if you've ensured that the mooring tackle meets safety standards and has been inspected for wear. Any mooring gear that has worn by one-third of its original diameter should be considered unsafe.

One of the drawbacks of staying at the mooring, like staying at the dock, is the threat of a storm surge. If the water level rises even moderately above present conditions, the mooring scope may not provide sufficient holding power. This can be combated by checking with expected storm surge reports prior to the hurricane.

Regardless of whether you choose to stay at the dock or mooring, there are some fundamental steps that need to be taken. The first is to minimize windage, or the amount of surface area that the wind can act against. The more surface area for the wind to act on, the greater the strain on your vessel and the dock or mooring. If possible, remove sails entirely and stow them belowdecks, especially roller-furler jibs. If it is not possible to remove sails, then it is imperative to fasten them as securely as possible. Next, look around for other possible objects that could result in added windage, including flags and pennants, and store them properly. Make sure that all ports are closed securely and that all funnels are removed and capped. Using stiff lines from both sides, secure the tiller or wheels that operate the rudders; do not leave coils of line on the deck without proper stops or other means of rendering them immovable; and take out all the slack from any running lines on the deck or mast. Finally, you must face the possibility that your vessel, or a vessel nearby, may break loose. In order to minimize the impact of loose vessels in a crowded harbor, it is important to remove and stow all protruding objects and set fenders on both sides, if at a mooring, or outside of a docked boat.

Hurricane Holes

If your boat is in a crowded anchorage zone, you may consider moving your vessel to a "hurricane hole" or area for safe anchorage. Small soft-bottom coves that are less crowded are traditional spots. Before making such a move, consider the fact that hurricane holes can become crowded with vessels seeking refuge from impending storms. This instantly eliminates one of the reasons for going to such places. If you do decide to utilize a hurricane hole, consider the following: Hurricane holes should be located before the storm season by consulting an inland chart. It is best to look for a location that has deep water (you may have to arrive at low tide) and is close. The best spots have a route that is free of highway and railroad bridges and has good protection, such as a high bluff, an outer reef, or tall trees on as many sides as possible. It is a good idea to visit potential hurricane holes prior to the hurricane season, test the bottom, and note the surroundings. Multiple hurricane holes should be tested and several options should be available in the event of a hurricane.

Arrive at a hurricane hole at least 12 hours prior to landfall, and set your anchor with at least a 7:1 scope (i.e., in 30 feet of water, 210 feet of anchor line is needed). Nylon is the best anchor line because of its elasticity. Chafing protection should be used where the anchor line passes through the anchor chute chocks. Experts recommend that you leave by means of a small boat once your vessel is securely anchored, and that all automatic switches have been double-checked.

If you elect to stay aboard, stay in touch with all weather advisories. It is important to have stocked up on fuel, water, food, ice, clothing, a portable radio and flashlight with extra batteries, and any prescription medicines. It might be necessary to put the engine in gear during the worst part of the storm

(continued)

to ease the strain on the anchor line, as well as to have someone stay awake on anchor watch at all times to prevent the boat from drifting. To help maintain your position, use a spotlight and/or radar at night. To see if water or debris is accumulating, and to make sure the pumps are operating, check the bilge regularly. Finally, traditional markers or navigation aids may have been rearranged by the storm. It is important, therefore, not to rely solely on those aids to guide you.

Do Not Go Offshore

Unless you are the owner of a large recreational vessel, 100 feet or greater, experts do not recommend that you go offshore. Hurricane conditions at sea are extremely violent. Going offshore should not be considered as a viable option for most recreational boaters. Remember, the objective is to minimize property loss without jeopardizing safety.

CHAPTER 8

Moorings

There are different types of permanent moorings, some created with several anchors, others with one or more heavy dead-weight concrete blocks. Of course, you must first find out the regulations in your area before you place your mooring. Usually a permit is necessary, and authorities may impose guidelines on the installation and characteristics of the mooring. Also, depending on local regulations, your mooring may or may

Some cruisers like to stay long-term in places such as this Tobago anchorage, and they have placed illegal permanent moorings between the islands. Check with local authorities before you set a mooring.

not be off-limits to other vessels in your absence. Check city and county ordinances in the area where you wish to moor.

One particular advantage to having a mooring is that, because it's made up of several anchors, this configuration may be considered a temporary mooring and is therefore not subject to local permits. Contact your local authority to confirm if this is the case.

MOORING BLOCKS

In contrast with embedded anchors, for which the pulling angle must be less than 8°, mooring blocks also work well with a short, almost vertical rode that keeps the swinging radius to a minimum.

Solid blocks are a mooring technique where weight really does matter. The heavier your concrete mooring block(s), the better the holding power. Because the load is imposed almost vertically, the weight must be at least equivalent to the maximum load. The mooring block's bottom surface should be as large as possible to create a suction-cup effect, which increases holding power. This suction effect is most successful in soft bottoms such as mud, and much less successful in coarse sand or rocky bottoms. Also, this holding power increases with time as the slab sinks deeper and deeper into the seafloor.

Assuming that the mooring will be set in relatively sheltered waters, it should be designed to withstand winds of 45 knots (Force 9) with the attached vessel (see Table 8-1).

To calculate the weight of the block, you must account for the density of the chosen material and its actual weight when immersed. Remember that the following materials retain only a percentage of their dry weight:

Steel = 86%

Concrete = 55%

Rock = 64%

TABLE 8-1. ESTIMATED AVERAGE LOAD ON MOORING BLOCKS DUE TO WIND

Boat Dimensions (ft./m)			Wind Load (daN[1])	
Length	Beam, motorboat	Beam, sailboat	Beaufort 9 (45 knots)	Concrete weight (kg), volume (m³)
14.7/4.5	5.9/1.8	1.5/0.46	225	410, 0.164
19.6/6	7.9/2.4	2.2/0.67	325	590, 0.236
24.6/7.5	9/2.75	7.9/2.4	445	810, 0.324
29.5/9	11/3.35	9/2.75	635	1,115, 0.446
34.5/10.5	12.9/3.95	9.84/3	820	1,490, 0.596
39.3/12	13.9/4.26	11/3.35	1,100	2,000, 0.800
49.2/15	16.4/5	12.95/3.95	1,450	2,635, 1.055
59/18	18/5.5	14.7/4.5	1,800	3,270, 1.300
68.9/21	19.6/6	17/5.2	2,500	4,545, 1.820
82/25	22/6.7	19/5.8	3,250	5,910, 2.365

[1] 1 daN = 2.25 pounds of force.

Because cement's holding power is only slightly above 50% of its dry weight, casting wire or other heavy steel elements into its bottom can increase its weight and thus holding power.

Tables 8-1 and 2-1 can give you an idea of the static load due to wind you should expect on a mooring given a particular boat type and length, as well as the weight of the immersed cement block necessary to hold this vertically exerted load. The second value in the last column of Table 8-1 gives an indication of the block's volume, assuming you use standard steel-reinforced concrete (if using only lightly reinforced concrete, multiply this value by 1.25). If you are establishing the mooring in a hurricane zone, these values should be multiplied by 4.

Consider setting up several medium-sized concrete blocks in the place of one large block to facilitate installation and maintenance. These blocks would then be linked up as a multiple-anchor mooring with an oversized chain.

If installing the mooring in a river or estuary, or anywhere with a large current change, twin deadweight anchors configured as a Bahamian moor (or two groups of twin blocks) may be the best solution with the boat secured between. One principal mooring line is vertically attached to one block, to which is attached a weighted messenger line, allowing the pickup of the secondary stern mooring.

Mooring Lines

Since the mooring line needn't be hauled aboard, oversizing can only be beneficial; since

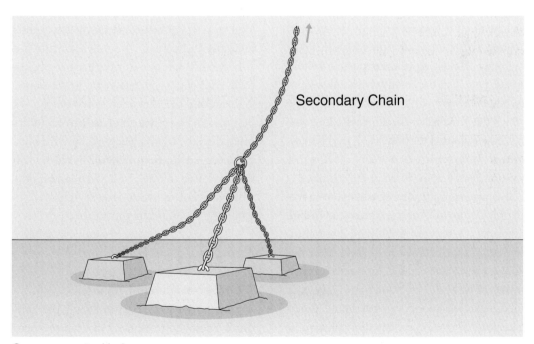

Concrete mooring blocks.

it rarely needs to be removed, a thicker line will better withstand continual use and chafe.

In a multiple-anchor mooring, attach the riding chains with the largest central shackle possible. The shackle is attached to what we will call a *storm-riding chain*. The chain length should be 1.5 times the high-water depth, with its working load at least the equivalent of the deadweight anchor. It will mostly sit at the seafloor and can serve as a shock absorber in strong winds. This chain is attached to what we call the *principal chain* by a shackle one diameter size bigger than the principal chain. The length of this chain should be equivalent to the sum of one high-water scope plus enough to encompass your free-board and attach to the buoy.

Confirm that all the component parts of this configuration, especially your shackles and swivels, have a safe working load equal to the weight of your concrete slab or deadweight anchor. This is especially true for your mooring buoy. Its floating volume must be around twice as much as the secondary chain's weight; the ideal is a buoy with a central tubing through which the principal chain can pass. Otherwise it is important that the buoy's ring load is transmitted to the chain by a metal shaft whose working load is at least that of the chain.

Regulations vary as to whether your mooring block may stay in the water year-round. Consider it a bittersweet blessing if you must remove it at the end of every season, since this allows you to inspect and maintain it much more easily. If you are allowed to leave your mooring in year-round, you still should inspect all aspects of it every year and don't allow more than two years to pass without refurbishing.

Do-It-Yourself Moorings

Once you have determined both the weight and volume of your mooring block, build a mold using solid wooden boards, making sure the mooring's bottom surface is as large as possible to increase the suction-cup effect. With muddy seafloors, this suction force will be greatest, and to maximize this, consider creating a spherical mound with sand at the bottom of your mold, then cover it with a plastic sheet. On sandy bottoms, the suction force is almost nonexistent, and it is advantageous to create the opposite; that is, to carve out a pyramidal cavity (again covered with a plastic sheet) so that the bottom of your deadweight will bury in the most ideal manner.

Use at least two $5/16$-inch welded rebar cages inside your mooring block. As a fastening eye, take the thickest possible steel wire and bend it into an omega shape (a central loop with straight ends). Bend the lower ends outward and cement them deep inside the concrete block to prevent the eye from being pulled out of the concrete by the vessel's force. Considering the concrete's heavy weight, it's best to order a truckload of cement to fill the mold directly. If possible, make sure the concrete is agitated to eliminate air bubbles. Give the block two to three days to dry, and if possible, an entire week (twenty-eight days would be theoretically the ideal).

Transporting and Positioning Mooring Blocks

The safest tranportation solution is to hire a company that specializes in lifting and handling these large objects and have them placed in the water by professionals. If the blocks are not too heavy (especially if you are using several in a triangular or star formation) and if you've been able to build them near your mooring spot, you could wait for low tide. You could then pull the deadweights as close to the water as possible and attach each one to two 50-gallon drums. When the water rises, the drums will float and you can drag them to the spot you wish to place them.

If the area is subject to an extreme tidal range, you can also place the block on the water's edge at low tide; once high tide arrives, use a very strong line to pull the block with the bow of the boat to the desired spot for immersion. We are talking here of an area of high tidal range; in some parts of Maine, the tidal range can be as much as 13 feet (4 m). In such a location, you can leave the concrete block on the sand at low tide, with a long rope and a buoy, and return at middle tide to attach the rope taut on the bow, them wait until the tide floats the concrete block. A boat 12 meters (39.3 ft.) long can easily lift a 1-ton concrete block.

With the block hanging on the bow, go to where you plan to set the deadweight mooring and cut the line attaching the block. This is easy, and not life-threatening. This should be done only with a powerboat (or a sailboat under motor) and with crew.

OTHER TYPES OF PERMANENT ANCHORS OR MOORINGS

Mushroom Anchors

A mushroom anchor buries in by its own weight. Once embedded in the seafloor, the concave surface resists the load. This anchor

A mushroom anchor works well in a soft bottom.

type only works in soft seafloors that allow deep penetration.

To set a mushroom anchor you need a motorboat powerful enough to twist the anchor into the sand. Release the mushroom anchor in the desired spot with a scope of 3:1 and circle around the anchor three times with the line taut. The anchor twists into mud and sand, and develops full holding power after approximately two weeks, so it must be installed well before you plan to use it.

Pyramid Anchor (Dor-Mor)

Based on the same principles as the mushroom anchor, the heavy weighted point of a pyramid anchor allows it to slowly penetrate and bury itself. Once well penetrated, its large flat surface resists the load (see photo next page).

Drilled Moorings for Coral and Hard Rock

In hard rock bottoms that provide no reliable anchor set, drilling a permanent mooring into the rock is an alternative. Drilled moorings

Dor-Mor pyramid anchor.

can also protect fragile coral reefs from damage, making them advantageous in environmentally sensitive areas. The procedure entails drilling a hole in the coral or rock and screwing in a threaded shaft about 1 foot (30 cm) long. The hole is then filled with concrete. Because these holding devices should only be installed by professionals, it is cost-effective to install several moorings at once.

Multiple-Anchor, Single-Point Moorings (Star Configuration)

This type of mooring uses a minimum of three anchors attached to three chains set at 120° from one another and centrally connected with a strong shackle. To set the anchors use a small, easily maneuverable motorboat and set each one individually in the desired spot, making sure your pulling angle is 120° off each other. Attach each chain to a buoy. Finally, have a diver connect the three chains with the shackle and a mooring line with a buoy attached at the surface.

One advantage of this system is its light weight. The mooring does not hold mainly with its weight, but with the surface resistance

of the deeply embedded anchors. For example, if we oversized the anchors for a mooring for a 30-foot (9 m) boat, we would make each anchor 66 pounds (30 kg) and altogether the anchors would weigh 198 pounds (90 kg). In comparison, a 198-pound (90 kg) concrete mooring would have difficulty holding a 10-foot (3 m) tender, let alone a 33-foot (10 m) sailboat in 50 knots of wind. This reduction in weight facilitates maintenance and eliminates the considerable challenge of installing or replacing a concrete block. If necessary, it is relatively easy to raise all three anchors to relocate or maintain your mooring.

The quality of this kind of mooring depends on the quality of the anchors used. The selection of three or more anchors for your permanent mooring differs from your boat's "portable" ground tackle because the anchors don't have be manageable and lightweight, and they only need to work effectively in one type of seafloor.

Before you think about skimping on the costs for this type of mooring however, first think of the value of the attached boat; next, calculate the installation cost of a block of concrete weighing several tons, along with its manufacturing and maintenance. Find out if a concrete block would achieve the same holding power, and finally, compare the results with the cost per year in a marina.

Helical Screw Anchors

First created in the early 1800s to support lighthouses in the Chesapeake Bay, helical anchors obtain their holding power from the seabed into which they are fastened.

Just as with a regular hardware screw, the denser the seabed and the more deeply the

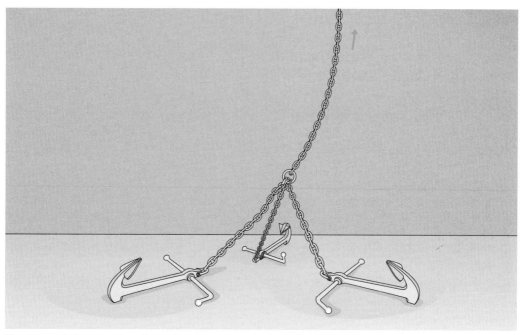

Mooring with three stock anchors placed in a triangular form (120° apart).

Helical screw anchors can be screwed into the seafloor by hand.

anchor is embedded, the more holding power this screw has to offer.

The advantage of screw anchors is they can be installed in environmentally sensitive areas such as coral reefs since the environmental impact of a screw mooring is relatively negligible.

Visible evidence of the screw mooring on the seabed is a mere footprint—only the metal head for securing the mooring line. The tackle rises directly to the water's surface with a buoy and does not contact the seafloor.

This anchor can be installed by hand at low tide. A similar larger anchor can be screwed into the seafloor from a hydraulic pump on a barge. Once deeply embedded, the holding power of these anchors is excellent.

A Theoretical Study in Rode Behavior

by Alain Fraysse

The safety of a boat and its crew depends on a few pieces of metal and rope that will hopefully prevent the boat from collision or running aground. When choosing a place to anchor, as well as sizing the anchoring gear, a wise skipper should not rely on luck to make sure that the anchor will hold if the weather conditions deteriorate. Some understanding of physics is invaluable.

Anchoring is based on the natural laws of physics and cannot be completely mastered unless an in-depth analysis of the soil around the anchor is made—just as oil platform engineers do (for more on seabed characteristics, see Chapter 1). In this appendix, we will focus on rode behavior, with special emphasis on a generally underestimated problem: the dynamic behavior of various types of rode under wind gusts.

If you tend to avoid to formulas, tables, graphs, etc., you may skip them and go directly to the conclusions of each section.

STATIC BEHAVIOR: HOMOGENEOUS RODE (MADE OF ONE MATERIAL)

Selecting anchor rodes for your boat is of primary importance, even if all your outings on the water last only a few hours. If your engine dies or any other emergency arises, knowing that you can drop an anchor and secure your boat is a necessity. You should choose anchor rodes based on your current and potential anchorages, your boat's windage, and its displacement.

Rode Requirements

In general, your anchor rode should fullfil the following requirements:

Requirement 1. Pull the anchor parallel to the bottom.

Requirement 2. Be easy to stow, deploy, and retrieve.

Requirement 3. Reduce the high peak loads caused by gusts and/or waves on the anchor and boat accessories.

Obviously, rigid materials such as steel bars or cables do not meet the third requirement. Until some currently unimagined space-age material is created, we are left with chain, nylon ropes, composite ropes, or some combination of these. (See Appendix 2 to learn more about unconventional rode materials.)

There are three different rode types to consider, each with its advantages and disadvantages: all-nylon rope, all-chain, and a combination nylon rope–chain rode. I will discuss the scientific, measurable characteristics of these three options to ascertain exactly which one would be best. I will use mathematical calculations and formulas. Don't just take my word for it; try the formulas out yourself and see if you're not convinced of my conclusions.

Theoretical Catenary

An anchor rode is not just a straight connection between the bow and the anchor. If you could swim down alongside it, you would see it start from the bow at a fairly vertical angle, then slowly level out until it blends smoothly into the bottom. This curvature, known as a *catenary*, is due to the weight of the rode, which causes the line to sag. This famous mathematical curve looks like a parabola, but its lower part is slightly flatter. The equation for this curve was established three centuries ago.

Homogeneous Rode Figure

An anchoring situation is somewhat different from the catenary described above (see the illustration next page).

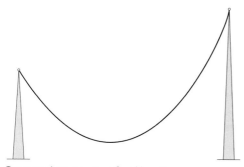

Catenary between two fixed locations.

- One of the hanging points (B at the bow roller) is mobile and pulled by a horizontal force (F) due to the wind pressure against the boat.

- The second point (A at the anchor pulling eye) is fixed on the bottom; the rode cannot hang below this point on a flat seafloor.

To keep things as simple as possible, I've made several assumptions:

- The anchor has been correctly set (see Chapters 6 and 7 on anchoring techniques).

- The rode is located in a vertical plane (R is the swinging radius).

- Since we are dealing with (for now) the static case, there are no waves that could induce vertical movements.

- The rode's stretch is negligible.

- Its friction on the bottom is negligible.

- Neither the boat nor the rode have inertia.

- The pulling force (F) is constant and located inside the rode plane.

- The system has reached its equilibrium point; i.e., the force (F) due to the wind pressure is exactly compensated for by an opposite force due to the weight of the rode.

Thanks to gravity, the rode acts as a pseudo-spring, even though I have just assumed it has no elasticity of its own (which is false for real nylon rode, but almost true for steel chain; see more on this below).

Obviously, the active rode length overboard (L) must be greater than the height (H)

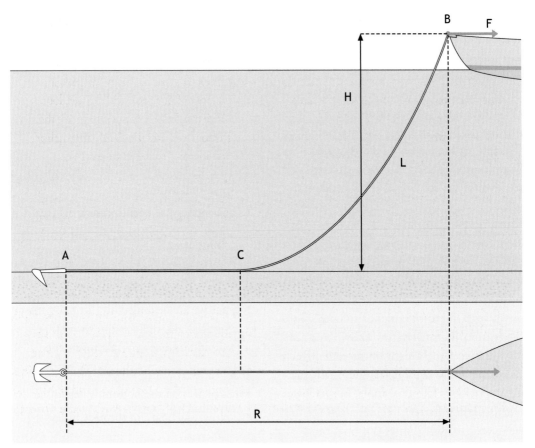

A typical anchor rode.

of the bow roller above the seabed, otherwise the anchor would not even reach the seafloor. Keep in mind that H = water depth + freeboard at the boat's bow (to review the importance of calculating this distance correctly, see the Importance of Scope section in Chapter 6). In shallow anchorages, this can be significant. For example, if the water depth is 2 meters (6 ft.) and the freeboard is 1 meter (3 ft.), H is 3 meters (10 ft.).

In these conditions, the rode figure varies according to four parameters:

1. Height (H)
2. Active rode length (L)
3. Rode weight (w) in the water, per length unit
4. Pulling force (F)

Let's try an example using a chain rode, where

H = 5 meters (16 ft.)

L = 15 meters (49 ft.) of 11 mm
   ($^7/_{16}$ in.) chain

w = 2.5 daN/m (1.7 lb./ft.) in seawater

Let's see what happens when F increases from 0 to higher values.

1. For F = 0 (gray curve), the rode is L-shaped; the upper part hangs vertically from the bow down to the seafloor and the rest lies on the bottom along the seafloor to the anchor.

2. When F increases (10 daN/22 lb., green curve), the boat moves backward, so the portion of the rode resting on the seafloor lifts up progressively. The shape of the part between the bow (B) and the contact point (C) with the bottom is a catenary. The load on the pulling eye remains horizontal and equal to F, so the anchor shaft remains horizontal too, and the holding power is unchanged.

3. When F reaches the critical value, or F_c (52 daN/116 lb., orange curve), the whole rode is lifted above the bottom. The rode is tangent to the bottom at the

shaft pulling eye, and the holding power is still unchanged.

4. Beyond F_c (i.e., 100 daN/220 lb., red curve), the load on the pulling eye is no longer horizontal with the seafloor. Once this force is enough to rotate the anchor by lifting the shank, the anchor's holding power begins to decrease.

5. If F continues to increase, the catenary becomes almost a straight line (black curve), and eventually the anchor pulls out (unless it's stuck behind a rock!).

What if we use nylon instead of chain? With a 22 mm ($^7/_8$ in.) nylon rode of the same length, the critical value F_c drops to 0.5 daN (1.2 lb.)! This is due to the 90% apparent weight loss of the nylon in seawater. Even with a 45-meter (150 ft.) line, F_c reaches a mere 6 daN (12 lb.). This explains why, in practice, it is impossible to keep an anchor flat on the bottom with an

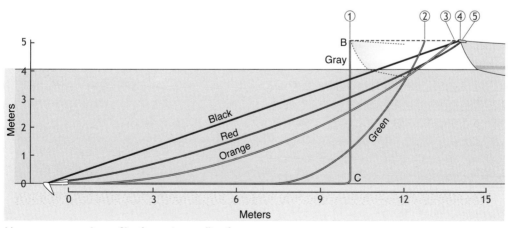

Homogeneous rode profiles for various pulling forces.

all-nylon rode as soon as the wind exceeds a few knots.

Fundamental Homogeneous Rode Equations

Given the rode's weight per length unit (w) and the height (H), a pulling force (F) lifts rode length (L_{up}):

$$L_{up} = \sqrt{H^2 + 2\frac{F}{w}H}$$

L_{up} is the minimum rode length to keep the shaft horizontal for a pulling force (F).

Conversely, the critical force (F_c) that lifts the whole rode length (L) is:

$$F_c = w\frac{L^2 - H^2}{2H}$$

F_c is the maximum pulling force to keep the shaft horizontal for a rode length (L). F_c is also the main factor that affects safety. It depends on the three parameters—H, L, and w—as follows:

- The critical force (F_c) is proportional to w. For example, for a given length (L), let us replace 8 mm ($^5/_{16}$ in.) chain with 10 mm ($^3/_8$ in.) chain. This increases the critical pulling force (F_c) by 44%, considerably improving holding capacity. Unfortunately, it also weighs down the vessel at the bow.

- F_c is approximately proportional to the square of length (L). Consequently, increasing L by, for example, 41% multiplies F_c by 2. The main drawbacks are a 41% increase of the weight carried on board, and a 41% increase of the swinging radius.

We can rewrite the first equation to calculate minimum scope (N—ratio L:H) to keep the shaft horizontal for a pulling force (F):

$$N = \sqrt{1 + 2\frac{F}{w}\frac{1}{H}}$$

This equation shows that, contrary to popular belief, the minimum scope depends on *both* parameters F and H.

An example will be more convincing. Using 8 mm ($^5/_{16}$ in.) chain, Table A1-1 uses the above equation to calculate the minimum scope that can withstand a horizontal force (F) of 89 daN (200 lb.).

Thus, choosing a minimum scope of 4:1 is adequate for a 9-meter (30 ft.) depth, but it is noticeably insufficient for a 4.6-meter (15 ft.) depth and overabundant for 18 meters (60 ft.).

This shows that with an all-chain rode, shallow anchorages need relatively large scopes, while deep anchorages make the best of moderate scopes.

TABLE A1-1. MINIMUM SCOPE TO WITHSTAND A FORCE OF 89 daN (200 lb.)

Height (H)	Minimum Scope (N)	Minimum Chain Length (L)
4.6 m (15 ft.)	5.6:1	26 m (84 ft.)
9 m (30 ft.)	4.0:1	37 m (120 ft.)
18 m (60 ft.)	2.9:1	54 m (176 ft.)

Incidentally, if we know the rode length (L) and the pulling force (F), we can use the first equation to calculate the height (H) for which F is critical; i.e., the maximum allowable height that does not lift the anchor shaft:

$$H = \sqrt{L^2 + \left(\frac{F}{w}\right)^2} - \frac{F}{w}$$

Angulation

If the pulling force (F) exceeds F_c, the rode is no longer tangent to the bottom at the shaft pulling eye; its angle, sometimes called *angulation* (see the illustration below), can be calculated with the following equation:

$$F(\alpha) = F_c \frac{\cos \alpha}{1 - \frac{L}{H} \sin \alpha}$$

This equation allows us to calculate the pulling force for any pulling angle (anchors are more or less tolerant of a moderate angulation, at the cost of reduced holding power; see the Determining Your Primary and Secondary Rode Lengths section in Chapter 4). We can verify that $F(0°) = F_c$.

In the all-chain example of the third equation (opposite), tolerating a 6° angulation instead of 0° would increase the acceptable load by 46%.

With an all-nylon rode, angulation is practically unavoidable, and keeping it at an acceptable value requires a very large scope. Since nylon rode has negligible weight in water, it follows an almost straight line from the anchor to the bow roller (see the illustration next page). Its slope tan α is virtually equal to the scope (N = L:H). In this case, whatever the (high) pulling force, the traditional 10:1 scope leads to a 5.7° angulation, which is acceptable for some modern anchors.

Pulling Force vs. Boat Drift

As we saw in Chapter 2, knowing the static relation between the pulling force and the position of the boat is of primary importance for predicting the movement of the boat and the strains that will affect the anchoring tackle

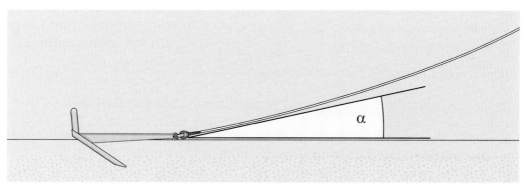

Angulation.

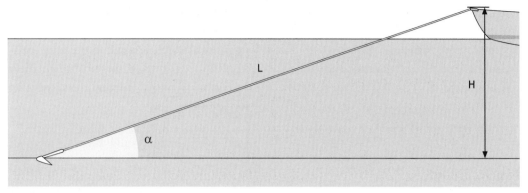

An all-nylon rode under load.

under wind gusts. For the all-chain rode in the third equation, this relation is charted in the graph below.

A striking characteristic of this relationship is its extreme nonlinearity: a given force variation causes much less drift at high pulling forces than at low ones. When the chain comes under heavy load, the pseudo-elasticity due to gravity vanishes, so the force necessary to move the boat backward increases exponentially.

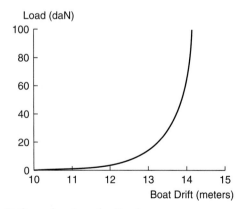

Drift as a function of pulling force.

Let's check both rode types against the criteria defined above (Requirements 1 and 2—see page 168); see Table A1-2.

Thus, except for moderate weather conditions, neither all-chain nor all-line rodes are truly ideal.

STATIC BEHAVIOR: HETEROGENEOUS RODE

Because it lacks weight in its lower extremity, it is difficult for an all-nylon rode to pull an anchor horizontally. On the other hand, the heavy upper part of an all-chain rode is unfortunately only effective in weighing down the bow of the boat. So, instead of spreading the weight evenly along the rode, putting more weight in its lower part and less weight in its upper part is an ideal approach.

In practice, two methods are commonly used:

1. Adding a heavy weight (sometimes called a kellet, sentinel, chum, or angel) to a nylon rode.

2. Using a moderate length of chain at the lower extremity, with a nylon line up to the bow—a hybrid rode.

TABLE A1-2. STATIC BEHAVIOR: HOMOGENEOUS RODE, REQUIREMENTS 1 AND 2

Criterion	All-Chain	All-Nylon
Pulls the anchor parallel to the bottom?	Yes	No, unless paying out a very long line
Easy to stow?	Yes, but very heavy	Yes
Easy to deploy and retrieve?	Yes (with a motorized windlass)	Yes

Kellet

Earlier, the second equation (page 172) gave the critical value F_c that lifts a homogeneous rode completely:

$$F_c = w\,\frac{L^2 - H^2}{2H}$$

If we add a weight (K) at distance (L_k) from the bow (see the illustration below), what improvement can we expect beyond F_c?

There is no simple expression of the result, but if we assume the scope is greater than 3:1, an acceptable approximation (with less than 6% error) is given by:

$$F_k \approx F_c + K\,\frac{L_k}{H} = F_c + KN\left(\frac{L_k}{L}\right)$$

This equation shows that the improvement equals the kellet weight (K) multiplied by the ratio L_k:H. Therefore, the best improvement is obtained by putting the kellet near the anchor, where the improvement equals the kellet weight (K) multiplied by the scope (N). By placing the same kellet in the middle of the rode, the improvement would only be half of that.

An all-nylon rode with a kellet close to the anchor has the same performance as an all-chain rode of the same length, with only half the total rode weight. This confirms that concentrating the weight down the rode, if possible, is much more effective than distributing the weight along the rode.

Unfortunately, very heavy kellets are difficult to handle. Their weight should be limited

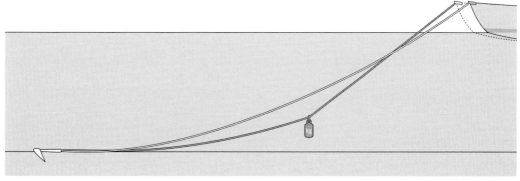

Kellet.

to around 22 kilograms (around 50 lb.), which is insufficient in severe wind conditions unless the scope is very long. It would be more effective to add this weight to the anchor (i.e, a heavier anchor). What's more, using a kellet does not significantly improve the swinging radius (R).

Combination Chain-Rope Rode

Using chain at the lower extremity of the rode is a better alternative. For other reasons we'll study in the dynamic behavior section below, nylon lines are generally preferred. Since the weight of nylon in seawater is relatively light, the nylon part of a hybrid rode looks like a straight line as soon as the pulling force exceeds a few pounds. In this sense, we can consider the additional line as an extension of a chain rode, used when the available chain length cannot keep the anchor flat on the bottom in the current depth and wind conditions (see the illustration below).

It is interesting to estimate the height gain that can be achieved this way for a given pulling force (F). Let's assume our chain-only rode length (L_{ch}) gets completely lifted at height (H_{ch}). If we insert a length of nylon line (L_{ny}) between the chain and the bow, the allowable height is increased by H_{ny}.

H_{ny} is approximately given by:

$$H_{ny} \approx L_{ny} \frac{2 L_{ch} H_{ch}}{L_{ch}^{2} - H_{ch}^{2}}$$

For example, if a 25-meter (82 ft.) all-chain rode allows a 5-meter (16 ft.) height, adding a 12-meter (39 ft.) nylon line allows an extra height of 10 meters (33 ft.). To achieve the same improvement by increasing the length of the chain-only rode, we would need 11 meters (36 ft.) of extra chain, with a much higher weight penalty than 12 meters (39 ft.) of nylon line, and a meager 1-meter (3 ft.) decrease of the swinging radius!

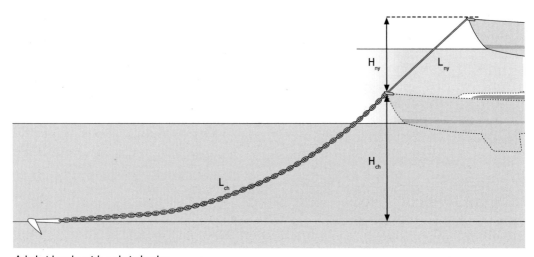

A hybrid rode with a chain leader.

This confirms that an all-chain rode is unnecessarily heavy, and that it can be replaced by a slightly longer hybrid rode for the same holding effectiveness.

The next question is, what is the best ratio of chain length to nylon length? Well, there is no absolute answer, because it results from a compromise between many criteria that may vary according to boats and skippers. Anyway, since the chain must be chosen before going to sea, the question really should be, what chain size and length should you buy?

In some countries, design standards specify minimum characteristics for anchor(s) and rode(s), given the length and/or displacement of the boat. If minimizing the onboard weight is of primary importance, choose the legal minimum. If more effectiveness takes priority, increase the size and/or length (if you use a motorized windlass, this helps handle the rode, too). Whatever length of chain you choose, however, you should include a portion of nylon line at the upper end of the rode, for the reasons explained in the dynamic behavior section below.

Rode Elasticity

Up to now, we have assumed that the rode material has no stretch, which obviously is not true; all material has some intrinsic elasticity. From the present static point of view, the most notable effect is a slight increase of the swinging radius. On the other hand, in dynamic situations when the pulling force becomes high, the rode elasticity can have significant effects (more on that later in the dynamic behavior section).

Consequently, it is important to keep in mind that the rode elongates as a function of the pulling force (F).

For a metal rod, as long as the load (T) does not exceed the elastic limit of the material (beyond which the device does not recover its initial length when the load returns to zero), the elongation is proportional to T. L has the following form, where

L_0 = the length for T = 0

A = the cross-sectional area of the rod

E = the elasticity module (the "stretchability" of a material, or how much longer it gets under a certain force without irreversibly changing shape)

$$L = L_0 \left(1 + \frac{T}{EA} \right)$$

For ordinary steel, E is typically 21,000 daN/mm². Thus, a 1,000 daN (2,200 lb.) load applied to a 10 mm (³/₈ in.) diameter rod gives a 0.06 % extension (i.e., 0.6 mm/m only).

All a bit unnecessary, yes? People know what *stretch* means. You don't have to define it mathematically but just give the percentages.

A chain the same size is slightly less stiff than a rod, so it will stretch approximately 20% more for the same load.

On the other hand, a nylon line is much more elastic (about 200 times more), but the extension is not proportional to the load at high values.

Pulling Force vs. Boat Drift

As I pointed out earlier, knowing the static relationship between pulling force and the horizontal position of the boat is important for predicting the boat's movement and the strain that will affect the ground tackle under wind gusts. The elasticity of the rode must be taken into account. Let's compare the curves for the examples above, where

water height = 10 meters (33 ft.)

primary rode = 36 meters (118 ft.) of 10 mm (3/8 in.) chain

secondary rode = 25 meters (82 ft.) of 10 mm (3/8 in.) chain + 12 meters (39 ft.) of 22 mm (7/8 in.) nylon

Thanks to the elasticity of its nylon portion, the hybrid rode shows more progressive behavior than an all-chain rode at high pulling forces (see the graph below), reducing shock loads under severe wind gusts much more effectively.

Conclusions

Let's compare both methods against the criteria defined earlier (Requirements 1 and 2)—see Table A1-3.

Theoretically, the nylon-plus-kellet solution gives the best effectiveness-to-weight ratio, but only if the kellet is close to the anchor. Unfortunately, handling a heavy kellet is difficult and dangerous. Most people who have deployed anchors on a slippery, pitching foredeck by hand can imagine the fiasco of deploying a 50-pound kellet overboard. It is evident from these equations that a kellet is not worth the effort, since a chain leader works better than a kellet, is easier to handle, and protects the rode from nylon abrasion.

So deploying a kellet turns out to be unsuitable in strong wind conditions unless the scope is very large. For the same onboard weight, a hybrid rode is slightly less effective,

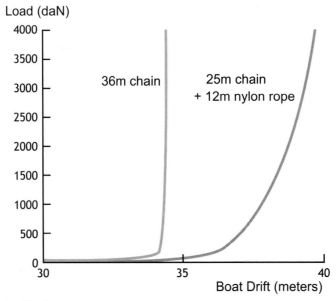

Drift as a function of pulling force.

TABLE A1-3. STATIC BEHAVIOR: HETEROGENEOUS RODE, REQUIREMENTS 1 AND 2

Criterion	Kellet	Hybrid (chain + nylon)
Pulls the anchor parallel to the bottom?	Yes, but limited by kellet weight (difficult to handle a 50 lb. kellet, for example)	Yes
Easy to stow?	No	Yes
Easy to deploy and retrieve?	No	Yes

but it has none of the drawbacks of the kellet option. Of course, adding a kellet to any combination of chain and nylon is not forbidden, but keep in mind the issues we just reviewed.

Now that we have examined the static behavior of an anchor rode, we are ready to tackle the consequences of wind gusts, which are responsible for most dragging situations.

DYNAMIC BEHAVIOR: HOMOGENEOUS RODE

As we learned in the Static Behavior section, an anchor rode should fulfill the following requirements:

Requirement 1. Pull the anchor parallel to the bottom.

Requirement 2. Be easy to stow, deploy, and retrieve.

Requirement 3. Reduce the high peak loads caused by gusts and/or waves on the anchor and boat accessories.

We've already reviewed Requirements 1 and 2; now we'll focus on Requirement 3.

As already pointed out, rigid devices (e.g., a steel bar) do not meet Requirements 1 and 2, so this discussion is confined to flexible devices. With flexible materials (i.e., chain,

nylon), the boat will move back and forth when the wind pressure changes. This motion is called *surging.* Due to a vessel's inertia, surging induces dynamic peak loads that can be much higher than the pulling forces that generate them, depending mainly on the rode material(s) and the pulling-force variations versus time.

Perfect Spring

Before studying various types of real rodes, it is interesting to look at the behavior of an idealized spring line securing a boat to a fixed point, such as a dock. Such a spring stretches proportionately to the load (T). If L0 is its length for T = 0 and σ is its stiffness, then its length (L) varies linearly versus T:

$$L = L_0 + \frac{T}{\sigma}$$

Its extension is:

$$\Delta L = \frac{T}{\sigma}$$

For example, a spring with stiffness 1,000 daN/m (686 lb./ft.) will stretch for 1 meter under a 1,000 daN load (or 1 ft. under a 686 lb. load). Let's tie a 5-ton boat (i.e., mass—M—equals 5,000 kg) to a dock with this spring. We start from the static equilib-rium position, where

$$L = L_0$$

$$T = 0$$

$$F = 0 \text{ (no wind)}$$

Step-Profiled Gust

What happens if a gust suddenly steps F up to $F_g = 400$ daN (900 lb.)? The illustration below shows the variations of the spring load, the velocity, and the position of the boat relative to the starting point.

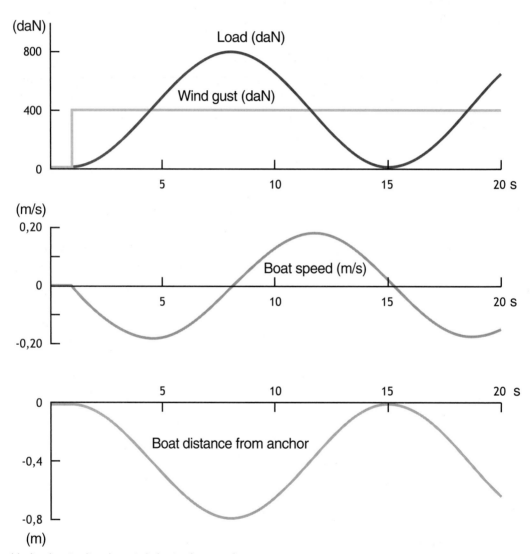

Idealized spring line dynamic behavior (step gust).

According to Newton's second law of motion, the boat begins to drift astern with acceleration:

$$\gamma = \frac{(T - F)}{M}$$

As the spring stretches, T increases until it becomes equal to F_g, which results in a null acceleration. At this moment, the boat is located at its static equilibrium position for the pulling force F_g

$$\Delta L_g = \frac{F_g}{\sigma}$$

0.4 m behind the starting point. But since its backward velocity reaches its maximum at

$$V_{max} = \frac{F_g}{\sqrt{\sigma M}}$$

0.18 m/s = 0.34 knot, the boat continues moving astern while losing speed. It reaches its apex position—

$$\Delta L_{max} = 2\,\frac{F_g}{\sigma} = 2\,\Delta L_g$$

0.8 m—with a null velocity and a maximum spring load of

$$T_{max} = 2\,F_g$$

800 daN (1,800 lb.).

Then the movement reverses: the boat accelerates forward, crosses the static equilibrium point, stops at the starting point, and the above sequence is repeated cyclically—the boat surges. The variations of all the parameters (position, velocity,

acceleration, and load) are sinusoidal with a period of

$$2\pi\,\sqrt{\frac{M}{\sigma}}$$

14 seconds. In practice, the friction of the water on the hull will dampen this oscillation, but not by much since the boat speed is not very high.

Contrary to what you might intuitively expect, neither the maximum load, T_{max} (twice the pulling force F_g), nor the apex position (twice farther the static position from the starting point) depends on the mass of the boat. Thus, high-displacement boats are not penalized in this situation.

An idealized spring line would be better than any other elastic device at limiting the dynamic peak load. In other words, nonlinear elastic or pseudo-elastic devices used as anchoring rodes (e.g., chains or nylon lines) will always suffer peak loads higher than twice the pulling force of the gust.

If the pulling force starts from a non-zero value, F_0, the general behavior is the same, but the maximum peak load is reduced by F_0, such as:

$$T_{max} = 2\,F_g - F_0$$

For example, if a steady wind applies a constant 100 daN (225 lb.) pulling force, the 400 daN (900 lb.) gust will induce a 700 daN (1,575 lb.) maximum peak load.

Trapezoidal-Profiled Gust

Back in the real world, a gust does not settle at its maximum level instantaneously, and it does not remain at this level indefinitely—otherwise it would not be a gust. A more realistic profile is a trapezoid. We can define the rise time, the duration at maximum value, and the decay time. But since we are mainly concerned about the maximum peak loads, we can ignore what happens beyond the first one.

In the illustration below, the gust rises from 0 to 400 daN (900 lb.) in 5 seconds. In this case, the maximum peak load is reduced by 10% compared with the step-profiled gust. Contrary to the step case, the boat's displacement has some influence; peak loads are higher for heavier boats, but the variations remain in the 20% range.

All-Chain Rode

Now our 5-ton boat is anchored in 5 meters (16 ft.) of water with 55 meters (180 ft.) of 8 mm (5/16 in.) chain. A steady wind applies a permanent force of 100 daN (225 lb.), which is already high, but gusts at twice the current velocity are expected, which means forces approximately four times higher—hence the very long scope. The critical load that lifts the whole rode is 393 daN (884 lb.), so a 400 daN (900 lb.) force could statically be withstood while maintaining a near-zero angulation.

The *dynamic* reality is quite different, as shown in the illustration opposite.

First, we can see that the variations of the parameters are no longer sinusoidal due to the high nonlinearity of the position-versus-force relation specific to chain. Second, for the same reason, the maximum peak loads are much higher than with a linear device (idealized spring line). In this example, they reach almost 1,600 daN (3,600 lb.), or four times the static force that generates them. Incidentally, 1,600 daN (3,600 lb.) is the maximum working load of a typical 8 mm steel chain. Beyond that point, chain would not recover its shape when the gust is over! In addition, the anchor will likely drag under such a load with the associated 4° angulation. Paying out more chain out won't help much; almost 100 meters (330 ft.) would be necessary to keep the anchor flat on the bottom, with load peaks still at 1,100 daN (2,500 lb.).

In an idealized spring line case, under a step gust the boat displacement has no influence.

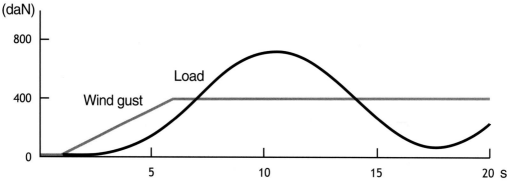

Idealized spring line dynamic behavior (trapezoidal gust).

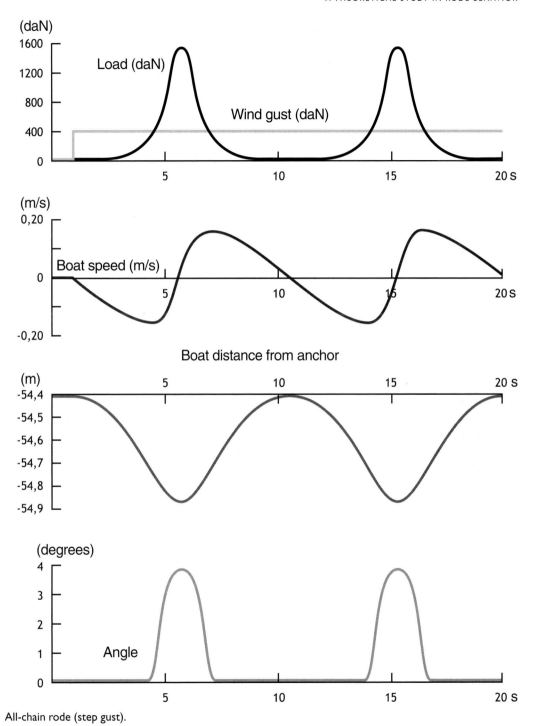

All-chain rode (step gust).

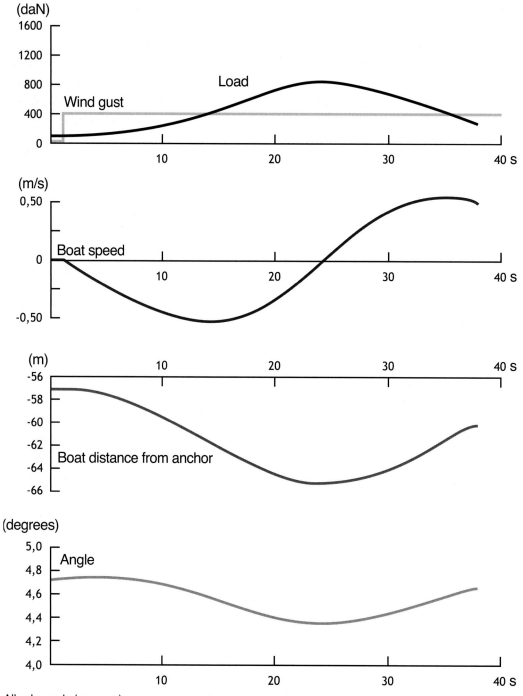

All-nylon rode (step gust).

Conversely, if the gust were trapezoidal with a 5-second rise time, the load would still peak at 1,350 daN (3,000 lb.) and the angulation would not decrease significantly. A 10-ton boat would get a 10% peak load increase.

Note that in the above examples, the natural (insignificant) elasticity of steel is taken into account (as discussed previously in the static heterogeneous rode section), otherwise the load peaks would be infinite.

All-Nylon Rode

Now let us try the opposite solution. We replace the chain with 18 mm ($^3/_4$ in.) nylon line of the same 55-meter (180 ft.) length. The results are shown in the illustration opposite.

We can see the behavior is much like that of a perfect spring with moderate stiffness. The problem is that despite the very long scope (11:1), the angulation remains around 4.5° whatever the load; the line is almost completely taut. Nevertheless, in good bottoms, anchors that are designed for this type of rode should hold effectively.

Dampening?

When an elastic device (either real, such as a spring line; or virtual, such as a chain that uses gravity) stretches, it stores energy in potential form. When it shrinks back, it restores this energy to the tied system in kinetic form but in the reverse direction—hence the oscillations. To counteract those oscillations, we must use a *dampening device*, which transforms the mechanical energy into any other form (for example, heat—as in friction dampers in automotive suspensions). For anchors, imagine dragging chains on the seabed, or using water parachutes. In reality, the relative speeds between an anchored boat and its environment (air, water, and bottom) are much too low for such devices to be effective while keeping them manageable in terms of size or weight.

Thus, unfortunately, surging seems unavoidable. This is why people can become just as seasick at anchor as they do on the high seas.

Conclusions

Let's check both rode types against the criteria defined at the beginning of this appendix—see Table A1-4.

An all-chain rode is therefore not conducive to handling peak loads, as it makes the ground tackle prone to dragging. On the

TABLE A1-4. DYNAMIC BEHAVIOR: HOMOGENEOUS RODE, REQUIREMENTS 1, 2, AND 3

Criterion	All-Chain	All-Nylon
Pulls the anchor parallel to the bottom?	Yes	No, unless paying out a very long line
Easy to stow?	Yes, but very heavy	Yes
Easy to deploy and retrieve?	Yes (with a motorized windlass)	Yes
Reduces peak loads?	No	Yes

other hand, although safe for peak loads, an all-nylon rode necessitates very high scopes that can be incompatible with tight anchorages. Even with an all-chain rode, strong gusts always require a very high scope to maintain the anchor (almost) flat on the bottom.

DYNAMIC BEHAVIOR: HETEROGENEOUS RODE

The results of our study of the dynamic behavior of homogeneous rodes have confirmed those of the static study:

- An all-nylon rode cannot get tangent to the bottom because it lacks weight in its lower part.
- Due to its lack of elasticity, an all-chain rode does not dampen severe peak loads under gusts. Besides, the cumbersome weight of its upper part is useless.

Now let us revisit the methods we studied in the static behavior section.

- Adding a heavy weight (kellet) down a nylon line.
- Using some length of chain in the lower part, with a line up to the bow (hybrid rode).

From a practical point of view, this rode can be divided into two categories:

1. A fixed but moderate length of chain permanently spliced to a long nylon line; whatever the water height, pay out all the chain plus the necessary length of nylon.

2. A long chain rode, which is paid out according to the water height, as usual, but which is then linked to the fixed point of the boat via a moderate length of nylon rope.

In the examples below, we are using the same water depth as in the previous examples (5 meters/16 feet), as well as the same long scope (11:1).

Long Line Plus Kellet

In the static study, we found that the effectiveness of the kellet is maximized when it is placed close to the anchor. In this case, the load, velocity, and position variations are the same as without a kellet (the elasticity prevails), but the angulation is significantly reduced: with a 25 kilogram (55 lb.) kellet down 55 meters (180 ft.) of nylon (18 mm/^{3}/$_4$ in. diameter), it peaks at less than 3°; see the illustration opposite.

However, to maintain a zero angulation all the way, a 73-kilogram kellet would be necessary!

Short Chain Plus Long Line

In a sense, such a rode can be considered a derivation of the line-plus-kellet version, in which the kellet is replaced with a length of chain. For a given chain weight, a short, wide-linked chain is better than a long, slender one because it puts the weight closer to the anchor. (This is why short-link chain is used for anchor rode.) Let's try 20 meters (66 ft.) of 10 mm (^{3}/$_8$ in.) chain, spliced to 35 meters (115 ft.) of 18 mm (^{3}/$_4$ in.) nylon; see the illustration on page 188.

Except for the shorter oscillation period, the load and velocity variations are about the same as with the line-plus-kellet rode. On the other hand, the position and angulation variations are significantly lower. Thus, for a small increase in the total onboard weight (18 kg/40 lb.), a chain section is more efficient

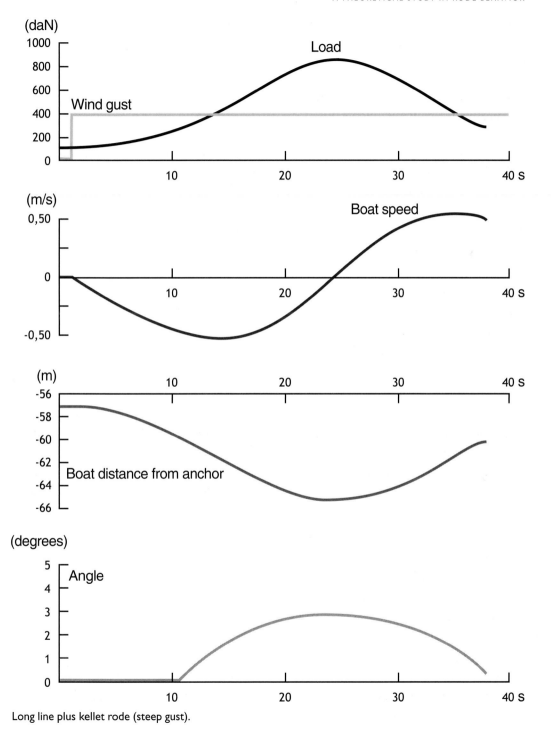

Long line plus kellet rode (steep gust).

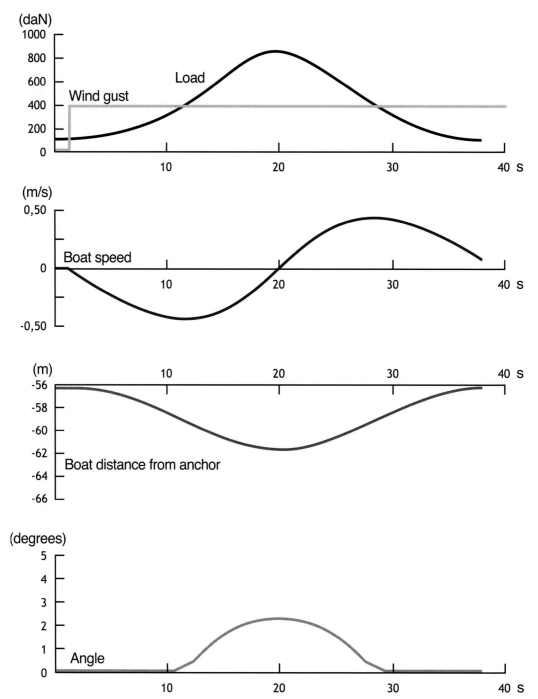

Short chain plus long line (steep gust).

than a kellet—and much easier to handle. What's more, the chain section, which lies on the bottom most of the time, is much less prone to chafe than a nylon one in aggressive environments such as those with coral heads.

Long Chain Plus Short Line

The problem with the above rodes is retrieving them in strong winds, even if some windlass manufacturers claim their models are designed to "swallow" rope as well as chain. On the other hand, a long chain with a matched windlass is ideal; but, as we ascertained previously, its lack of elasticity does not allow for dampening severe peak loads.

Assuming the parameters are the same as above, let us first pay out 45 meters (147 ft.) of chain. Then, by any appropriate means, such as a chain hook or a standard snap hook, we take up a link of chain with 10 meters (33 ft.) of nylon. The other end of the nylon rope is tied to the mooring bitt, which takes a load off the windlass and helps prevent unpleasant rattling at the roller, too. Thus, we still have a 55-meter (180 ft.) rode, but it includes a short elastic section; see the illustration next page.

The oscillations are twice as fast, the peak loads and angulation are barely increased, but the velocity and the swinging radius are significantly reduced. The price for increased comfort and safety is a moderate increase in onboard weight—16 kilograms (36 lb.) more than when using short chain plus a long line.

In addition, this solution is well adapted to deeper water, provided the available chain is permanently spliced to a nylon extension.

For example, if you have 55 meters (180 ft.) of chain, you can splice an equal length of nylon to it to get a king-size rode. When you don't need to pay out the whole chain, use the hook with the additional short line to take up the chain. If the whole chain is necessary, simply pay out more rode, up to 110 meters (360 ft.).

Conclusions

Let's check all three solutions against the criteria defined at the top of the dynamic behavior section (Requirements 1, 2, and 3), plus various criteria—see Table A1-5 on page 191.

Obviously, the long chain plus short nylon line is the winner, except for small boats that have onboard weight problems. Actually, there is no boundary between the hybrid-rode versions. You can choose any chain-nylon mix within a wide range (say, from 40:60 to 80:20) with no significant performance differences.

In practice, this involves having two rode elements at your disposal before attempting to anchor:

1. A long hybrid rode, typically 50:50 ratio. The nylon section should be spliced into the last links of the chain so that it does not jam in the windlass (see the left photo on page 191 and also Chapter 4).

2. An auxiliary 9- to 15-meter (30 ft. to 50 ft.) nylon rope, ending with a chain hook. Use this to take up the chain when the water height and/or the wind conditions do not require paying out all of the chain section of the rode (see the right photo on page 191 and also Chapter 5).

In any case, there should be at least 10 meters of nylon in the active rode, or more

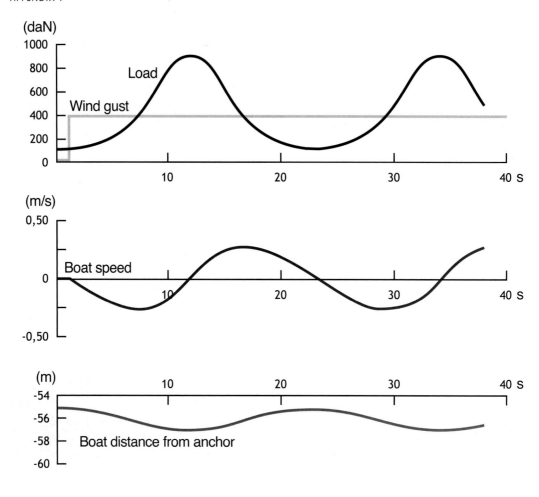

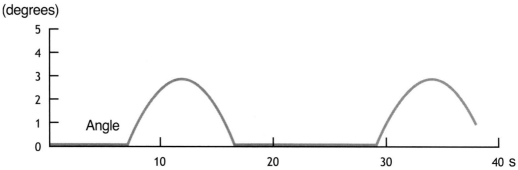

Long chain plus short line (steep gust).

TABLE A1-5. DYNAMIC BEHAVIOR: HETEROGENEOUS RODE

Criterion	Long Line + Kellet	Short Chain + Long Line	Long Chain + Short Line
Pulls the anchor parallel to the bottom?	Yes, but limited by kellet weight	Yes	Yes
Easy to stow?	No (kellet)	Yes	Yes, but very heavy
Easy to deploy and retrieve?	No (kellet setup and removal)	Moderately (transition between chain and line)	Yes (with a motorized windlass)
Reduces peak loads?	Yes	Yes	Yes
Minimizes swinging radius?	No	Moderately	Yes
Abrasion resistant (to bottom chafe)?	No	Mostly	Yes

precisely, between the mooring bitt and the chain section.

Please remember that even with a heavy rode, strong gusts always require a very high scope to maintain the anchor (almost) flat on the bottom.

Waves also require higher scopes. Since they lift the bow, they increase the effective height to consider when deciding how much rode to pay out (see the Importance of Scope section in Chapter 6).

Chain-nylon chain splice.

Chain hooks.

Unconventional Rode Solutions

Chain and rope have been, and remain, the leading contenders in the "rode race." After much research and testing, we have found that a combination of the two, together with the proper connectors, makes a better rode than either chain or rope alone. At present, three-strand twisted and eight-strand plaited nylon are the standard choices for the rope portion of the rode, but this may not remain the case indefinitely. Considering the many modern improvements in anchor gear resulting from scientific research and testing, it would be surprising if the future did not hold some sort of material breakthrough that will revolutionize rode systems as we know them today.

In the meantime, we thought we'd take a bold step and introduce some potentially effective rode options that either exist on the market today or will be available in the near future.

FLAT-STRAP CONSTRUCTION (WEBBING)

A flat nylon strap, typically used for outdoor climbing is particularly advantageous at the stern, where storing a rode can be difficult. The flat strap may have the same strength as a rope, but it can be stored much more easily on a spool. According to manufacturers, a 2-inch strap has a breaking strength of 6,000 pounds. It offers less elasticity than braided rope of the same strength, however, and you must regularly inspect the seams at the extremities of the strap, since the stitching can disintegrate due to chafing and wear. The strap cannot be used with a windlass when spliced with chain, but in combination with a chain leader may serve as an ideal rode for an aluminum anchor at the stern.

WHY NOT EXPERIMENT WITH A WIRE LEADER?

When an anchor is lowered, the chain leader frequently piles up on top of it before the vessel backs down enough to straighten the chain. This loose chain may prevent the rode from optimally performing one of its most important functions—exerting a unidirectional pull on the anchor for thorough entrenchment.

It may seem like an outlandish idea to add yet another element to your ground tackle, but we have seen promising results when a rigging wire cable leader is added between the anchor and the chain leader. Our experimental setup used stainless steel rigging wire, which should probably be replaced with galvanized steel cable for long-term use in salt water. This would match the metal of the cable with the

A flat-strap rode is easy to coil on a spool at the stern, but it is less elastic than a nylon line.

├─────────── 50 cm (1.6') ───────────┤

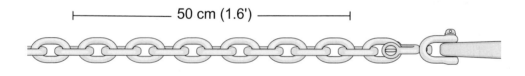

Projected chain surface

Projected wire surface

The shaded areas indicate the approximate difference in surface area between the chain and wire. A surface area of 180 cm² along the first 50 cm (1.6 ft.) of chain leader prevents the anchor from digging deeper into the ground. A flexible stainless steel wire leader with equal breaking strength (1 x 19, or ³/₈ in./10 mm) shows just 40 cm² of surface area. Both ends of the chain leader should be equipped with adequate wire terminals to create a safe connection without a breakpoint between the anchor and the chain leader.

galvanized chain leader and anchor, reducing the possibility of galvanic corrosion.

The cable doesn't have to be long to have a dramatic affect. A $^3/_8$-inch anchor chain is about $1^1/_4$ inches wide. Replacing just 20 inches of this chain with $^5/_{16}$-inch-diameter stainless steel wire (see Table 4-1) would dramatically reduce the footprint of chain piled atop the anchor, allowing the chain to pull deeper instead of piling up. When retrieving ground tackle, a skipper needn't worry about it fitting in a windlass, since the piece would be too short to reach the windlass gypsy on deck. That is another advantage of the system: instead of a heavy chain on deck scratching your topsides, the cable provides an elegant, smooth "tightwire" on the foredeck.

The result is deeper anchor penetration and increased holding power. The extremities of the cable should be fitted with terminals that can easily be affixed to the anchor at one end and the chain on the other.

ROPES WITH HIGH ELASTICITY

Ropes can currently be manufactured with a high elasticity coefficient (i.e., an elongation of more than 300%). Using this new kind of rope as part of a rode configuration confers numerous advantages similar to those derived by mountaineers from the very elastic ropes they use.

First, this rope makes a rather low scope (3:1) feasible. Although this results in less than optimal pulling angles at low wind speeds, the remaining holding power of the anchor is ample for the conditions. Meanwhile, with a shorter scope, the vessel's swinging radius is reduced. This is a very desirable setup in a crowded anchorage when there is no wind, when boats tend to swing in all directions due to tides or current.

Because of its elasticity, the anchor line elongates dramatically as winds increase, increasing the scope to as much as 9:1, so you do not have to pay out more rode. This reduces the pulling

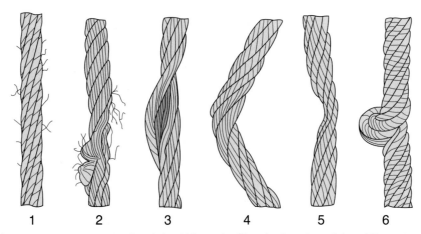

Wire leaders require constant control, and should be replaced at the first signs of decay. These signs can be any of the following: broken wires (1), broken strands (2), opened strands (3), bends (4), compression damage (5), and hockles (6). Other signs include elongation (after extensive strain), abrasion, and corrosion.

TABLE A2-1. COMPARISON OF CHAIN AND FLEXIBLE ELASTIC LINE

Wind/Weather Conditions	Chain	Flexible Elastic Line
Calm weather conditions	Low holding angle; excellent holding	High holding angle; minimal holding
Average wind	Holding angle increases; holding power diminishes	Holding angle decreases; holding power increases
Strong wind	Holding angle at its maximum; anchor holding minimal; no shock absorption	Holding angle at its minimum; anchor holding maximal; shock absorption

angle at the anchor, increasing the anchor's holding power when it is needed most. A very flexible yet strong line also reduces shock loads on the entire anchor gear (see Table A2-1).

LEAD-CORED LINE

Lead-cored nylon line is comprised of small, end-to-end cylinders of lead covered with two or more layers of woven fibers. Though this line is not commonly available in the United States, it is marketed in some countries as the indispensable complement to an aluminum anchor. We, however, see several disadvantages from using this line in your anchor rode.

First, although the lead does—as intended—add a small amount of weight to the line, the difference is not dramatic. The total weight of a 120-foot (36.5 m) lead-filled line with a diameter of 14 mm is 28 pounds since the lead filling is usually laced into only the first 30 feet; a 14 mm unleaded line of the same length weighs 8.3 pounds. It does incrementally improve the pulling angle of the rode, of course, but a lead-filled line is still only one-fourth the weight of an equal length of chain of the same breaking strength. In other words, the slightest gust of wind negates any significance of this slight addition of weight to a nylon line.

Second, the lead pieces laced into the anchor line add no chafe protection; if anything, they can exacerbate friction against the seafloor since this type of line tends to lie closer to the seafloor than a lighter unleaded line.

Third, the lead pieces decrease elasticity and its desired dampening effect.

Finally, there's the cost factor: 15 feet (4.5 m) of chain leader plus 15 feet (4.5 m) of nylon line costs 40% less than the same length of lead-filled line.

In sum, a good nylon anchor line with just 15 feet (4.5 m) of chain leader improves the setting angle just as well as a leaded anchor line. This 15 feet of chain leader is heavier than the leaded anchor line—putting weight in the place where weight should be, near the anchor shaft. The chain then contends with the chafing seafloor, while the soft, unleaded nylon anchor line above delivers the necessary elasticity.

We believe there is plenty of room for experimentation and innovation in finding solutions to anchoring problems and encourage readers to experiment intelligently, observe, and share their results with other mariners. Keep your eye on marine publications for new developments in the next decade.

Conversion Table

CONVERSION OF METRIC TO U.S. CUSTOMARY/IMPERIAL UNITS

Metric Unit	U.S./Imperial Unit
1,000 meters (m)	3,280.8 feet (ft.)
500 m	1,640.4 ft.
200 m	656.2 ft.
150 m	492.1 ft.
100 m	328.1 ft.
75 m	246.1 ft.
60 m	196.8 ft.
50 m	164.0 ft.
25 m	82.0 ft.
20 m	65.6 ft.
12 m	39.4 ft.
10 m	32.8 ft.
8 m	26.2 ft.
7 m	23.0 ft.
6 m	19.7 ft.
5 m	16.4 ft.
4.5 m	14.8 ft.
4.0 m	13.1 ft.
3.5 m	11.5 ft.
2.5 m	8.2 ft.
2.0 m	6.6 ft.
1.5 m	4.9 ft.
1 m	3.3 ft.
0.9 m	35.4 in.
0.6 m	23.6 in.
0.5 m	19.7 in.
300 mm	11.8 in.
200 mm	7.9 in.
1 knot/1.854 kilometers per hour/0.515 meter per second	1 nautical mile per hour/1.15 miles per hour
1 joule	0.7375 ft. lb.

Manufacturers and Distributors

It would be impossible to create an exhaustive list of all manufacturers, importers, and distributors for every type of anchor and all types of accompanying gear. We have tried, however, to collect as up-to-date a list as possible. Some of the equipment listed here was not discussed in the book, but we have listed it in an effort to make the list as comprehensive as possible. Since some company names are different from the product names, we have listed the products as well.

Where possible, we give you the contact information for the manufacturer and, when applicable, the distributor or North American importing company.

ACCO Chain Products
1416 East Sanborn Street
Winona, MN 55987
800-553-8056
www.accochain.com
Chain

Alphacar Trading
12 Pomporovsky Street
Rishon Lezion 75354
Israel
972-54-4777045
www.anchor-safe.com
Anchor-Safe wireless remote-control chain
  counter

Anchor Concepts, Inc.
P.O. Box 98476
Raleigh, NC 27624
888-282-2535; 919-845-1940
www.hydrobubble.com
HydroBubble anchor

Anchorlift USA
1671 NW 144th Terrace, Suite 103
Sunrise, FL 33323
866-946-3527; 954-838-0701
www.anchorliftusa.com
Windlasses and accessories

Anchor Marine & Industrial Supply
P.O. Box 58645
Houston, TX 77258
800-233-8014; 713-644-1183
www.anchormarinehouston.com
Anchors, chain, fittings

Anchor Right International
P.O. Box 843
Melbourne, Victoria 3941
Australia
61-(0)3-5984-4700
http://anchorright.net
SARCA anchor

Australian Yacht Winch Company
4 Narang Place
St Marys, New South Wales 2760
Australia
61-(0)2-9623-2448
www.arco-winches.com
Hutton-Arco winches

Baldt Anchor and Chain
801 West 6th Street
Chester, PA 19013
610-447-5200
www.baldt.com
Baldt anchor

Bosun Supplies Company
P.O. Box 86
Arnold, MD 21012
888-433-3484
www.bosunsupplies.com
Chain, accessories, hardware, fittings

Carefree of Colorado
2145 West 6th Avenue
Broomfield, CO 80020
800-243-3097; 303-469-3324
www.powerwinch.com
Powerwinch

Creative Marine Products
P.O. Box 2120
Natchez, MS 39120
800-824-0355; 601-442-1630
www.creativemarine.com
Super Max anchor

CruzPro Instruments
35 Keeling Road, #A4
Henderson, Auckland 1008
New Zealand
64-(0)9-838-3331
www.cruzpro.com
Chain counters

DCL Mooring and Rigging
4400 North Galvez Street
New Orleans, LA 70117
800-228-7660; 504-944-3366
www.dreyfussupply.com
Anchors, chain, wire rope, fittings

Deep Blue Marine AG
Engenbühl 130
CH-5705 Hallwil
Switzerland
41-(0)62-767-7799
www.deepblue.ch/marine
U.S. distributor:
Ascend Marine
10441 Dutchtown Road
Knoxville, TN 37932
865-777-2215
BlueNet chain counter

Digger Anchor Company
40154 Highway 71
Sauk Centre, MN 56378
800-653-1499
www.diggeranchor.com
Digger anchor

Dor-Mor
P.O. Box 461
Claremont, NH 03743
603-542-7696
www.dor-mor.com
Dor-Mor pyramid anchors

Euro Products
1557 NW Ballard Way
Seattle, WA 98107
800-577-3877; 206-784-9848
www.europroductsinc.com
Hardware, chain, wire rope

Fehr Bros. Industries
895 Kings Highway
Saugerties, NY 12477
800-431-3095; 845-246-9525
www.fehr.com
Chain, wire rope, hardware

Flotation Technologies
20 Morin Street
Biddeford, ME 04005
207-282-7749
www.flotec.com
Mooring products

FOB SAS
B.P. 14
29801 Brest Cedex 09
France
www.fob.fr
33-(0)2-98-02-04-17
FOB anchor

Fortress Marine Anchors
1386 West McNab Road
Fort Lauderdale, FL 33309
800-825-6289; 954-978-9988
www.fortressanchors.com
Fortress anchor

Galley Maid
60 NE 110th Street
Okeechobee, FL 34972
863-467-6070
www.galleymaid.com
Windlasses

Greenfield Products
P.O. Box 99
Greenfield, OH 45123
800-582-6287; 937-981-2696
www.greenfieldproducts.com
PVC-coated anchors and accessories

Hans C-Anchor
Tierra Verde, FL 33715
727-565-1355
www.hansanchor.com
Stealth anchor

Hazelett Marine
P.O. Box 600
Colchester, VT 05446
802-863-6376
www.hazelettmarine.com
Elastic mooring system

Helix Mooring Systems
P.O. Box 723
Belfast, ME 04915
800-866-4775; 207-338-0412
www.helixmooringsystems.com
Helix anchors

Hydromar
Nieuwzandweg 1
1771 MZ Wieringerwerf
Netherlands
31-(0)227-54-96-00
Winches, windlasses

Ideal Windlass Company
P.O. Box 430
East Greenwich, RI 02818
401-884-2550
www.idealwindlass.com
Windlasses

Imtra
30 Samuel Barnet Boulevard
New Bedford, MA 02745
508-995-7000
www.imtra.com
Lofrans and Muir windlasses

Inland Marine
2 Atlantic Street
South Dartmouth, MA 02748
508-644-5445
www.mushroommooring.com
Mushroom anchors, chain, hardware

Kingston Anchors
143 Hickson Avenue
Kingston, Ontario K7K 2N8
Canada
613-549-2718
www.kingstonanchors.com
QuickSet anchor

Lewmar
www.lewmar.com
Anchors, winches, windlasses, hardware

Lighthouse Manufacturing
2944 Rubidoux Boulevard
Riverside, CA 92509
951-683-5078
www.lighthouse-mfg-usa.com
Windlasses

Paul E. Luke, Inc.
15 Luke's Gulch
East Boothbay, ME 04544
207-633-4971
www.peluke.com
Luke Storm (fisherman-type) anchor

Manson Anchors
P.O. Box 104 035
Lincoln North
Henderson, Auckland
New Zealand
64-(0)9-835-0968
www.manson-marine.co.nz
Manson Supreme anchor

Marine Fenders International
909 Maher Avenue
Wilmington, CA 90744
310-834-7037
www.marinefendersintl.com
Fenders

Maxwell Marine
2907 South Croddy Way
Santa Ana, CA 92704
714-689-2900
www.maxwellmarine.com
Winches

North East Rigging Systems
277 Baker Avenue
Concord, MA 01742
978-287-0060
www.nerigging.com
Anchors, hardware, windlasses

North West Marine Dist.
26940 26th Avenue
Aldergrove, British Columbia V4W 2Y6
Canada
604-607-7901
www.northwestmarine.ca
Chain and hardware

NoTECO Division, Mele Companies, Inc.
1712 Erie Street
Utica, NY 13501
888-674-4465; 315-733-4600
www.noteco.com
Bulwagga anchor

Plastimo/Navimo USA, Inc.
7455 16th Street East, Suite 107
Sarasota, FL 34243
866-383-1888
www.plastimousa.com
Manta and Kobra anchors, Goïot hardware

PSI Marine
3075 Shattuck, Suite 801
Saginaw, MI 48603
800-780-6094; 989-695-2646
www.tideslide.com
TideSlide mooring products

Quick USA
509 McCormick Drive
Glen Burnie, MD 21061
410-768-5991
www.quickusa.com
Chain counters, chain, windlasses

Richter Anchors
2207 Songbird Court
Plymouth, WI 53073
800-507-7386
www.richteranchors.com
Richter anchor

Rigging Only
P.O. Box 264
Fairhaven, MA 02719
508-992-0434
www.riggingonly.com
Anchors, chain, windlasses, winches, fittings

Rocna Anchors
P.O. Box 242
Albany Village, Auckland 0755
New Zealand
64-(0)9-413-5286
www.rocna.com
Rocna anchor

Safe Harbor Marine
570 Heron Point Lane
Bellingham, WA 98229
360-647-7611
www.safeharbormarine.com
Docking and anchoring equipment

Scandvik
P.O. Box 68
Vero Beach, FL 32961
800-535-6009
www.scandvik.com
Andersen winches, hardware

Schoellhorn-Albrecht Machine Company
575-105 Rudder Road
St. Louis, MO 63026
314-351-3333
www.schoellhorn-albrecht.com
Windlasses, winches, hardware

Seaflex, Inc.
102 Columbia Drive, #210
Cape Canaveral, FL 32920
310-548-9100
www.seaflex.net
Seaflex Mooring System

Sea Tech & Fun s.a.r.l.
B.P 103
40 Ibn Safouane
2036 La Soukra, Tunisia
www.spade-anchor.com
Spade and Sword anchors

Slide Anchor
1751 Industrial Boulevard
Lake Havasu City, AZ 86403
928-855-1108
www.slideanchor.com
Anchors

South Pacific Windlass Australia
7 Anella Avenue, Unit 24
Castle Hill, New South Wales 2154
Australia
61-(0)2-9659-2889
www.southpacific.com.au
Windlasses

Spartan Marine
340 Robinhood Road
Georgetown, ME 04548
800-325-3287; 207-371-2542
www.spartanmarine.com
Hardware

Stainless Outfitters
161 Saunders Road
Barrie, Ontario L4N 9A3
Canada
800-268-0395; 705-725-1779
www.stainlessoutfitters.com/marine.htm
Stainless steel anchor carriers

Suncor Stainless
70 Armstrong Road
Plymouth, MA 02360
508-732-9191
www.suncorstainless.com
Stainless steel anchors, chain, hardware, wire rope

Swiss Tech America
1550 Huddersfield Court
San Jose, CA 95126
888-800-9574; 408-505-7245
www.swisstech-america.com
WASI Bügel anchor, Swiss Tech products

Tie Down Engineering
5901 Wheaton Drive
Atlanta, GA 30336
800-241-1806; 404-344-0000
www.danforthanchors.com; www.tiedown.com
Danforth anchors and chains, Hooker anchors

Wagner Products Company
P.O. Box 221001
St. Louis, MO 63122
314-966-4444
www.wagnerproducts.com
Powerpointe sand and mud anchor

Washington Chain & Supply
P.O. Box 3645
Seattle, WA 98124
800-851-3429; 206-623-8500
www.wachain.com
Anchors, chain, fittings

WASI
Postfach 24 01 53
D-42231 Wuppertal
Germany
49-(0)202-26320
www.wasi-maritim.com
U.S. distributor: see Swiss Tech America

Wenling Jingang Anchor Windlass Factory
No. 835, Jingang Development Zone
Binhai, Wenling, Zhejiang
China
86-576-8288-1276
www.jgwindlass.com
Windlasses

Windline
234 West 146th Street
Gardena, CA 90248
310-516-9812
www.windline.com
Anchoring accessories

XYZ Marine Products
575 Main Street, #1514
New York, NY 10044
212-486-3912
www.xyzanchor.com
XYZ anchor

About the Authors

ALAIN POIRAUD

Raised in France, Alain Poiraud is trained as a biomedical engineer and has worked with several international firms. His area of expertise is the development of artificial hearts and valves.

He sailed on France's Atlantic coast as a young boy and participated in the Tour de France sailing races. He navigated for many decades in France, designing and building his steel ketch *Hylas*. In the early 1990s, he embarked on a voyage through the Mediterranean, where he found the inspiration to reinvent anchoring.

Since many of the anchorages in the Mediterranean have weed-covered seafloors, he spent years researching and testing various anchor types. His systematic curiosity, coupled with an inventive spirit, led him to develop a new anchoring technology. The Spade anchor was born and quickly won several prizes, including first place in *Practical Sailor* magazine's top-ten product ranking in 1999, a DAME (Design Award METS) award at the 2000 Marine Equipment Trade Show (METS), and another top-ten product ranking from *Practical Sailor* in 2001. The

Spade has won many international comparison tests in several magazines. In 2003, the Spade was joined by the Sword, which built upon the experience of its predecessor.

He is the author of *Tout savoir sur le mouillage*, distributed by Loisirs Nautiques (December 2003).

He is currently exploring South America on *Hylas*, and maintains a website at www.hylas.ws.

ERIKA AND ACHIM GINSBERG-KLEMMT

In 1993, with a CQR as a wedding gift, cruisers Erika and Achim Ginsberg-Klemmt sailed their steel ketch *Pangaea* through the Mediterranean, Atlantic, Caribbean, and along the U.S. East Coast. On the second leg, a Bruce anchor joined their ground tackle through Panama, the Galápagos, the Marquesas, and Hawaii.

Their "technomadic" vision of life inspires their website, www.pangaea.to. Launched in 1997, it was the first cruising website updated live via a Pactor amateur radio link.

In spring 2004 they embarked on a "rum route" voyage from the Catalonian coast, sailing on their second *Pangaea*, a Dalu 47 aluminum sloop from Meta, the shipyard of Bernard Moitessier's *Joshua*. This time, they were accompanied by their children Antonia and Ari, and later by Maeva Margarita, who was conceived on the island of her middle name and born aboard in Longboat Key, Florida. On this cruise, only new-generation anchors equipped their yacht, along with their trusty Aries self-steering.

Sarasota, Florida, is their present home port, although they admit you ain't a land-lubber until the title is signed.

Achim is an impassioned engineer and bluewater anchorer. Raised in Hamburg, Germany, his first sail was made from his grandmother's bedsheet. His mother looked on in shock and worry as he took to the ocean in a rubber dinghy on the Baltic Sea. After studying engineering in Germany and France, he developed software for optical spectrophotometers, geophysical sonar systems for underwater cartography, and most recently for X-ray image analysis systems.

Educated at UC Berkeley, the Sorbonne, and St. John's College Graduate Institute, Erika is an impassioned writer of everything from poetry to technical articles. She has worked as a trilingual tour guide, translator, web developer, journalist, lecturer, and teacher. Bluewater sailing was the logical continuum of a wanderlust that has run through Erika's soul since her carefree days growing up in Laguna Beach, California. She is the mother of three children who know *Pangaea* as their floating home.

Index

Numbers in **bold** indicate pages with illustrations